Good Housekeeping Institute has been caring about good cooking for over 40 years. In the Institute's unique testing kitchens recipes are devised, cooked and tasted and then tested over and over again to guarantee that you get perfect results.

With Good Housekeeping cookery books you buy more than a collection of recipes – you buy a share of the Institute's long experience and an open invitation to ask the experts for advice on your cookery problems.

All you have to do is to write to Good Housekeeping Institute, Chestergate House, Vauxhall Bridge Road, London, S.W.1.

This series of Good Housekeeping cookery books contains all the best of the huge collection of recipes which have been cooked, tested and photographed in Good Housekeeping Institute.

GOOD HOUSEKEEPING LIBRARY OF COOKING

A complete list of titles

MEAT COOKERY

SALADS, VEGETABLES AND FRUITS

FISH AND SHELLFISH

SWEETS, PUDDINGS AND DESSERTS

POULTRY AND GAME
Eggs and Cheese

SAVOURIES, SNACKS AND APPETISERS
With a supplement on Picnics

CAKES, PASTRIES AND BREADS

DRINKS, COCKTAILS AND HOMEMADE WINES

JAMS, PRESERVES AND HOMEMADE SWEETS
With a supplement on Home Freezing

THE COMPLETE COOK
Menus, Methods and Equipment

Poultry and Game Eggs and Cheese

GOOD HOUSEKEEPING LIBRARY OF COOKING

SPHERE BOOKS LTD.
30/32 Grays Inn Road, London W.C.1

First published in Great Britain in 1969
by Sphere Books

© National Magazine Co., Ltd., 1969

Set in Times New Roman

Four-colour illustrations printed by
Acorn-Typesetting and Litho Services Ltd.
Feltham, Middx.

Text printed and bound by C. Nicholls & Company, Ltd., Manchester.

Contents

NOTE: Unless otherwise indicated, recipes give 4 average servings.

List of Colour Plates

CHAPTER 1

Introduction

After meat and fish – each of which forms the subject of a separate book in this series – poultry, eggs and cheese are our most important main-dish foods. Game is not such an everyday food, but game birds are naturally linked with poultry from the cookery point of view – indeed, in many dishes they are interchangeable.

Detailed notes on the choice, preparation and carving of poultry and game are given in the Supplement, but we give here a definition of the terms, "poultry" and "game", followed by brief general notes on the main methods of cooking.

Poultry includes chickens (fowl), guinea-fowl, ducks, geese and turkeys. Nowadays a large amount of frozen poultry is available, which means that there is a good all-the-year-round supply. (See the notes on frozen poultry in the Supplement, page 166). Most poultry is now sold ready for cooking, that is, cleaned or drawn, plucked and where necessary trussed. However, we give in the Supplement full details of these processes. Both fresh and frozen chickens, ducks, and occasionally turkeys, are available in separate joints as well as whole.

Game is the name given to those wild birds and animals which are hunted and killed for food, but which at certain times of the year are protected by law. There are also some wild birds which though not technically known as game, are also protected. For convenience' sake we include here pigeons, though only the wood or wild pigeon counts as game, and rabbits, which though not protected, so closely resemble hares from the cookery point of view, that it would be impracticable to separate them.

CHICKEN, GUINEA-FOWL
A very young chicken (poussin or broiler) is usually grilled, fried or baked, though of course there is no reason why it should not also be used in casserole dishes and so on.

The large broilers and also the birds sold as roasting fowl both look and taste very appetising when roasted. The smaller ones are not usually stuffed, and even for a full-grown bird this is not essential, but many people like to stuff a chicken to keep its shape and make it go further, as well as to add extra flavour.

Birds over a year old are usually best cooked by a method which will soften the connective tissues, so they are excellent in any sort of stew or casserole, for which a prime roaster is not required. However, it is a mistake to use a really elderly bird for these dishes, since an old fowl should never be cut before cooking – if it is to retain any flavour and succulence, it requires to be left whole while given long, slow simmering, steaming or pressure-cooking. Birds which are being casseroled or stewed may be cooked in stock, red or white wine, cider or sherry, or a mixture of wine or cider and stock. The wine or cider not only gives a delicious flavour, but it also helps to make the chicken flesh tender – there is no need to use much of it, and often the end of a bottle can be used up in this way.

Guinea-fowl can be cooked in many ways suitable for chicken, but as the bird lacks fat, see that the flesh does not dry out when it is roasted. Baste frequently and if possible either bard or lard it with fat bacon or strips of fat (see Supplement for details) alternatively, the guinea fowl may be cooked in aluminium foil or in well greased greaseproof paper. For casseroles and stews guinea-fowl may be treated just like chicken.

TURKEY, DUCKS, GEESE

Whole turkeys are most commonly roasted, stuffed with one or two kinds of forcemeat. Cut joints (or leftover parts of the bird) can be made into a variety of casserole dishes and so on.

Ducks may be roasted or casseroled, braised, etc. They are usually cooked or served with some sharp-flavoured ingredient such as oranges or apples, to offset their richness. The usual stuffing, sage and onion, also helps to counteract this effect.

Geese are probably more often roasted than made into casseroles and similar dishes; since they are rich in fat, they demand the same kind of stuffing and accompaniments as ducks.

GAME BIRDS

Generally speaking, the more simply game is cooked, the better. For young birds there is no better way than roasting, but for older ones, which are likely to be tough if plainly roasted, braising and casseroling are better methods.

Since game birds lack fat, it is usual to cover the breast before roasting with pieces of fat bacon and to baste them frequently with fat during the cooking; sometimes a knob of butter or a piece of juicy steak is put inside the bird before it is roasted, to keep it pleasantly moist.

HARE AND RABBIT
Hares may be roasted, fricasseed or braised, but probably the best-known dish in which they figure is "jugged" hare – see the recipe in Chapter 3, page 53.

Rabbits may be cooked in similar ways, and indeed in almost any way suitable for other kinds of meat – only young tender ones should be roasted or fried. They make a good pie filling and adapt well to such cold dishes as jellied moulds.

VENISON
This is the meat of the red-deer. The haunch is the prime cut, and this and the other better-quality cuts roast or fry well; for the back or breast, however, slow methods of cooking are best.

MADE-UP DISHES
Poultry and game are particularly easy to use up in all kinds of pies, savouries, salads and cold dishes. Imposing party galantines and moulds can also be made with them. Soups and broths are another delicious by-product of a poultry or game meal. See the relevant chapters for recipes.

EGGS AND CHEESE
We give the chief methods of cooking these two invaluable foods, with the best-known recipes for main meals and snacks.

RECIPE NOTES
We include a number of recipes of foreign origin; where necessary these have been modified sufficiently to make them practicable for use in this country, available ingredients being substituted for items that would not be obtainable here.

In general, recipes give four servings unless otherwise indicated. With a roast bird such as a chicken, duck or turkey, one would of course usually find that there was a certain amount of flesh left on the carcase, which may be used in made-up dishes or soup.

A rough-and-ready guide is that when birds are served whole, one should reckon $\frac{1}{2}$ to $\frac{3}{4}$ lb. (oven-ready weight) per person; for made-up dishes, 3–6 oz. (boned) per person, according to whether the dish is for a main meal or a snack and also depending on whether or not it includes other satisfying ingredients such as rice.

CHAPTER 2

Roast poultry and game

Both traditional dishes and some less usual variations are included in this chapter, as well as a few recipes for baked and barbecued chicken. See chapter 10, page 139, for bacon rolls, stuffings, gravy and other accompaniments.

ROAST CHICKEN
Oven temperature: fairly hot (400°F., mark 6)
If the bird is frozen, allow it to thaw out completely, then remove the bag of giblets. Wash the inside of the bird and stuff it at the neck end with herb stuffing, sausage-meat or another stuffing as you wish. Don't stuff too tightly, as the bread or rice in the forcemeat mixture tends to swell and might cause the skin of the bird to split. To add extra flavour you can put an onion, a thick lemon wedge or a knob of butter in the body of the bird. Brush the chicken with melted butter or oil and sprinkle with salt and pepper. Put it in a shallow roasting tin, and if you like put a few strips of streaky bacon over the breast to prevent the bird from becoming too dry.

Cook in the centre of the oven, basting from time to time and allowing 20 minutes per lb. plus 20 minutes. Put a piece of greaseproof paper over the breast if the flesh shows signs of becoming too brown. Alternatively, wrap the chicken in foil before roasting, making the join along the top; allow the same cooking time, but open the foil for the final 15–20 minutes, to allow the bird to brown.

Serve with roast potatoes and a green vegetable or – for a change – a tossed green salad. Bacon rolls, forcemeat balls, small chipolata sausages, bread sauce and thin gravy are usual accompaniments for roast chicken.

Note: An older bird can be roasted if you first steam or boil it for about 2 hours, to make it tender; it is best to do this the previous day, so that the chicken has time to get cold before it is stuffed. Roast for 30–45 minutes to make it crisp, brown and really hot.

ROAST BROILER
Oven temperature: fairly hot (400°F., mark 6)

The bird will be already prepared for cooking – apart from stuffing, if required. As a very young bird is delicately flavoured, you may not want to stuff it, so try just rubbing the inside of the chicken with a piece of crushed garlic and adding a knob of butter. Any of the usual stuffings may be used, but preferably nothing too strongly flavoured. Loosen the chicken's wings, so that you can pull up the flap of skin over the breast and fill the cavity, making the breast a good shape but remembering not to stuff too tightly. Pull the flap down again and secure it with a skewer.

Put the chicken in a roasting tin, cover the breast with fat bacon and put some dripping over the rest of the bird. Roast for 45–50 minutes in the centre of the oven, according to size (about 15 minutes longer if bird is stuffed); baste occasionally.

Serve the chicken with bread sauce and gravy; garnish if desired with bacon rolls and chipolata sausages.

ROAST SPRING CHICKEN
Oven temperature: fairly hot (400°F., mark 6)

Spread a small spring chicken or young roasting chicken with softened butter and put a knob of butter inside. Wrap in buttered paper and cook in the centre of the oven for about ½–¾ hour, according to size; remove the paper for the last 15 minutes to brown the breast, and baste with hot butter during the cooking. Serve with bacon rolls, etc.

FRENCH-STYLE ROAST CHICKEN

A 2½–3 lb. chicken	Melted butter
3 oz. butter	2 rashers of bacon
Salt and pepper	¼ pint chicken stock
5–6 sprigs of tarragon	(or white wine)
or parsley	

Oven temperature: fairly hot (375°F., mark 5)

Prepare the bird as for ordinary roasting.

Cream the butter with a good sprinkling of salt and pepper and put the butter and sprigs of herb inside the bird. Brush the breast with melted butter and cover with the rashers of bacon. Place the bird in a roasting tin and add the stock. Bake in the centre of the oven, basting with the stock every 15 minutes; allow 20 minutes per lb. plus 20 minutes. Remove the bacon during the last 15 minutes of the cooking to brown the breast. Retain the stock to make gravy.

11

ALMOND CHICKEN

1 roasting chicken, jointed
and skinned, or 4 chicken
joints, skinned

1 egg, beaten
4 oz. ground almonds
2 oz. butter

Oven temperature: fairly hot (400°F., mark 6)

Brush the joints with egg and roll them in the ground almonds, pressing these well in. Melt the butter in a shallow roasting tin and bake the chicken in this towards the top of the oven for ¾–1 hour, until tender; baste once or twice during the cooking. Serve with a green or mixed salad.

Alternatively, serve with almond sauce. To make this, brown 2 oz. blanched and shredded almonds in ½ oz. butter, season with salt and pepper and add ¼ pint double cream; heat, but do not boil.

LEMON-GLAZED CHICKEN

4 chicken joints
Seasoned flour
1 oz. butter

1 oz. blended white fat
Parsley or lemon to garnish

For the Glaze

2 tbsps. oil
3 tbsps. lemon juice
1 tbsp. chopped onion

Salt and pepper
A pinch of powdered
thyme

Oven temperature: moderate (350°F., mark 4)

Wipe the chicken portions and toss them in seasoned flour (a paper or polythene bag is useful for this). Melt the butter and white fat in a shallow roasting tin or baking dish large enough to take the chicken portions without overlapping. Place the chicken skin side down in the fat and bake for 25 minutes; turn them and cook for a further 20 minutes.

Blend together the ingredients for the glaze, spoon it over the chicken and continue to cook for a further 15 minutes, basting once during the cooking. Test the chicken to make sure it is cooked. Serve with a little of the glaze and garnish with parsley or lemon.

BAKED CHICKEN IN A BASKET

4 chicken joints
4 oz. butter
1 egg, beaten
2 oz. white bread-crumbs

1–2 oz. Parmesan cheese,
grated
1 onion, skinned and thinly
sliced, to garnish

Oven temperature: hot (425°F., mark 7)

Prepare the chicken. Melt the butter in a shallow baking tin in the oven. Coat the chicken pieces with beaten egg and the bread-crumbs mixed with the cheese. Place them in the tin and cook for ½ hour; turn them over and cook for a further ¼ hour, or until crisp, brown and tender. Drain well. Dish up in

12

a large wicker basket lined with napkins and garnish with onion rings. Serve with a salad tossed in salad cream and piled on a bed of lettuce or endive.

BAKED CHICKEN LEGS AND CRANBERRY DIP

6 chicken legs	3–4 oz. dry bread-crumbs
2 eggs, beaten	$\frac{1}{4}$ lb. cranberry jelly
$\frac{1}{2}$ level tsp. salt	$\frac{1}{2}$ tsp. prepared mustard
A pinch of black pepper	1 tbsp. vinegar

Oven temperature: moderate (350°F., mark 4)

Dip the chicken legs in beaten and seasoned egg and coat with bread-crumbs. Place on a greased baking tray and bake in the centre of the oven for 1 hour. Crush the cranberry jelly with a fork and mix in the mustard and vinegar; chill and serve with the chicken. (Serves 6.)

CHICKEN WITH OYSTERS (U.S.A.)

A 3-lb. ready-to-cook chicken, cut in eighths	$\frac{1}{4}$ level tsp. powdered dried sage
1$\frac{1}{4}$ level tsps. salt	$\frac{1}{2}$ lb. shelled oysters
$\frac{1}{2}$ level tsp. pepper	$\frac{1}{4}$ pint double cream
4 oz. butter	$\frac{1}{2}$ level tsp. powdered dried basil
$\frac{1}{4}$ pint milk	

Oven temperature: fairly hot (375°F., mark 5)

In the autumn, when the wonderful New England oysters are just coming into season, some Yankees like to smother their chicken in a kind of oyster stew.

Sprinkle the chicken with half the salt and pepper. Heat the butter in a large pan and sauté the chicken pieces (uncovered) for 10 minutes, turning them once. Put into a baking dish measuring about 12 by 7$\frac{1}{2}$ by 2 inches, pour the milk over the top and sprinkle with the rest of the salt and pepper and the sage. Cover with aluminium foil and bake in the centre of the oven for 1$\frac{1}{4}$ hours. Uncover the dish, add the drained oysters, cream and basil, cover and bake for a further 15 minutes, or until the sauce is hot. Serve in soup plates, with a fork and spoon. (Serves 8.)

MUSHROOM-BAKED CHICKEN

A 10-oz. can of condensed mushroom soup	$\frac{1}{4}$ of a pkt. of sage and onion stuffing mix
$\frac{1}{4}$ pint milk	2 oz. butter
4 frozen chicken joints	

Oven temperature: fairly hot (400°F., mark 6)

Mix the soup and milk together and pour some into a basin. Dip the chicken joints in this and then toss them in the dry stuffing mix. Put the joints on a baking tray, top each with

½ oz. butter and bake in the centre of the oven for 1 hour. Heat the rest of the soup and milk and serve poured over the chicken.

CHICKEN PARCELS

4 chicken quarters	4 level tbsps. Demerara
2 oz. melted butter	sugar
3 medium-sized onions,	1–2 tsps. vinegar
skinned and sliced	Paprika pepper

Oven temperature: fairly hot (400°F., mark 6)

Cut 4 pieces of foil each large enough to cover a portion of chicken. Brush each piece of chicken with melted butter, dip the slices of onion in the sugar and divide them between the pieces of foil. Place the chicken portions on top of the onion and sprinkle with vinegar and paprika. Lightly fold the foil over the chicken, place the parcels on a baking tray or in an ovenproof dish and bake just above the centre of the oven for about 45 minutes, or until the chicken is tender. Remove the pieces from the foil and serve topped with the sliced onion.

ROAST GUINEA FOWL

Oven temperature: fairly hot (400°F., mark 6)

Singe, draw and wipe the bird (see Supplement, page 163) and truss it for roasting. Roast in the centre of the oven for 45–60 minutes (or longer, according to size), basting frequently with butter or dripping. Garnish with watercress and serve with thin gravy and an orange or mixed green salad or with bread sauce.

ROAST TURKEY

(see colour picture No. 1)

If the bird is frozen, let it thaw out completely before cooking: allow 20–30 hours in a cool larder for a bird up to 12 lb.; over this weight it takes up to 48 hours. Remove the bag of giblets from the body cavity. Wash and wipe the bird and stuff it at the neck end; herb stuffing, or chestnut stuffing is commonly used: allow 1 lb. made stuffing for a bird up to 14 lb.; or twice this amount for a larger bird. For the body cavity, sausage-meat or sausage stuffing is generally used: allow 1–2 lb., according to size. Occasionally, sausage-meat and another stuffing are put in alternately, giving variegated layers when the bird is carved. (See the chapter on Sauces and Stuffings.)

Make the turkey as plump and even in shape as possible, then truss it with the wings folded under the body and the legs tied together. Before cooking the bird, spread it with softened dripping or butter; the breast may also be covered with strips of fat bacon. If you are going to cook it by the quick method (see below) it is best to wrap the bird in aluminium foil to prevent the flesh drying and the skin hardening. Foil is not recommended for the slow method, however, as it tends to give a steamed rather than a roast effect.

For the slow method cook in a warm oven (325°F., mark 3), for the quick method cook in a very hot oven (450°F., mark 8), calculating the time according to the chart below.

Approx. Cooking Times by Slow Oven Method

6–8 lb. bird	3–3½ hours
8–10 lb. bird	3½–3¾ hours
10–12 lb. bird	3¾–4 hours
12–14 lb. bird	4–4¼ hours
14–16 lb. bird	4¼–4½ hours
16–18 lb. bird	4½–4¾ hours

Approx. Cooking Times by Quick Oven Method

6–8 lb. bird	2¼–2½ hours
8–10 lb. bird	2½–2¾ hours
10–12 lb. bird	2¾ hours
12–14 lb. bird	3 hours
14–16 lb. bird	3–3¼ hours
16–18 lb. bird	3¼–3½ hours

Unless the bird is cooked in foil, baste regularly. In either case, turn it once, for even browning. If foil is used, unwrap it for the last ½ hour, so that the bird may be well basted and then left to become crisp and golden.

Small sausages, forcemeat balls, rolls of bacon and water-cress may be used to garnish the turkey. Serve it with brown gravy and bread sauce. Cranberry or some other sharp sauce can also be served. Sliced cooked ham or tongue is a favourite accompaniment, with of course vegetables such as roast potatoes and sprouts.

ROAST STUFFED TURKEY, LISBON STYLE

1 turkey, 7–8 lb.	¼ level tsp. powdered
½ lb. fillet of pork	cinnamon
½ lb. ham or lean bacon	A little grated nutmeg
1 onion, skinned and chopped	Paprika pepper
A little olive oil for	Salt
frying	6 oz. fresh white bread-crumbs
12 olives, stoned	3 egg yolks
A pinch of powdered mace	

Oven temperature: warm (325°F., mark 3)

Prepare the turkey for roasting; cook the giblets for 15 minutes in boiling salted water, drain and mince them, together with the pork and ham. Fry the onion slowly in the olive

15

oil; add the minced meats, stoned olives, spices and seasonings and continue cooking for 5 minutes. Add this mixture
to the bread-crumbs, stir well and bind with the egg yolks, then
leave to get quite cold. Stuff the turkey, truss for roasting,
shaping it carefully, and roast for about 3 hours, basting at
intervals, until the flesh is tender when tested.

ROAST GOOSE
Oven temperature: fairly hot (400°F., mark 6)
If the bird is not ready prepared, note these special points:
Pluck the goose according to the notes in the Supplement
(page 163) and remove the stumps from the wings. Cut off
the feet and wing tips at the first joint. Cut off the head, then,
forcing back the neck skin, cut off the neck where it joins the
back. Draw the bird as described for other poultry and clean
the inside with a cloth wrung out in hot water. Put a thick fold
of cloth over the breast-bone and flatten it with a mallet or
rolling pin. Stuff with sage and onion stuffing or a fruit stuffing. (See Sauces and Stuffings chapter, page 139.)

Working with the breast side uppermost and tail end away
from you, pass a skewer through one wing, then through the
body and out again through the other wing. Pass a second
skewer through the end of the wing joint on one side, through
the thick part of the leg, through the body and out the other
side in the same way. Pass a third skewer through the loose
skin near the end of the leg, through the body and out the
other side in the same way. Enlarge the vent, pass the tail
through it and fix with a small skewer. Wind string round the
skewers, keeping the limbs firmly in position, but avoid passing the string over the breast of the goose. Tuck the neck skin
in under the string.

Sprinkle the bird with salt, put in a baking tin (on a rack or
trivet, as goose tends to be fatty) and cover with the fat taken
from inside, then with greased paper. A sour apple put in the
roasting tin during the cooking adds flavour to the gravy.

Roast for 15 minutes per lb. plus 15 minutes, basting frequently. To cook by the slow method, roast in a moderate oven
(350°F., mark 4) for 25–30 minutes per lb. Remove the paper
for the last 30 minutes, to brown the bird.

Serve with giblet gravy (made in the roasting tin after the
fat has been poured off) and apple or gooseberry sauce.
Apple rings which have been dipped in lemon juice, brushed
with oil and lightly grilled, also make an attractive garnish.

ROAST DUCK
Oven temperature: fairly hot (400°F., mark 6)
Pluck, draw and truss in the usual way (see Supplement, page
163), except that the wings are not drawn across the back; tie

16

the legs with fine string. Unless the bird is a young duckling stuff it with sage and onion stuffing at the tail end. Sprinkle the breast with salt and pepper. Cook just above the centre of the oven, allowing 20 minutes per lb. Remove the trussing strings and skewers; serve the bird garnished with watercress and accompanied by apple sauce, potatoes, peas and thin brown gravy. Orange salad is also a favourite accompaniment for roast duck. (See Chapter 10.)

ROAST DUCK, SEVILLE STYLE

A duck
4 Seville oranges
2 level tsps. arrowroot
¾ pint giblet stock (see p. 165)

2 tsps. lemon juice
2 tsps. sherry
Caster sugar

Oven temperature: fairly hot (400°F., mark 6)

Roast the duck in the usual way. Wash and peel off the thin outer skin of 2 of the oranges, blanch it in boiling water for a few minutes, then shred it into thin strips. Blend the arrowroot with a little cold stock, then boil the rest and stir in the arrowroot. Cook, stirring carefully, for 3 minutes. Add the lemon juice, the juice of the 2 peeled oranges and the sherry. Finally add the shredded orange peel.

Make a salad by peeling and slicing the remaining 2 oranges very thinly and sprinkling with a little caster sugar. Serve the roast duck with the Seville sauce poured over and surrounded by the orange salad.

DUCK WITH BIGARADE SAUCE

A roasting duck
½ oz. butter
Salt and pepper
¼ pint white wine
4 oranges (use bitter ones when available)

1 lemon
1 level tbsp. sugar
1 tbsp. vinegar
2 tbsps. brandy
1 level tbsp. cornflour
1 bunch of watercress

Oven temperature: hot (425°F., mark 7)

Rub the breast of the duck with the butter and sprinkle with salt. Put the duck in the roasting tin with the wine and cook in the centre of the oven for 15 minutes per lb., basting occasionally with the wine. Squeeze the juice from 3 of the oranges and the lemon. Wash 1 orange and grate the rind from it. Melt the sugar in a pan with the vinegar and heat until it is a dark brown caramel. Add the brandy and the juice of the oranges and lemon to this caramel and simmer gently for 5 minutes. Cut the remaining orange into segments. When the duck is cooked, remove it from the roasting tin, joint it and place the pieces on a serving dish. Drain the excess fat from the roasting tin and add the grated rind and the orange sauce to the sediment. Blend the cornflour with a little cold water, stir it into the sauce, return the tin to the heat, bring to the boil and cook for 2–3 minutes, stirring. Season the sauce and pour over the joints. Garnish with the orange wedges and watercress.

DUCK WITH CHERRIES

A roasting duck
½ oz. butter
Salt
½ pint stock
1 orange, washed
3–4 lumps of sugar

1½ oz. caster sugar
1 wineglass port
1 lb. red cherries, stoned
1 pint Espagnole sauce (see p. 141) or good gravy

Oven temperature: hot (425°F., mark 7)

Rub the breast of the duck with the butter and sprinkle with salt. Put the duck in the roasting tin with the stock and cook in the centre of the oven for 15 minutes per lb., basting occasionally with the liquid. Meanwhile, rub the skin of the orange with sugar lumps to obtain the zest and put the lumps in a pan with the caster sugar and the port. Squeeze the orange and add the juice to the sugar in the pan; allow the sugar to dissolve slowly, add the cherries, cover and simmer gently for about 5 minutes.

The duck should still be slightly pink when cooked; remove it from the oven and cut into joints. Place the joints on a serving dish and keep hot. Strain the syrup from the cherries and keep the fruit hot. Add the syrup to the Espagnole sauce and spoon some of the mixture over the duck. Arrange the cherries at either end of the serving dish and serve the remaining sauce separately.

DUCK WITH FRENCH GOOSEBERRY SAUCE

A duck
½ pint gooseberry
  purée
1 oz. sugar

½ oz. butter
1 tsp. lemon juice
1 wineglass medium-dry
  sherry

Oven temperature: hot (425°F., mark 7)

Place the cleaned and trussed duck in a roasting tin and cook for 1 hour (or till tender) towards the top of the oven, basting every 20 minutes with the fat that runs out. Mix the gooseberry purée, sugar, butter and lemon juice and heat slowly. Before serving, add the sherry and serve this sauce separately.

ROAST GROUSE

Oven temperature: fairly hot (400°F., mark 6)

After hanging (see Supplement, page 163), pluck, draw and truss the bird, season inside and out and lay some fat bacon over the breast. Put a knob of butter inside the bird and place it on a slice of toast. Roast in the centre of the oven for 30 minutes, basting frequently. After 20 minutes roasting, remove the bacon, dredge the breast with flour, baste well and cook for a further 10 minutes.

Remove the trussing strings before serving the bird on the toast on which it was roasted. Garnish with watercress and serve with thin gravy, bread sauce, fried crumbs and matchstick potatoes. A lettuce or watercress salad may also be served. (See Chapter 10, page 139, for accompaniments.)

ROAST ORTOLANS
Oven temperature: hot (425°F., mark 7)
Pluck and singe the birds, but leave the "trail" inside. The crop may be drawn through a hole made in the back of the neck, and the head and neck may be removed. Cover the breasts with vine leaves and wrap the birds in thin rashers of fat bacon. Cook in the centre of the oven for 12–15 minutes, basting frequently. To dish, leave the vine leaves and bacon on, and place each bird on a croûte of fried bread or buttered toast. Thin gravy, fried crumbs and chipped potatoes are the correct accompaniments. See Chapter 10.

ROAST PARTRIDGE
Oven temperature: very hot (450°F., mark 8)
Select a young bird; pluck, draw and truss it, season the inside with pepper and salt, replace the liver and add a knob of butter. Cover the breast with pieces of fat bacon. Roast the bird in the centre of the oven for 10 minutes, then reduce the oven to fairly hot (400°F., mark 6) and roast for a further 10–20 minutes, according to size; partridge must be well-done.

The usual accompaniments are fried crumbs or game chips and a tossed salad or bread (or orange) sauce. A garnish of lemon quarters and watercress (seasoned and sprinkled with a few drops of vinegar) is often added. (See Chapter 10 for accompaniments.)

ROAST PHEASANT
Oven temperature: very hot (450°F., mark 8)
Pheasant requires to be well hung, otherwise the flesh is dry and tasteless; it needs on an average 10–11 days – rather less should the weather be "muggy", up to 3 weeks if frosty.

Pluck, draw and truss the bird and cover the breast with strips of fat bacon, Roast in the centre of the oven for 10 minutes, then reduce the heat to fairly hot (400°F., mark 6) and continue cooking for 30–40 minutes, according to the size of the bird, basting frequently with butter. About 15 minutes before the cooking is completed, remove the bacon, dredge the breast of the bird with flour, baste well and finish cooking.

Remove the trussing strings, put the pheasant on a hot dish and garnish with watercress. Serve with thin gravy, bread sauce, fried crumbs and chipped potatoes; a tossed green salad may also be served. (See Chapter 10, page 139.)

STUFFED PHEASANT

A pheasant
½ lb. sausage-meat
2–3 chicken livers
1 chopped truffle, if
   available
Salt and pepper
A little chopped parsley
1 egg yolk

A very little cream or
   top of the milk
Bacon for barding
1 glassful Madeira or
   sherry
2 tsps. tomato purée
Nutmeg
Fried croûtons

Oven temperature: fairly hot (375°F., mark 5)
Prepare the bird in the usual way, then making a stuffing with the sausage-meat, chicken livers, truffle (if used), seasoning, parsley, egg yolk and cream or top of the milk; the mixture should be fairly stiff. Stuff the bird with this filling, cover it with bacon and roast it in the centre of the oven for about 45 minutes. After about 30 minutes, add the wine, tomato purée, more seasoning and a little grated nutmeg, with a little hot water if required. Finish the cooking, basting the bird often with the sauce. To serve, remove the bacon, place the pheasant on a dish, garnish with croûtons and pour the sauce over all.

PHEASANT AND MACARONI

A pheasant
8 oz. macaroni
4 tomatoes, skinned and
   sliced

½ pint veal stock
6 oz. Parmesan cheese,
   grated
Salt and pepper

Oven temperature: very hot (450°F., mark 8)
Roast a well-larded pheasant (p. 167); baste frequently. Meanwhile gently simmer the macaroni and tomatoes in the veal stock until cooked. Add the cheese and continue cooking for a few minutes. Season to taste. Cut up the pheasant into neat joints, then put it together again and stand it on a bed of the macaroni. Serve with fried potatoes and watercress.

ROAST PIGEON

Oven temperature: very hot (450°F., mark 8)
Select young birds for roasting and allow 1 per person, unless they are very large. Pluck and draw them, singe if necessary and truss them. Spread with some softened butter and tie a piece of fat bacon over the breasts. Roast in the centre of the oven for 15–20 minutes, according to size, basting well and

removing the bacon before cooking is completed, to allow the breast to brown.

Add a garnish of watercress and serve gravy or a sauce separately. If liked, the pigeons may be halved before serving.

ROAST PTARMIGAN: Cook as for grouse. Allow 1 bird for 2 people.

ROAST JAPANESE QUAIL
Oven temperature: hot (425°F., mark 7)

Pluck and singe the birds but do not draw, as they are eaten whole. Allow 1 bird per person. Cut off the head and neck and take out the crop. Place each bird on a round of fried bread and cover the breast with thin rashers of fat bacon. Roast in the centre of the oven for 12–15 minutes, basting with butter. Serve on the bread with the bacon left in place; thin gravy, fried crumbs and chipped potatoes are the usual accompaniments. (see Chapter 10.)

Note: Wild quail may no longer be shot and sold, but Japanese quail, reared on special farms, may be marketed in the ordinary way.

ROAST WILD DUCK
(See colour picture No. 2)
Oven temperature: hot (425°F., mark 7)

One teal will serve 1–2 people; other wild ducks – e.g., mallard – as a rule will serve 2–3 people.

Hang for a few days only, then pluck, draw and truss like a domestic duck. Spread with softened butter and roast in the centre of the oven, basting frequently. Allow 20 minutes for teal, 30 minutes for mallard and wigeon – they should on no account be over-cooked. Halfway through, pour a little port or orange juice over the birds. Garnish with watercress and sliced orange (optional) and serve with thin gravy and orange salad or with Bigarade sauce. (See Chapter 10, page 139.)

WILD DUCK WITH RAISIN STUFFING

2 wild duck	Chopped nuts (optional)
6 oz. fresh white bread-crumbs	Salt and pepper
4 sticks of celery, chopped	1 egg, beaten
1 onion, skinned and chopped	½–¾ pint hot milk
6 oz. seedless raisins	Slices of fat bacon
	Orange-flavoured gravy
	Watercress to garnish

Oven temperature: hot (425°F., mark 7)

Prepare the birds. Combine the bread-crumbs, the celery, onion, raisins and chopped nuts (if used). Season and bind

21

together with the beaten egg and the milk. Stuff the birds with this mixture and sew up or secure with small skewers. Place pieces of bacon over the birds and roast in the centre of the oven for about 20–30 minutes, taking care not to over-cook them. Serve with a good gravy, with some orange juice added, or with a simple salad made by tossing sliced peeled oranges in a French dressing. Garnish with watercress if available.

ROAST WOODCOCK, SNIPE, PLOVER

Oven temperature: fairly hot (375°F., mark 5)

Allow 1 bird per person. Pluck and singe the birds. Don't draw them, but skin the head and neck and remove the eyes before trussing. Cover each bird all over with softened butter, then put it on a round of toast. Cover the breasts with rashers of fat bacon and roast in the centre of the oven for 15–20 minutes. Serve the birds on the toast, garnished with lemon and watercress. Thin gravy, fried crumbs and game chips (or if preferred, a salad) are the usual accompaniments. (see Chapter 10, page 139.)

ROAST STUFFED HARE

A young hare	½ pint water or stock
Fat bacon	Bread sauce (see Chapter 10,
Dripping for basting	p. 139)
¼ oz. flour	

For the Stuffing

4 oz. fresh white bread-crumbs	1 tsp. dried thyme
	A squeeze of lemon juice
2 oz. chopped suet	Salt and pepper
2 tsps. chopped parsley	A few drops of piquant sauce
Grated lemon rind	Egg or milk to mix

Oven temperature: moderate (350°F., mark 4)

Prepare the hare in the usual way. Wash the heart, liver and kidneys, put into cold water and bring to boiling point, then strain, discarding the water. Chop finely and put into a large basin with the other stuffing ingredients, mix thoroughly and stir in beaten egg or milk to blend. Stuff the cavity in the hare with this forcemeat and sew up, leaving a fairly long thread at each end. Cut the sinews in the hind legs at the thigh, bring the legs forward and press closely against the body: the fore-legs must be bent back in the same way. Use 2 fine metal skewers to keep them in position, or if preferred, a trussing needle and string. The head must be raised – in order to keep it in position, put a skewer through the mouth and fix down on to the back. The hare is much improved in appearance and flavour if some fat bacon is tied on the back and the whole hare is completely covered with greased paper during the cooking time.

The average time taken to cook the hare is 1½–2 hours, and it should be basted every 15 minutes. Fifteen minutes before it is ready, remove the paper and bacon, baste and allow to brown, then lift it on to a hot dish and take out the skewers and string. Drain away the surplus fat and add the flour, brown it, then add about ½ pint stock or water to make a thick gravy; boil for 5 minutes and strain this round the hare. Serve with bread sauce.

ROAST SADDLE OR BARON OF HARE
Oven temperature: moderate (350°F., mark 4)
Very young hares may be roasted whole, but for larger hares the body alone is used, being known as saddle or baron of hare. Cut off the saddle close to the shoulders. (Reserve the rest of the hare to jug or make into soup.) Prepare some veal forcemeat (see Chapter 10, page 139). If liked, the heart, liver and kidneys may be added to the forcemeat; wash them well, put into a pan of cold water, bring to boiling point, strain and chop finely. Stuff the hare, fold the skin over and sew in position. Lay slices of fat bacon over the back, cover with greased greaseproof paper, put in a tin with some knobs of dripping and roast in the centre of the oven for 1½–2 hours, according to size. Baste frequently, as the flesh is apt to be dry. Fifteen minutes before the cooking is completed, remove the paper and bacon, baste the hare and allow to brown. Remove the skewers and string before dishing up. Serve with thick gravy and red-currant (or guava) jelly.

ROAST VENISON
Oven temperature: warm (325°F., mark 3)
The best joint for roasting is the saddle, but for a smaller piece use the loin or a fillet cut from the saddle. The custom used to be to cover the joint with a paste made by mixing flour and water to a stiff dough (allow about 3 lb. flour to a saddle) and rolling it out to ½ inch in thickness, but nowadays the meat is usually brushed generously with melted fat or oil and loosely wrapped in foil. Roast in the centre of the oven, allowing 25 minutes to the lb.; 20 minutes before the cooking is completed, remove the foil or the paste, dredge the joint with flour and return it to the oven to brown. Serve hot, with a thickened gravy and red-currant or cranberry jelly.

CHAPTER 3

Casseroles, hot-pots, stews, fricassees

The great majority of poultry recipes probably come into this category, but many of them of course are variations on a basic theme. Boiled chicken, though not strictly speaking a casserole dish, is also included in this chapter.

The number of servings given by a casserole dish is fairly elastic especially when a whole chicken (or other bird) is used as base. In general, these recipes serve at least 4 people, unless otherwise stated.

Note: For method of cooking rice, and for accompaniments, see Chapter 10, page 139.

HERBS FOR FLAVOURING
Many of these recipes suggest flavouring the liquor or sauce with a bouquet garni – a small bunch of herbs tied together in muslin or with a thread round the stalks. Here are two versions:

TRADITIONAL BOUQUET GARNI

A bay leaf
A sprig of parsley
A sprig of thyme
A few peppercorns (optional)

tied with a small piece of leek leaf; if peppercorns are included use muslin – see below

You can of course choose other herbs, or include some dried ones – mixed or otherwise.

BOUQUET GARNI USING DRIED HERBS

A small bay leaf
A pinch of mixed dried
  herbs
6 peppercorns

1 clove
A pinch of dried
  parsley

Tie the herbs together in a small square of muslin with a string

24

or cotton, leaving a long end free to tie the bouquet garni to the handle of the saucepan.

CASSEROLE OF CHICKEN

2 medium-sized onions, skinned and sliced	1 tbsp. oil
2 sticks of celery, scrubbed and chopped	1 oz. butter
	4 chicken joints
¼ lb. mushrooms, washed and sliced	3 level tbsps. flour
	¾ pint chicken stock
2 oz. bacon, rinded and chopped	A 15-oz. can of tomatoes
	Salt and pepper

Oven temperature: moderate (350°F., mark 4)

Lightly fry the onions, celery, mushrooms and bacon in the oil and butter for about 5 minutes, until golden brown. Remove from the pan with a slotted spoon and line the bottom of the casserole with the vegetables. Fry the chicken joints in the oil and butter for 5 minutes, until golden brown. Put the chicken in the casserole on the bed of vegetables. Stir the flour into the remaining fat and cook for 2–3 minutes; gradually stir in the stock and bring to the boil. Continue to stir until the mixture thickens and add the tomatoes, with salt and pepper to taste. Pour this sauce over the chicken joints, cover and cook in the centre of the oven for ¾–1 hour, until the chicken is tender.

CASSEROLED CHICKEN AND RICE

6–8 oz. long-grain rice	½ pint chicken stock or soup
A 4-lb. boiling chicken, jointed and skinned	2–3 tbsps. white wine (optional)
1 pimiento, sliced	3 cloves
2 sticks of celery, scrubbed and chopped	1 bay leaf
	Salt and pepper

Oven temperature: moderate (350°F., mark 4)

Par-boil the rice for 5 minutes, then put alternate layers of rice, chicken, pimiento and celery in a greased ovenproof dish. Heat together the stock, wine, cloves and bay leaf and pour over the chicken. Check the seasoning. Cover with a lid and cook in the centre of the oven for 2½ hours. (Serves 6–8.)

CHICKEN À LA CRÈME

A roasting chicken, jointed	3 level tbsps. flour
2 small onions, skinned and sliced	¼ pint dry white wine
	¼ pint stock
1 oz. butter	A bouquet garni
1 tbsp. oil	¼ pint single cream
Salt and pepper	

Fry the chicken joints and onion slices in the butter and oil for about 5 minutes, until a light golden brown. Season the chicken with salt and pepper, cover and continue to cook slowly until tender, turning the pieces once – about 20 minutes. Remove the chicken and onion from the pan. Stir the flour into the fat remaining in the pan and cook for 2–3 minutes. Gradually stir in the wine and stock, bring to the boil and continue to stir until the sauce thickens. Add the bouquet garni, return the chicken joints and onions to the sauce and simmer for a further 10–15 minutes. Remove the bouquet garni and place the chicken on a serving dish. Add a little of the sauce to the cream and blend to a smooth mixture; return the blended mixture to the pan and re-heat without boiling. Pour the sauce over the chicken joints.

CHICKEN BOURGUIGNONNE

A chicken
Butter for frying
3–4 button onions, skinned
3 rashers of bacon, rinded and diced
A bouquet garni

Salt and pepper
1 glass of red Burgundy
2 oz. mushrooms, washed and sliced
Mashed potatoes

Joint the chicken, put it in the butter with the onions and diced bacon and fry until brown. Add the bouquet garni, salt, pepper and wine, cover with a lid and simmer gently until the chicken is tender – about 30 minutes. Meanwhile fry the mushrooms; 10 minutes before the end of the cooking time remove the bouquet garni and add the mushrooms. Serve in a border of mashed potato.

CHICKEN CHEESE

4 joints of chicken
4 oz. butter
A small piece of onion, skinned and chopped
A pinch of dried thyme
$\frac{1}{4}$ pint stock
3 level tbsps. cornflour

$\frac{1}{4}$ pint dry cider
2–3 tbsps. single cream
4 oz. strong Cheddar cheese, grated
Salt and pepper
2 level tsps. mild mustard

Fry the chicken joints in the hot butter, turning them frequently, until tender – about 20 minutes. Remove them, put into an ovenproof dish and keep hot. Meanwhile simmer the onion with a good pinch of thyme in the stock until tender – about 10 minutes. Strain the stock and return it to the pan. Blend the cornflour with a little cold water; add a little of the hot stock and mix, then return the mixture to the pan. Bring to the boil, stirring all the time, and stir in the cider. Remove the pan from the heat and stir in the cream, half the cheese and the seasonings. Pour the sauce over the chicken portions, sprinkle with the remaining cheese and grill under a very hot grill until golden brown.

CHICKEN CHASSEUR

4 joints of chicken
1 level tbsp. seasoned flour
1 tbsp. oil
1 oz. butter
1 onion, skinned and chopped
2 oz. mushrooms, washed and
   sliced

2 tomatoes, skinned, seeded
   and diced
¼ pint Espagnole sauce
2 tbsps. white wine
Salt and pepper
Chopped parsley

Oven temperature: moderate (350°F., mark 4)

Coat the chicken joints in seasoned flour and fry in the oil and butter for about 5 minutes, until golden brown. Remove the chicken joints from the pan and put into a casserole. Fry the onion and mushrooms in the oil and butter for 5 minutes, until golden brown; add the tomatoes, Espagnole sauce (see Chapter 10, page 139), wine, seasoning and pour over the chicken joints. Cover and cook in the centre of the oven for ¾–1 hour, until tender. Place the chicken joints on a serving dish, pour the sauce over them and sprinkle with parsley.

CHICKEN EVERGLADES

4 chicken joints
1 oz. butter
1 tbsp. oil
4 slices of ham
¼ lb. mushrooms, washed and
   sliced
A small pkt. of frozen peas

1 clove of garlic, skinned
   and crushed
3 level tbsps. flour
¼ bottle of white wine
¼ pint stock or water
Salt and pepper

Fry the chicken joints in the butter and oil for about 5 minutes, until golden brown. Put them in a casserole and cover each with a slice of ham. Fry the mushrooms in the oil and butter for about 5 minutes, remove from the pan and add to the casserole, with the peas and crushed garlic. Stir the flour into the fat remaining in the pan and cook for 2–3 minutes. Stir in the wine and stock or water gradually, bring to the boil and stir until it thickens; season with salt and pepper and pour over the chicken joints. Cover and cook in the centre of the oven for ¾–1 hour, until the chicken joints are tender.

CHICKEN FRICASSEE

A 2½-lb. boiling chicken,
   jointed
2 medium-sized onions,
   skinned and finely chopped
2 carrots, peeled and finely
   sliced
¼ lb. mushrooms, washed and
   sliced
A bouquet garni

Salt and pepper
2 oz. butter
2 oz. flour
4 rashers of streaky bacon,
   rinded and rolled
1 egg yolk
3 tbsps. single cream
Juice of ½ a lemon
Chopped parsley to garnish

Place the chicken joints, vegetables, just enough water to cover and the bouquet garni in a large saucepan. Add salt and pepper and bring slowly to the boil; simmer gently for 1 hour, or until the chicken is tender. When the chicken is cooked, remove it from the heat, strain off the stock and put it on one side. Remove the chicken meat from the bones and cut it into cubes. Melt the butter, stir in the flour, cook for 2–3 minutes and remove from the heat. Measure off 1 pint of the strained stock, gradually stir it into the roux, bring to the boil and continue to stir until the sauce thickens. Add the meat and vegetables and heat through for about 2 minutes. Grill the bacon rolls. Blend together the egg yolk and cream, add a little of the sauce to the mixture and blend to a smooth cream. Return the blended mixture to the sauce and heat through gently, without boiling. Add the lemon juice. Pour the fricassee into a serving dish and garnish with the bacon rolls and chopped parsley.

CHICKEN JAMBALAYA

½ a cooked chicken
2 onions, skinned and sliced
1 green pepper, seeded and chopped
2 sticks of celery, scrubbed and sliced
2 tbsps. oil
¼ lb. mushrooms, washed and sliced

¾ lb. tomatoes, skinned and quartered
¼ pint chicken stock
¼ pint dry white wine (optional)
6 oz. long-grain rice
¼ lb. ham, chopped
Salt
Pepper

Cut the chicken flesh into cubes. Sauté the onions, pepper and celery in the oil until they are golden brown. Add the mushrooms, tomatoes, stock, wine and rice and cook gently on top of the stove until the rice is tender (15–20 minutes). Add the chicken and ham and heat through. Season to taste.

CHICKEN LOUISETTE

4 chicken joints
1 tbsp. oil
2 oz. butter
1 onion, skinned and sliced
1 clove of garlic, skinned
1 oz. flour
¼ pint stock
¼ pint medium white wine

A bouquet garni
½ a cucumber, peeled and sliced
2 oz. ham, chopped
Salt and pepper
2 egg yolks
3 tbsps. single cream

Sauté the chicken joints in the oil and 1 oz. of the butter until they are golden brown, then remove from the pan. Add the onion and garlic to the fat and continue to brown. Sprinkle on the flour and cook for 1 minute. Gradually add the stock and wine, bring to the boil and cook until thickened. Replace the chicken joints, add the bouquet garni and simmer on top of the stove for 20–30 minutes. Cook the cucumber in the remaining butter. Add the ham and seasoning and simmer for a further 4–5 minutes. When the chicken joints are tender strain off the liquor. Mix the egg yolks and cream and add a little of the chicken liquor to blend. Add this mixture and the remaining chicken liquor to the pan containing the cucumber and ham and heat very gently until the sauce thickens. Place the chicken joints on a serving dish and pour the sauce over.

As a variation, mushrooms may replace the cucumber.

CHICKEN MARENGO

4 chicken joints
3–4 tbsps. oil
2 carrots, peeled and sliced
1 stick of celery, scrubbed and chopped
1 onion, skinned and chopped
2 oz. streaky bacon, rinded and chopped
3 level tbsps. flour

½ pint chicken stock
A 15-oz. can of tomatoes
2 tbsps. sherry
Salt and pepper
A bouquet garni
¼ lb. mushrooms, washed and sliced
Chopped parsley

Oven temperature: moderate (350°F., mark 4)

Fry the chicken joints in the oil for about 5 minutes, until golden brown, remove them from the pan and put into a casserole. Fry the vegetables and bacon in the oil for about 5 minutes until golden brown; remove them from the pan. Stir the flour into the remaining fat, cook for 2–3 minutes and gradually stir in the stock; bring to the boil and continue to stir until it thickens. Return the vegetables to the pan and add the tomatoes, sherry, salt and pepper. Pour this sauce over the chicken joints, add the bouquet garni and sliced mushrooms and cook in the centre of the oven for ¾–1 hour, until the chicken joints are tender. Remove them to a warm serving dish. Strain the sauce from the casserole over them and sprinkle with chopped parsley.

CHICKEN POACHED IN TOMATO

A chicken
A little flour
Fat for frying
12 small onions, skinned and sliced

2 sticks of celery, sliced
2–3 carrots, peeled and sliced
Salt and pepper
½ pint tomato purée

Joint the chicken, dredge the pieces with flour and sauté in the hot fat until well browned all over. Pour away the fat and add the onions, celery, carrots, salt, pepper and tomato purée. Simmer gently for ¾–1 hour, until the chicken is tender, and serve with dry boiled rice.

29

CHICKEN POACHED IN WHITE WINE

A chicken
A bay leaf
Parsley
White wine to cover
2 oz. butter

2 oz. flour
Salt
1 tbsp. cream or
top of the milk

Cut the chicken into joints and put these into a shallow sauce-pan. Add a bay leaf and a sprig of parsley. Pour in enough white wine to cover the chicken almost entirely. Simmer very gently for 40 minutes, until the chicken is tender, then lift out the chicken, drain it and place in a serving dish. Make a sauce as follows: Melt the butter, add the flour and gradually stir in 1 pint of the strained wine; add salt, bring to the boil and add the cream or top of the milk. Pour this over the bird and serve at once.

CHICKEN RICE WITH PIMIENTOS

A chicken
Dripping
2 onions, skinned and sliced
Stock or water
A piece of orange peel
2 red peppers (pimientos),
seeded and chopped

1 lb. tomatoes, skinned and
chopped
1 clove of garlic, skinned
and crushed
Salt and pepper
A pinch of herbs
6 oz. long-grain rice

Brown the chicken in the dripping with the sliced onions; when it is golden brown all over, add stock to cover, with the orange peel, and simmer until tender – about 40 minutes. Add the peppers and tomatoes to the hot fat, season with the garlic juice, salt, pepper and herbs, and cook till tender. Boil the rice in some of the chicken stock, drain and put on a dish. Carve the chicken, arrange on the rice and cover the surrounding rice with the tomatoes and peppers.

CHICKEN PILAU

1 oz. butter
1 onion, skinned and
sliced
1 clove of garlic, skinned and
crushed (optional)
4 rashers of streaky bacon,
rinded and chopped
An 8-oz. can of tomatoes,
drained (or 4 tomatoes,
skinned and sliced)

6–8 oz. long-grain rice
1 tbsp. currants (optional)
1–1¼ pints stock (from a
bouillon cube)
8 oz. cooked chicken meat –
use ½ a cooked chicken
1 tbsp. parsley, chopped
1 tbsp. lemon juice
Salt and pepper

Melt the butter and fry the onion, garlic and bacon for 5 minutes. Add the tomatoes and the rice and continue cooking until the rice is transparent. Add the currants and stock and simmer uncovered for about 10 minutes. Add the cut-up chicken and cook for a further 10–20 minutes, or until the liquid is absorbed and the rice tender. Stir in the parsley and lemon juice, check the seasoning and serve at once.

CHICKEN RISOTTO

Left-over cooked chicken
A bouquet garni
Salt and pepper
1½ pints chicken stock
2–3 onions, skinned
4 oz. mushrooms, washed
1½ oz. dripping
8 oz. long-grain rice
4 bananas
Fat for frying
Grated cheese

Cut the chicken flesh into neat pieces and boil the bones with the bouquet garni, seasoning and water to make the stock. Cut up the onions and half the mushrooms and fry in the dripping, then add the rice and fry until it is opaque. Add the boiling stock and some salt and cook gently until the liquor is absorbed and the rice tender; do not stir while it is cooking, but if necessary fork it gently. Lay the chicken on top of the rice for about 10 minutes, to heat through. Fry the remaining mushrooms and the bananas for a garnish. Put the rice and chicken on a heatproof dish, sprinkle with cheese and brown under the grill. Serve with green salad.

CHICKEN SOUS LA CLOCHE

1 small chicken, drawn
and trussed
¼ pint white wine
¼ pint chicken stock
4 oz. mushrooms, sliced
Salt and pepper
A bay leaf
1½ oz. butter
1½ oz. flour
½ pint milk
Cooked asparagus tips
(fresh or cannd)

Oven temperature: moderate (350°F., mark 4)

Place the chicken in a casserole and add the wine, stock, mushrooms, a little salt and a bay leaf. Cover and cook in the centre of the oven for about 1¼ hours, or until tender. Drain off the liquid – it should make about ½ pint – and retain the mushrooms. Melt the butter, add the flour, stir over a low heat for 1–2 minutes to make a roux. then gradually stir in the milk and the chicken liquid. Bring to the boil, season well and add the asparagus and mushrooms. Boil for 2–3 minutes and pour over the chicken (after removing the strings).

CHICKEN STEW

A 4-lb. chicken
2 onions, skinned and chopped
1 oz. lard
1 level tsp. paprika pepper
½ pint stock or water
Salt and pepper
2 green peppers, seeded and
sliced
4 tomatoes, skinned
¼ pint sour cream
¼ pint milk
1 oz. flour

31

Cut up the chicken, reserving the liver and the gizzard, and wash the pieces in cold water. Fry the onions until golden brown in the hot lard. Sprinkle the paprika pepper over the onions, stir, add the stock or water and bring to the boil. Add the chicken, the sliced liver, the partially cooked gizzard, cut into pieces, and a little salt. Cover the pan and simmer until the chicken is almost tender. Now add the green peppers and tomatoes, and continue to cook until the chicken is quite tender. Mix the sour cream with the milk and blend with the flour; add this thickening to the chicken stew and bring to the boil. Season to taste before serving. (Serves 6–8.)

CHICKEN AND WALNUTS – 1

A 3½–4 lb. roasting chicken, jointed	A 6-oz. can of water chestnuts, drained and diced (optional)
2 tbsps. sherry	1 pint chicken stock
2 level tsps. caster sugar	2 level tbsps. cornflour
3 tbsps. oil	4 oz. halved walnuts
8 oz. button mushrooms, washed and sliced	1 oz. butter

Oven temperature: moderate (350°F., mark 4)

Place the chicken in a dish, pour the sherry and caster sugar over it and leave it to marinade for 1–2 hours. Heat the oil in a frying pan and brown the drained chicken pieces. Place the mushrooms and the chestnuts in a large casserole. Arrange the chicken pieces on top, pour the chicken juices and chicken stock into the casserole, cover and bake in the centre of the oven for 2 hours. Drain off the liquor, keep the chicken hot and thicken the liquor with the cornflour. Brown the walnuts in melted butter for 4–5 minutes and drain. Dish up the chicken and vegetables, pour some of the gravy over them (serving the rest separately) and garnish with the browned walnuts. (Serves 7–8.)

CHICKEN AND WALNUTS – 2

1 small cauliflower	¼ lb. mushrooms, halved
2 oz. shelled walnuts, quartered	½ lb. cooked chicken
4 oz. butter	2 level tbsps. flour
1 large onion, skinned and sliced	¾ pint chicken stock
	1 level tsp. yeast extract
	Salt and pepper

Prepare the cauliflower and divide into sprigs. Fry the nuts in the fat until light brown and crisp, then drain. Gently fry the cauliflower sprigs, onion and mushrooms until tender – 15–20 minutes – then add the chicken, cut into small pieces. Mix the flour with about 2 tbsps. stock and add to the vegetables, with the remaining stock, yeast extract and seasoning. Bring to the boil, simmer for about 10 minutes and just before serving, add the nuts. Serve with boiled rice. (Serves 3–4.)

CHICKEN WITH ALMONDS

4 chicken joints
2 oz. butter
1 tbsp. oil
2 onions, skinned and sliced
3 tomatoes, skinned and chopped
¾ pint stock (made from a bouillon cube)
A pinch of ground cinnamon
Salt and pepper
2 oz. blanched almonds, chopped or slivered
2 oz. sultanas
6–8 oz. long-grain rice, boiled
Parsley

Wipe and trim the chicken joints and fry in the butter and oil until they are browned on all sides. Add the onions and tomatoes and fry for a further 5 minutes, shaking the pan so they do not stick to the bottom. Add the stock, pinch of cinnamon and seasoning. Cover with a lid or large plate and simmer for about 20 minutes. Add the almonds and sultanas and continue cooking for a further 15–20 minutes. Serve with a border of boiled rice and decorate with parsley.

CHICKEN WITH NOODLES (CHINESE)

4 oz. fine egg noodles
4 oz. cooked chicken
3 sticks of celery
2 oz. mushrooms
2 oz. bean sprouts
2 tbsps. oil
½ pint chicken stock
1½ level tbsps. cornflour
2 tbsps. water
2 tbsps. soy sauce
Salt and pepper

Boil the noodles in a generous amount of water for 10 minutes; turn them into a colander, rinse in cold water and leave to drain. Cut the chicken and vegetables into shreds. Heat the oil in a pan, add the shredded vegetables and toss and cook for a minute. Add the chicken and toss for another minute. Add the stock, stir well, cover the pan, turn down the heat and simmer for 10 minutes. Add the cornflour, mixed to a paste with water and soy sauce, and stir continuously until the sauce is smooth and thick. Season to taste, then stir in the noodles; when the mixture is very hot, turn it into a deep dish. (Serves 2–3.)

CHICKEN WITH MUSHROOMS (CHINESE)

A 3-lb. chicken
1 tbsp. soy sauce
15 dried mushrooms, soaked
1 medium-sized bamboo shoot
2 water chestnuts
Oil for deep frying
5 slices of fresh ginger
1 level tsp. salt
1 pint water
½ level tsp. sugar
⅛ level tsp. pepper
2 onion stalks, cut into 1-inch pieces
2 level tsps. cornflour blended with 3 tbsps cold water

Halve the chicken and rub inside and out with soy sauce. Slice the mushrooms, bamboo shoot and water chestnuts into shreds. Put about 1 inch oil into a deep frying-pan and when it is very hot fry the chicken on each side for 2 minutes; drain the chicken and set aside. Drain off the oil. In the oily pan sauté the ginger with the salt for 1 minute; add the water, mushrooms, water chestnuts, bamboo shoot, sugar, pepper and onion stalks. Place the chicken in this mixture, cover, lower the heat and simmer for 15 minutes. Remove the chicken, chop into pieces 1½ inches by 1 inch and arrange on a serving dish. Stir the blended cornflour into the gravy and when it is clear and thick pour the whole mixture over the chicken and serve at once. (Serves 5–6.)

CHICKEN AND PORK WITH RICE (SPANISH)

A chicken
½ lb. lean pork
¼ pint olive oil
2 large onions, skinned
    and chopped
2 cloves of garlic, skinned
    and chopped

8–12 oz. long-grain rice
3 tomatoes
2 red peppers
1½ pints stock
A pinch of saffron
½ gill sherry

Oven temperature: moderate (350°F., mark 4)
Cut the chicken into neat joints and the pork into small pieces. Heat the olive oil in a shallow frying-pan and fry the chicken and pork until they are golden brown; then remove them and put them in a casserole. Fry the onion and garlic in the olive oil until they are lightly browned, taking care that the fat does not become too hot. Add the rice and cook for 2 minutes, then add the sliced tomatoes and red peppers and cook for another 2 minutes. Pour this mixture over the chicken in the casserole, add the boiling stock, saffron and sherry and cook in the centre of the oven or simmer over a gentle heat until cooked – about 1 hour. (Serves 6.)

COQ AU VIN

3 oz. bacon, rinded and
    chopped
6 oz. mushrooms, washed
    and sliced
15 button onions, skinned
    and sliced
½ oz. butter
1 tbsps. oil
A small roasting chicken

4 tbsps. brandy
3 level tbsps. flour
½ bottle red wine
¼ pint stock
1 level tbsp. sugar
A bouquet garni
A pinch of ground nutmeg
Salt and pepper

Oven temperature; moderate (350°F., mark 4)
Fry the bacon, mushrooms and onions in the butter and oil for about 3–4 minutes, until lightly browned; remove from

the pan. Fry the chicken on its breast and underside for 8–10 minutes, until golden brown. Pour the brandy over the chicken, remove the pan from the heat and "flame" it by igniting the liquid in the saucepan with a match. Remove the chicken from the pan when the flames have died down and place it in a casserole. Stir the flour into the fat remaining in the pan and cook for 2–3 minutes. Stir in the wine and stock gradually, bring to the boil and continue to stir until the mixture thickens; add the sugar, herbs and seasonings. Add the cooked vegetables to the casserole and pour the sauce over the chicken. Cover and cook in the centre of the oven for ¾–1 hour, until tender. Before serving, remove the bouquet garni.

PINEAPPLE CHICKEN CASSEROLE

A chicken (jointed) or 4 chicken joints	An 8-oz. can of pineapple chunks
1 oz. seasoned flour	2 thin slices of lemon
2 oz. butter	4 oz. blanched almonds, chopped and toasted
¼ pint stock and pineapple juice	

Oven temperature: moderate (350°F., mark 4)

Trim the chicken and dredge it with seasoned flour. Melt the butter and brown the chicken well on all sides. Place it in a casserole with the stock and pineapple juice, cover and bake for about ½ hour in the centre of the oven. Remove from the oven and add the pineapple and lemon. Cover and replace in the oven for another 15 minutes; test for tenderness. Sprinkle the almonds over the chicken and cook uncovered for 5 minutes, until lightly browned.

SWEET-SOUR CHICKEN (CHINESE)

1 oz. fat	1 onion, skinned
2 cloves of garlic, skinned and crushed	¼ pint (approx. a 6-oz. can) of condensed chicken soup
1 chicken breast, sliced	1 level tbsp. flour
4 chicken livers, quartered	2 level tbsps. sugar
2 carrots, peeled	3 tbsps. soy sauce
1 cucumber, peeled	3 tbsps. vinegar
2 tomatoes, skinned	

Heat the fat and sauté the crushed garlic until browned. Add the chicken breast and livers. Slice the carrots into ½-inch slices. Split the cucumber lengthwise and cut into pieces ⅛ inch thick. Cut the tomatoes into eighths and the onion in ¼-inch wedges. Add to the meat mixture with the soup, cover and simmer until tender – about 20–30 minutes. Blend the remaining ingredients and pour over the chicken mixture, then cook for 2–3 minutes. Serve in a bowl, with rice and noodles. (Serves 3–4.)

CHICKEN CHOP SUEY (U.S.A.)

A 3½–4½ lb. ready-to-cook
  chicken, cut up
2½ pints boiling water
3 chicken bouillon cubes
6 oz. long-grain rice
6 whole black peppercorns
8 oz. celery, sliced

1 medium-sized onion,
  skinned and sliced
2 tbsps. soy sauce
A 1-lb. can of bean sprouts,
  drained and rinsed in cold
  water
3 level tbsps. cornflour

The day before the Chop Suey is required, put the chicken in a pan with the water and bouillon cubes, cover and simmer for 2–3 hours, or until fork-tender, then cool quickly. Cut the meat from the bones and refrigerate the meat and the broth.

About ½ hour before serving, cook the rice and keep it hot. Measure the broth (there should be 2–2¼ pints) and reserve ½ pint of it. To the rest of the broth add the peppercorns, celery and onion and cook, uncovered, until the vegetables are tender but still crunchy – about 10 minutes. Add the soy sauce, chicken and bean sprouts. Cook for 3–4 minutes. Mix the cornflour with the remaining ½ pint broth, add to the chicken mixture and cook, stirring, until smooth and slightly thickened. Serve at once on hot rice. (Serves 8.)

To vary, replace the chicken by turkey or 3–4 cups cooked veal or pork, in thin strips.

CHOW-MEIN STYLE: Serve the chicken on a deep heated platter, garnished with cooked spring onions. Substitute canned Chow Mein noodles for the rice.

Note: Chop Suey, an American adaptation of Chinese food, was originally devised on the Pacific sea-board.

CHICKEN IN ORANGE SAUCE
(see colour picture No. 4)

4 frozen chicken joints
Seasoned flour
2 oz. butter or
  margarine
2 tbsps. cooking oil
½ pint chicken stock (made
  from a bouillon cube)

Juice and grated rind of 1
  large orange
1 tbsp. lemon juice
1 level tbsp. flour
¼ lb. white grapes, skinned
  and seeded
Salt and pepper

Thaw the chicken and wipe it dry, then toss it in the seasoned flour. Heat 1 oz. of the fat with the oil in a saucepan; brown the chicken evenly and drain the pieces. Pour off any surplus fat and wipe out the pan. Replace the chicken in the pan, add the stock, grated orange rind and fruit juices and bring to the boil. Cover the pan and simmer for 40–50 minutes, until the chicken is tender. Place the chicken on a serving dish and keep warm. Soften the remaining butter and blend with the flour to a paste. Whisk into the chicken liquor, a small amount at a time. Bring the liquor to the boil and stir until thickened – about 3 minutes. Add the grapes and check the seasoning. Pour over the chicken.

BRAISED CHICKEN

A boiling fowl
Dripping
2 rashers of bacon
1 carrot
1 onion
2 sticks of celery
A piece of turnip

A bouquet garni
Salt and pepper
¾ pint stock
1 oz. flour
Fried mushrooms and
    watercress to garnish

Oven temperature: fairly hot (400°F., mark 6)
Joint the fowl, cut into convenient-sized portions and fry until brown in a little dripping. Prepare and dice the bacon, carrot, onion, celery and turnip and put at the bottom of a stewpan or casserole. Add the bouquet garni and the fried pieces of chicken. Season and add the stock, which should just cover the chicken. Cover and cook until tender in the centre of the oven or on top of the stove; this will take about 1½–2 hours. Remove the pieces of chicken and keep them hot. Strain the liquor and thicken with the flour blended with a little cold water. Mound the vegetables on a hot dish and arrange the chicken on top, pour the sauce over and garnish the dish with fried mushrooms and watercress sprigs.

MEXICAN-STYLE CHICKEN WITH RICE
(see colour picture No. 4)

4 chicken joints, fresh or
    frozen (thawed)
2 level tbsps. seasoned
    flour
4 tbsps. cooking oil
1 medium-sized onion, skinned
    and finely chopped
A 16-oz. can of peeled
    tomatoes

A 6-oz. can of pimientos,
    diced
2 chicken stock tablets
8 stoned olives
6 oz. long-grain rice
½ lb. sausages
Salt and pepper
A small pkt. of frozen
    peas

Thaw the chicken and wipe dry, then toss in seasoned flour, Heat the oil in a 6–7 pint saucepan and brown the chicken joints evenly; keep them warm. Add the onion to the pan and brown lightly. Drain the tomatoes and make the juice up to ¾ pint with water. Add the tomatoes, liquid, pimientos, crumbled stock tablets, olives, rice and the sausages, cut in ½-inch slices. Stir well and season. Arrange the chicken on top, cover and simmer for 30 minutes, stirring the rice once or twice with a fork to prevent sticking. Check the seasoning, add the peas and simmer for a further 15 minutes.

PAELLA

6–8 mussels. fresh or bottled
2–4 oz. Dublin Bay prawns
  (or frozen scampi)
1 small cooked lobster
1 small chicken
4 tbsps. olive oil
1 onion, skinned and chopped
1 green pepper, seeded
  and chopped

1 clove of garlic, skinned
4 tomatoes, skinned and
  chopped
8–12 oz. long-grain rice
2–3 pints chicken stock
  (made from a cube)
Salt and pepper
A little powdered saffron
A small pkt. of frozen peas

This famous Spanish dish takes its name from the pan in which it is cooked – a shallow oval metal dish with handles at each side. There are few hard-and-fast rules about making a paella, although the following ingredients are traditionally included – chicken, lobster, shellfish of various kinds, onion, green or red peppers and rice. Paella is rather elaborate and somewhat expensive to prepare in this country, but it makes an attractive party dish.

Shell or drain the mussels and peel the prawns, if fresh. Remove the lobster meat from the shell and dice it, retaining the claws for decorating. Cut the meat from the chicken into small pieces. Put the oil into a large paella or frying-pan and fry the onion, green pepper and crushed garlic for 5 minutes, until soft but not browned. Add the tomatoes and chicken pieces and fry until the chicken is lightly browned. Stir in the rice and add half the stock, the seasoning and saffron (blended with a little of the stock). Bring to the boil, then reduce the heat and simmer for about 20–25 minutes, until the chicken is tender and the rice just cooked. Stir in the mussels, prawns, lobster meat and peas and simmer for a final 5–10 minutes, until heated through. Serve garnished with a few extra strips of green pepper or pimiento and the lobster claws. Mussels in their shells can also be used as a garnish. (Serves 6–8.)

CURRY OF COLD ROAST CHICKEN
(see colour picture No. 5)

Cut the cold chicken into neat pieces, removing all bone, gristle, etc. Make a curry sauce (see Chapter 10, page 139), add the chicken and heat gently for a few minutes, but without boiling, until the chicken is thoroughly hot. Stir in a little cream if you have some and check the seasoning. Serve in a border of boiled rice, either on individual plates as seen in the picture, or on a large dish. Serve with side dishes chosen from those pictured – sliced tomato, sliced banana, rings of red and green peppers, sliced hard-boiled egg, gherkins, chutney, pickles and relishes, sliced or grated fresh coconut garnished with chopped green and red peppers.

CHICKEN CURRY

12 oz. long-grain rice
2 lb. chicken, jointed
1 clove of garlic, skinned
1 oz. whole coriander
3 onions, skinned and halved
2 level tsps. salt
¾ lb. butter or margarine
½ oz. whole black peppercorns

½ oz. whole cumin seed
3 oz. sultanas
3 oz. raisins, seeded
1 grain of saffron mixed with
  2 tsps. water
2 oz. almonds, browned and
  salted

Wash the rice and leave it in water for at least 3–4 hours before cooking. Boil the chicken in about 1¼ pints water with the garlic, coriander seeds (tied in muslin), onions and salt, until fairly tender – about 2 hours – then remove from the pan. Strain the broth and measure it; if less than 2 pints, make up with water.

Put the butter or margarine into a large saucepan, chop and add the cooked onions and fry gently over a low heat until brown; add ½ pint water and continue to cook until this evaporates. Add the chicken and fry for a short time, add the peppercorns and cumin seeds and fry these for 2–3 minutes. Add the chicken broth and let it boil, then add the rice and sultanas and half the raisins, mix well and sprinkle in the saffron. Cover tightly and cook over a very low heat until the water has completely evaporated. Pile in a dish and garnish with the remaining raisins and the almonds. (Serves 4–5.)

CHICKEN "DOPYAZA"

2 lb. chicken joints, skinned
1 level tsp. ground ginger
1 level tsp. salt
2 lb. onions, skinned
1 clove of garlic, skinned and
  crushed
5 level tbsps. ghee or butter

Seeds of 1 cardamon
1 level tbsp. ground turmeric
1½ level tbsps. ground cumin
1 level tbsp. ground coriander
¾ pint yoghourt
½ pint water
8 peppercorns

Oven temperature: warm (325°F., mark 3)

If possible, use an enamelled iron casserole. Wipe the chicken joints, prick with a fine skewer, rub in the ginger and salt and leave for 30 minutes. Roughly chop 1 lb. of the onions. Fry in the fat until evenly browned, then add the garlic; remove the onion and drain it. Cook the cardamon seeds in the fat for 1 minute. Place the chicken in the fat with the turmeric, cumin, coriander and yoghourt and cook until the yoghourt is almost absorbed. Pound the cooked onions (or pulp them in an electric liquidiser), add the water and pour over the chicken joints. Slice the rest of the onions thinly, put on top with the peppercorns, cover the pan tightly and cook towards the bottom of the oven for 1 hour. Serve with rice. (Serves 4–5.)

The name *dopyaza* means "twice onion" and as a general

rule in these curries onions should be added in two different forms at two stages of the cooking, as in this recipe. However, a number of authentic recipes do not follow this method.

BOILED CHICKEN

Prepare the bird as described in the Supplement, page 163. Tie the legs together and fold the wings under the body. Rub the bird over with lemon juice to preserve the colour, put it in a large pan and just cover with cold water; add a little salt, an onion stuck with 3–4 cloves, a carrot and a bouquet garni. Bring to the boil and simmer for 3–4 hours if the bird is a genuine boiling fowl; for the usual chicken, 45 minutes is enough. Drain the bird and keep it hot while making a parsley, egg or white sauce with ½ pint of the chicken stock and ½ pint milk. Serve the chicken coated with the sauce.

Many people like to serve boiled ham as an accompaniment, to give extra flavour.

Alternatively, the bird may be served cold, either whole and coated with a chaudfroid sauce or sliced and accompanied by salad. It makes excellent sandwiches.

The meat from a boiled chicken is often used to make a fricassee; take the flesh from the bones, dice it and mix with a white sauce made with half milk and half chicken stock.

See Chapter 10, page 139, for sauce recipes.

BRAISED DUCKLING AND TURNIPS

A duckling	Salt and pepper
Stock	1 lb. young turnips
2 oz. butter or margarine	1 tbsp. chopped parsley

Joint the duckling and braise it in a little stock over a low heat, with half the fat and seasoning to taste. Boil the turnips until they are just tender and then sauté them lightly in the remaining butter or margarine, without colouring them. Sprinkle with parsley, pile in the centre of a hot dish, and arrange the joints of duckling round the edge. Skim and strain the liquor and serve it separately in a sauce boat.

BRAISED DUCK WITH PINEAPPLE

A small can of pineapple chunks	Dripping
½ pint cheap white wine	½ pint thick brown sauce (see chapter 10, p. 139)
A duckling	1 tsp. tomato ketchup

Oven temperature: hot (425°F., mark 7)

Drain the pineapple and soak it in the wine overnight. The next day, brown the duck with some dripping in the centre of the oven for about 40 minutes, then drain off all the fat. Drain the wine from the pineapple, mix it with the brown sauce and tomato ketchup and pour over the duck; cover the whole baking tin with aluminium foil or a lid and return it to a fairly hot oven (375°F., mark 5) for ¾–1 hour. Before starting to dish up, put the pineapple pieces in a saucepan to heat while you carve the bird; put the duck on a hot dish, garnish with pineapple and cover with sauce. (Serves 4–6.)

CANARD MONTMORENCY

A duckling (about 5–6 lb.), quartered	A 14-oz. can of stoned black cherries
1 level tsp. salt	3 level tsps. flour
Pepper	2 tbsps. stock made from the duck giblets
1 oz. butter	
4 tbsps. Madeira	

Sprinkle the duck joints with the salt and pepper. Melt the butter in a large saucepan and brown the joints on all sides. Remove from the pan and drain off the fat; replace the duckling and pour the Madeira and 4 tbsps. of the cherry juice over. Cover and simmer for 40 minutes, or until tender. Remove the joints from the pan, drain on kitchen paper and keep them warm. Skim the fat from the juice, blend the flour with the stock and stir into the juices in the pan. Bring to the boil, add the cherries and heat through. Check the seasoning. Arrange the duckling on a serving dish and coat with the sauce. (Serves 5–6.)

DUCK AND ORANGE CASSEROLE

A duckling, jointed	¼ lb. mushrooms, sliced
Seasoned flour	1–2 oz. flour
½ oz. fat	¾ pint stock
2 onions, skinned and chopped	¼ pint orange juice
	1 orange, washed

Oven temperature: moderate (350°F., mark 4)

Coat the duck joints with the seasoned flour and fry in the fat for 8–10 minutes, until well browned. Transfer to an ovenproof casserole. Fry the onions and mushrooms lightly in the hot fat for about 3 minutes, remove from the pan and add to the casserole. Stir the flour into the remaining fat and brown over a very low heat, stirring all the time. Remove from the heat, gradually stir in the stock and orange juice and bring to the boil; continue to stir until it thickens. Pour over the duck, cover and cook in the centre of the oven for about 1 hour.

Peel off the coloured part of the orange rind with a vegetable peeler and cut it into very thin strips. Divide the orange itself into segments, removing any pith or pips. Simmer the strips of rind in water until tender – about 5 minutes; drain well and sprinkle over the cooked duck joints. Garnish with the orange segments before serving. (Serves 4–6.)

CASSEROLE OF DUCK WITH RICE
(PORTUGUESE)

A duckling, jointed
2 onions, skinned and chopped
2–3 carrots, peeled and sliced
1 tbsp. chopped parsley

Salt and pepper
½ pint stock
8 oz. long-grain rice
¼ lb. Portuguese sausage (*chourico*)
Fat for frying

Oven temperature: moderate (350°F., mark 4)

Place the duckling, onions, carrots, parsley and seasoning in an ovenproof casserole, with the stock. Cover and cook in the centre of the oven for 1½ hours. Drain off the stock and make up to ¾ pint with water if necessary. Keep the casserole warm. Place the rice and stock in a pan and bring to the boil, cover and simmer for 12–15 minutes, or until the rice is tender and the liquid absorbed: add more liquid if the mixture becomes too dry. Slice the sausage and fry in a little hot fat until browned; drain. Arrange half the rice in the serving dish, cover with the duckling joints and top with the remaining rice. Garnish with the sausage slices.

DUCK IN RED WINE

A duckling (about 5–6 lb.)
½ a clove of garlic, skinned and crushed
2 oz. flour
¾ pint red wine
2 oz. mushrooms, washed and sliced

A bay leaf
Sprigs of parsley
½ level tsp. dried thyme
1 level tsp. salt
1 lb. small onions, skinned
1 lb. small carrots, scraped

Oven temperature: moderate (350°F., mark 4)

Remove the skin and fat from the duck and put them with the giblets into a pan; cover with water and simmer for 1 hour. Skim off the fat from the surface and let the stock cool. Cut the duck into joints. Heat 2 tbsps. of the duck fat in a pan, then brown the duck joints on all sides. Remove them from the fat and put in a casserole. Add the crushed garlic to the fat, fry for 1 minute and stir in the flour. Add the wine, mushrooms, herbs and salt. Bring to the boil, stirring constantly until the sauce thickens. Put the prepared onions and carrots into the casserole, pour the sauce over, cover and cook in the centre of the oven for ¾–1 hour, until tender. (Serves 5–6.)

DUCK À LA BOURGEOISE

A duckling
¼ pint red wine
½ pint Espagnole sauce (see chapter 10, p. 139)

14 button onions
Fat for frying
¼ lb. green grapes
Creamed potato

Oven temperature: moderate (350°F., mark 4)

Joint the duck and remove as much fat as possible. Place in a roasting tin and cook for 15 minutes in the centre of the oven. Add the wine to the Espagnole sauce, re-thicken if necessary, then add the duck. Simmer very gently until tender – about 20 minutes. Meanwhile skin the onions and fry in a covered pan until golden brown and soft. Skin the grapes and remove the pips. Pipe a border of creamed potato round a serving dish, place the duck in the centre and pour the sauce over. Garnish with the scalded grapes and the onions. (Serves 4–6.)

DUCK À LA CIRO

A duck, roasted
4 raw cooking apples
Sauternes wine
2 oz. mushrooms
1½ level tbsps. chopped onion
Salt, pepper, nutmeg and
  powdered thyme

2 level tbsps. parsley
  butter
2 level tsps. grated orange
  rind
2 oz. fried crumbs
2 level tsps. grated lemon
  rind

Oven temperature: fairly hot (375°F., mark 5)

Slice the apples and keep hot. Peel, core and slice the apples, place in a bowl, cover with Sauternes and marinade for ½ hour. Arrange the apple slices in the bottom of a cassserole and over them place the washed and sliced mushrooms. Sprinkle with onion, season with salt, pepper, nutmeg and thyme and dot the surface with parsley butter. Place the sliced duck neatly on top. Add the orange rind to the marinade and pour over. Cover tightly and cook in the centre of the oven for 35 minutes, or until the apples are soft. Remove the lid and sprinkle the top with the crumbs and lemon rind. (Serves 4–6.)

DUCK À LA PORTUGAISE

A duckling
1 tbsp. oil
1 oz. butter
1 small onion, skinned and
  chopped
1 green pepper, seeded and
  finely chopped
½ lb. tomatoes, skinned
  and quartered

1 canned pimiento, finely
  chopped
1 oz. flour
¼ pint chicken stock
¼ pint red wine
A bouquet garni
A dash of paprika
Salt and pepper

Oven temperature: moderate (350°F., mark 4)

Joint the duck and sauté in the oil and butter until the joints are golden-brown; remove from the heat and place in a 2-pint casserole. Sauté the onion and green pepper in the remaining fat until lightly browned. Add the tomatoes and pimiento and sprinkle in the flour; cook for 1–2 minutes. Gradually add the

43

stock and wine and bring to the boil. Add the bouquet garni, a dash of paprika and seasoning to taste. Pour over the duck joints and cook in the centre of the oven for 1–1½ hours, or until the duck is tender. Remove the bouquet garni before serving. (Serves 4–6.)

DUCKLING WITH GRAPES
(see colour picture No. 6)

2 ducklings
1 small onion, skinned
1 clove
1¼ pints water
2 lb. old potatoes
2 egg yolks
1 oz. butter, melted
3 level tsps. tomato paste
3 oz. dripping

1 oz. flour
Salt and pepper
Brown colouring
½ lb. green grapes, peeled and seeded
2 tbsps. red-currant jelly
A few cooked green peas to garnish

Cut the birds into neat pieces. If the giblets are available, simmer them with the onion and clove in the water to make a good stock: otherwise, use a chicken stock tablet. Peel and cook the potatoes, drain well and sieve them. Beat the egg yolks, melted butter and 2 tsps. of the tomato paste into the potato and pipe or pile around a serving dish; pipe also a few small separate shapes for garnish. Fry the pieces of duck in the dripping until brown, then set them aside while the sauce is made.

Pour off all but 1 tbsp. of the fat, add the flour and cook gently until it is lightly browned. Add the remaining tomato paste and the giblet or chicken stock, season well and if necessary colour with browning. Bring to the boil and skim well. Put in the duck pieces and simmer for 1–1½ hours. Bake the potato garnish towards the top of a hot oven (425°F., mark 7); arrange the duck pieces on the dish and sprinkle with the prepared grapes. Check the seasoning of the sauce, add the jelly, boil for a minute and strain over the dish. Add the potato shapes and green peas. Serve with buttered new potatoes and green beans. (Serves 6–8.)

BLANQUETTE OF TURKEY

½ lb. cooked turkey
1 medium-sized onion, skinned and chopped
1½ oz. butter
3 level tbsps. flour
¾ pint chicken stock

Salt and pepper
A pinch of mace
1 egg yolk
2 tbsps. single cream
2 tsps. lemon juice
Toast to garnish

Remove all the skin and bone from the turkey meat and cut it into cubes. Cook the onion lightly in the butter for 5 minutes without colouring; stir in the flour and cook for a further 2–3 minutes. Gradually stir in the stock, bring to the boil and continue stirring until it thickens. Add the turkey meat, season well, add the mace and heat the turkey thoroughly. Remove the sauce from the heat. Blend the egg yolk, cream and lemon juice to a smooth cream; stir in a little of the sauce, return the blended mixture to the pan and reheat without boiling. Turn the blanquette into a serving dish and serve with small triangles of fresh toast. (Serves 2.)

TURKEY CACCIATORA

1 small onion, skinned and chopped	Salt and pepper
1 clove of garlic, skinned and chopped	½ lb. cooked turkey, cut in cubes
1 carrot, peeled and cut in thin rings	1 level tbsp. flour
1 bay leaf	A pinch of basil and a pinch of allspice, mixed
Olive or cooking oil	2 tbsps. red wine
An 8-oz. can of tomato juice	A small pkt. of frozen peas
	4 oz. short-cut macaroni

Cook the onion, garlic, carrot and bay leaf in 2 tbsps. oil for about 10 minutes. Add the tomato juice and season, then simmer for 20 minutes. Remove the bay leaf. Coat the cubed turkey with flour, basil and allspice, then fry it gently in a little more oil. Pour the tomato sauce over the turkey, add the wine and peas and simmer for 10 minutes. Cook the macaroni in boiling salted water for 10–15 minutes. Arrange on a dish and pour the turkey mixture over it. (Serves 3.)

This is a delicious way of using up turkey leftovers.

TURKEY AND CRANBERRY CASSEROLE

2 medium-sized onions, skinned and chopped	2 tbsps. chopped parsley
2 oz. butter or dripping	A pinch of thyme
½ lb. mushrooms, washed and sliced	Salt and pepper
	4 oz. long-grain rice
½ lb. cooked turkey, diced	1 level dessertsp. curry powder
4 oz. cooked ham, diced	½ pint chicken stock
4 oz. leftover stuffing	4 oz. cranberry sauce (or jelly)

Oven temperature: moderate (350°F., mark 4)
Sauté the onions in 1 oz. butter until tender. Add the mushrooms and sauté for 2 minutes. Put into an ovenproof casserole and add the turkey, ham, crumbled stuffing, herbs and seasoning in layers. Brown the rice in the pan with the remaining butter and the curry powder; add to the casserole and pour in the stock. Cook in the centre of the oven for about 30 minutes, or until the rice is tender and the liquid absorbed. Garnish with the cranberry sauce (or jelly) arranged in a border round the dish. (Serves 3.)

GIBLET AND CHESTNUT STEW

Turkey or goose giblets
A little lard
1 oz. small onions, skinned
1 oz. flour
½ pint water

2-3 tbsps. tomato paste
Salt and pepper
1 lb. chestnuts
½ lb. sausages, grilled
Chopped parsley

Cut the giblets into small pieces and fry them lightly in the hot lard. Add the onions, and when they have browned, sprinkle in the flour and add the water, tomato paste and seasoning. Simmer for 45 minutes and meanwhile prepare the chestnuts; make slits in the skins, boil the nuts for about 10 minutes, then skin them and cook until they are half-done. Add the half-cooked nuts to the giblets after the first 45 minutes and continue to cook gently until they are tender. Place the grilled sausages in the stew and warm them through. Skim off any fat from the gravy and serve the stew on a hot dish, garnished with parsley.

Note: Canned or dried chestnuts could also be used.

GUINEA-FOWL AND RED CABBAGE

A guinea-fowl
Butter or dripping for frying
1 small red cabbage,
  finely shredded
1 lb. chestnuts, peeled

1 lb. apples, peeled,
  cored and sliced
1 glass red wine
1 glass stock
Salt and pepper

Truss the guinea-fowl and brown it in the butter or dripping in a flameproof casserole. Remove, then fry the red cabbage. Add the chestnuts and the apples. Place the bird on top, add the red wine, stock and seasoning to taste. Cover and cook for 1½-2 hours, until both the cabbage and the chestnuts are cooked.

SALMI OF POULTRY OR GAME
(see colour picture No. 8)

1 duck or 1-2 game birds in
  season, roasted
1 orange
1 shallot, skinned and chopped
1½ pints chicken stock
¼ pint rough red wine

½ pint Espagnole sauce
  (see chapter 10, p. 139)
1 tbsp. port
Red currant jelly
2 oz. white grapes,
  skinned

Cut the bird or birds into joints, remove the skin and break up the carcase into small pieces; put into a saucepan. Wash and peel the orange and divide into sections. Add the orange peel, shallots and stock to the game; bring to the boil and simmer for ½ hour. Mix together the wine, Espagnole sauce and ¼ pint of the strained stock. Place the joints in a pan, add the mixed stock and sauce and simmer until heated through. Arrange the joints on a serving dish. Add the port to the sauce and reduce until the mixture is of coating consistency. Pour over the game and garnish with sections of orange, red currant jelly and grapes.

CASSEROLE OF PARTRIDGE

2 medium-sized onions, skinned and sliced
2 sticks of celery, scrubbed and sliced
¼ lb. mushrooms, washed and sliced
4 oz. bacon, rinded and chopped
1 tbsp. oil
1 oz. butter
2 partridges, plucked, drawn and jointed
3 level tbsps. flour
¾ pint stock
A 15-oz. can of tomatoes, drained
Salt and pepper
¼ pint red wine

Oven temperature: moderate (350°F., mark 4)
Fry the onions, celery, mushrooms and bacon in the oil and butter for about 5 minutes, until golden-brown. Remove from the pan with a slotted spoon and line the bottom of an oven-proof casserole with them. Fry the partridge joints in the oil and butter for about 5 minutes, until golden brown. Remove from the pan with the slotted spoon and put in the casserole on the bed of vegetables. Stir the flour into the fat remaining in the pan and cook for 2–3 minutes. Gradually stir in the stock, bring to the boil, and continue to stir until it thickens. Add the tomatoes, salt, pepper and wine, pour the sauce over the partridge joints, cover and cook in the centre of the oven for about 1 hour, until the partridge joints are quite tender. (Serves 4–6.)

PARTRIDGE WITH CABBAGE

2 partridges, plucked, drawn and trussed
Butter or bacon fat
1 medium-sized firm cabbage
4–6 oz. streaky bacon
Salt and pepper
1 carrot, peeled and roughly chopped
1 onion, skinned
2–3 cloves
A bouquet garni
Stock
Smoked sausages (optional)

Oven temperature: moderate (350°F., mark 4)
This is one of the best ways of serving old partridges; the red-legged or "French" type can be cooked very well in this manner.

Fry the partridges in butter or bacon fat until golden brown. Cut the cabbage in quarters, removing the outside leaves and any hard pieces of stalk, wash it well, cook for 5 minutes in boiling salted water, then drain. Line a casserole with the bacon and lay half the cabbage over it, with seasoning to taste. Put the partridges on the top, with the carrot, the onion stuck with the cloves and the bouquet garni; add the rest of the cabbage and more seasoning. Cover with stock, put on a lid and cook in the centre of the oven for 1–1½ hours, or until the birds are tender.

As a variation, 1–2 lightly fried smoked sausages are sometimes added to the casserole mixture before it is put into the oven.

To serve, remove the partridges, bacon and sausages (if used) from the casserole, cut the birds into neat joints and the sausages into pieces; remove the carrot, onion and bouquet garni and cut the cabbage in shreds with a sharp knife. Serve the cabbage with the pieces of partridge on top of it and the bacon and sausage around. (Serves 4–6.)

CASSEROLE OF PHEASANT – 1

1 pheasant, plucked, drawn and jointed	2 oz. flour
1 tbsp. oil	½ pint chicken stock
1 oz. butter	¼ pint orange juice
¼ lb. mushrooms, washed and sliced	¼ pint very dry white wine
	1 orange, washed

Oven temperature: moderate (350°F., mark 4)
Fry the pheasant on both sides in the oil and butter for 5–6 minutes, until well browned. Remove from the pan with a slotted spoon and transfer to a 2-pint ovenproof casserole. Fry the mushrooms lightly for 4–5 minutes, remove from the pan with a slotted spoon and add to the casserole. Stir the flour into the fat remaining in the pan and cook for 2–3 minutes. Remove the pan from the heat and gradually pour in the stock, orange juice and white wine; bring to the boil, stirring until it thickens, and pour into the casserole. Cook for 1 hour in the centre of the oven, until the pheasant is tender. Meanwhile peel the zest from the orange with a vegetable peeler and cut into thin strips with a sharp knife. Divide the orange itself into segments. Simmer the strips of rind in water until they are soft and sprinkle over the casserole before serving. Garnish with the orange segments.

CASSEROLE OF PHEASANT – 2

1 pheasant	¾ pint stock
2 oz. butter	¼ lb. button mushrooms, washed
¼ lb. cooked ham, diced	
Salt	4 tbsps. red currant jelly

Oven temperature: moderate (350°F., mark 4)
Fry the bird on all sides in the melted butter until browned. Put in an ovenproof casserole, add the ham, salt, and stock and cook in the centre of the oven for 2 hours. Add the mush-

rooms after about 1½ hours and stir in the jelly just before serving.

PHEASANT WITH CHESTNUTS

1 pheasant, plucked, drawn and jointed	¾ pint stock
1 tbsp. olive oil	1 wineglass Burgundy
1 oz. butter	Salt and pepper
½ lb. chestnuts, peeled	Grated rind and juice of
2 medium-sized onions, skinned and sliced	½ an orange
	2 tsps. red currant jelly
3 level tbsps. flour	A bouquet garni
	Chopped parsley

Oven temperature: moderate (350°F., mark 4)
Fry the pheasant in the oil and butter for about 5–6 minutes, until golden brown. Remove from the pan with a slotted spoon and put in a casserole. Fry the chestnuts and onions in the oil and butter for about 5 minutes, until golden brown, and add to the pheasant. Stir the flour into the remaining fat and cook for 2–3 minutes. Remove the pan from the heat and gradually add the stock and wine; bring to the boil and continue to stir until it thickens. Season and pour over the pheasant. Add the orange rind and juice, red currant jelly and bouquet garni, cover and cook in the centre of the oven for 1 hour, until the pheasant is tender. Remove the bouquet garni before serving and adjust the seasoning, if necessary. Sprinkle with chopped parsley.

CANNED PHEASANT EN CASSEROLE

4 oz. bacon, chopped	1 level tbsp. red currant jelly
A 3-oz. pkt. of thyme and parsley stuffing	Lemon juice to taste
2 oz. lard	A 1-lb. can of small whole onions, drained
A 3-lb. can of whole roast pheasant in Burgundy jelly	1 oz. butter
3 level tbsps. cornflour	Chopped parsley to garnish

Oven temperature: hot (425°F., mark 7)
Mix the bacon with the stuffing and add just enough water to give a fairly stiff consistency; leave to stand for 5 minutes. Shape into 20 balls, place in a small baking dish with the melted lard and put in the top of the oven. Drain and joint the pheasant, arrange in a large ovenproof casserole, cover and put in the centre of the oven for 15–20 minutes. Blend the cornflour with a little of the stock from the can, add to the remaining stock and bring to the boil. Add the red currant jelly and lemon juice. Simmer gently whilst frying the onions in the butter for 3–4 minutes, till coloured. When the bird is heated through, add the onions, pour the sauce over and top with the stuffing balls. Sprinkle with parsley.

SPANISH CASSEROLED PHEASANT

1 pheasant	1 onion, skinned
¼ pint red wine	½ lb. tomatoes
½ pint chicken or game	Salt and pepper
stock	Slices of fried bread
2 oz. diced Spanish raw ham	

Joint the pheasant, put it in a flameproof casserole with the wine, stock, ham, sliced onion and tomatoes, salt and pepper, and simmer over a low heat until the pheasant is cooked – 45 minutes to 1 hour. Dish the joints of pheasant on the pieces of fried bread and keep hot. Reduce the sauce, sieve it, reheat, and pour over the pheasant. Serve at once.

CASSEROLE OF PIGEON

2–3 pigeons, plucked, drawn and jointed	1 onion, skinned and chopped
2–3 tbsps. oil	3 level tbsps. flour
2 oz. bacon, rinded and chopped	1 pint chicken stock
2 carrots, peeled and sliced	1 tbsp. tomato paste
	Salt and pepper
	Creamed potatoes

Oven temperature: moderate (350°F., mark 4)

Fry the pigeon joints in the oil for about 5 minutes, until golden brown, remove from the pan with a slotted spoon and put into an ovenproof casserole. Fry the bacon, carrots and onion in the remaining oil for about 5 minutes, until golden brown. Remove the vegetables from the pan with a slotted spoon and add to the casserole. Stir the flour into the remaining fat in the pan and cook for 2–3 minutes. Remove the pan from the heat and gradually stir in the stock. Bring to the boil, continue to stir until it thickens and add the tomato paste and seasoning. Pour the sauce over the pigeon joints, cover and cook in the centre of the oven for about ¾–1 hour, or until the pigeon is tender. Add a border of creamed potatoes.

CASSEROLE OF PIGEON AND CHESTNUTS

2 pigeons	1 pint stock
2 level tbsps. seasoned flour	½ lb. chestnuts
Fat for frying	4 chipolata sausages
1 large onion, skinned	Salt and pepper

Halve the pigeons, remove the feet and wash and dry the birds. Dip them in the seasoned flour, then fry them in hot fat until they are golden brown and place them in an ovenproof casserole. Slice the onion, fry it until it is light brown and arrange it round the pigeons. Add the stock, cover with greaseproof paper or a lid and simmer slowly for about 2 hours. Roast and peel the chestnuts and fry the sausages; add these to the pigeons 10–15 minutes before serving and simmer all together. Reseason as required and serve with a green salad.

PIGEONS À LA CATALANE

2–3 pigeons	¼ pint chicken stock
1 tbsp. oil	¼ pint dry white wine
1 oz. butter	1 strip of orange peel
1 oz. ham, roughly chopped	3 cloves of garlic, skinned
1 oz. flour	A bouquet garni
1 level tbsp. tomato paste	Salt and pepper

For the Stuffing

Pigeon livers, chopped	1 clove of garlic, skinned and
4 oz. fresh bread-crumbs	chopped
2 oz. ham, chopped	1 egg, beaten
1 tbsp. chopped parsley	

Oven temperature: moderate (350°F., mark 4)

Prepare the pigeons. Make the stuffing by combining the livers, bread-crumbs, ham, parsley and garlic with the beaten egg. Stuff the pigeons and sauté them in the oil and butter until golden brown, then transfer them to a 3-pint ovenproof casserole. Sprinkle the chopped ham over the pigeons. Blend the flour with the fat remaining in the pan and make a roux. Gradually add the tomato paste, stock and wine, bring to the boil and cook for 1 minute. Remove from the heat and pour over the pigeons. Add the orange peel, garlic, bouquet garni and seasoning, then cook in the centre of the oven for 35–45 minutes. Remove the bouquet garni before serving.

BRAISED PIGEONS WITH GOLDEN SPAGHETTI

2 pigeons	Stock
2 oz. bacon, rinded and	A bouquet garni
chopped	Salt and pepper
1 carrot, peeled and chopped	6 oz. spaghetti
A piece of turnip, peeled	Salted water
and chopped	2 oz. butter
2–3 sticks of celery, scrubbed	Tomatoes or watercress
and chopped	to garnish
1 onion, skinned and chopped	

Oven temperature: moderate (350°F., mark 4)

Cut the pigeons in half down the back. Cut up the bacon and vegetables into small pieces and put into a stewpan or ovenproof casserole, then place the portions of pigeon on the top. Add almost enough stock to cover, the bouquet garni and seasoning, cover and cook till the pigeons are almost tender – about 1–1½ hours. Put into a greased baking tin, with the stock strained over them, and cook in the centre of the oven until the stock is reduced to a glaze and the pigeons are brown. Meanwhile boil the spaghetti in salted water until tender and drain. Cut the butter into small pieces and add to the spaghetti, turning this so that the butter coats it thoroughly, making it golden and glistening. Serve the pigeons with the spaghetti on a hot dish and garnish with tomatoes and watercress. Alternatively, the pigeons may be served with asparagus and melted butter.

PIGEONS WITH CHESTNUTS (CHINESE)

3 pigeons (breast part only)	1 tbsp. soy sauce
Flour	1 tbsp. sherry
3–4 tbsps. oil	Salt and pepper
1 level tbsp. cornflour	2 spring onions
1 pint chicken stock	10 water chestnuts
1 level tsp. sugar	

Oven temperature: moderate (350°F., mark 4)

Halve each piece of pigeon, flour and fry in oil for about 10 minutes. Remove and keep hot. Add the cornflour to the remaining oil in pan, stir well, then add the stock, sugar, soy sauce and sherry, with seasoning to taste. Cut up the onions and slice the water chestnuts, then add both to the sauce. Bring to the boil, pour over the pigeons and cook in the centre of the oven for 20–30 minutes.

TIPSY PIGEONS

8 black olives	4 oz. bacon, rinded and
4 tbsps. sherry	chopped
2 pigeons, plucked and drawn	3 level tbsps. flour
2 tbsps. oil	½ pint chicken stock
1 large onion, skinned and	2 tbsps. brandy
sliced	Salt and pepper
4 slices of garlic sausage	

Oven temperature: moderate (350°F., mark 4)

Marinade the olives in the sherry for 2 hours. Fry the pigeons in the oil until golden brown – about 5 minutes. Remove from the pan with a slotted spoon and put into an ovenproof casserole. Fry the onion, garlic sausage and bacon in the remaining fat until golden brown – about 5 minutes. Remove from the pan with a slotted spoon and add to the casserole, with the sherry and olives. Stir the flour into the fat remaining in the pan and cook for 2–3 minutes. Gradually stir in the stock, bring to the boil and stir until it thickens. Add the brandy, season and pour the sauce over the pigeons. Cover and cook in the centre of the oven for 45 minutes, until tender.

RICH GAME CASSEROLE

A can or bottle of pheasant	4 tbsps. port wine
or other game	1 dozen button mushrooms
¾ pint Espagnole sauce	A little fat
(see chapter 10, p. 139)	6 glacé cherries

This is a good recipe for use when game is not in season.

Divide the bird into joints and remove the skin. Put the pieces into a heavy, flameproof casserole. Cover with the sauce, wine and mushroom stalks and simmer slowly for about 30 minutes. Sauté the mushroom caps in the fat. Arrange the pieces of game on a hot dish. Strain the sauce, skim off any excess fat and pour the sauce over the joints. Garnish with the sautéed mushrooms and the cherries.

HARE IN RED WINE (GERMAN)

A small hare	$\frac{1}{2}$ lb. small onions, skinned
6 oz. bacon, rinded	2 cloves, 2 bay leaves,
2–3 tbsps. dripping	2 peppercorns
2 oz. flour	Salt and pepper
1 pint stock or water	2 glasses of red wine

Oven temperature: cool (300°F., mark 2)

Cut the hare into small pieces, taking the flesh off the bones when practicable. Cut the bacon into thin strips and mix with the hare. Heat the dripping in a thick stewpan and fry the meat, turning it frequently until brown; take it out and keep hot. Stir in the flour and add the stock. Transfer, with the meat, sliced onions, herbs and seasonings, to a casserole and cook gently towards the bottom of the oven for about 3 hours. Add the wine and continue to cook until the liquor is thick; remove any excess fat. Serve in the casserole, with a piped border of creamed potato.

JUGGED HARE

A hare	1 carrot, peeled and sliced
2 oz. bacon, rinded and chopped	$1\frac{1}{2}$ pints stock
	A bouquet garni
1 oz. lard or dripping	Juice of $\frac{1}{2}$ a lemon
1 onion, skinned and stuck with 2 cloves	3 level tbsps. flour
	1 tbsp. red currant jelly
1 stick of celery, scrubbed and sliced	1 glass of port or red wine (optional)

Oven temperature: warm (325°F., mark 3)

Prepare the hare (see the Supplement, page 168), retaining the blood; wipe and joint. Fry the joints with the bacon in the lard until they are lightly browned (about 2 minutes). Transfer to a deep casserole and add the vegetables, enough stock to cover the joints, the bouquet garni and lemon juice. Cover and cook in the centre of the oven for 3–4 hours, or until tender.

A few minutes before serving, blend the flour with a little cold water to a smooth cream, stir in the blood of the hare and add to the casserole, with the jelly and wine (if used). Re-heat without boiling and serve with red currant jelly and forcemeat balls (see Chapter 10, page 139).

53

PIQUANT HARE

4 hare legs
Bacon for larding
1 half-bottle white
  wine
1 glassful wine vinegar
2–3 carrots, peeled and sliced
2–3 small onions, skinned
  and sliced
1 bay leaf

Tarragon leaves
Sprigs of parsley
Sprigs of thyme
Coarsely ground pepper
3 tbsps. olive oil
1 tbsp. dry mustard
1 dessertsp. tomato sauce
A little flour
2–3 tbsps. single cream

Wipe over the hare legs and lard them with the fat bacon, then prepare a marinade with the wine, vinegar, carrots, onions, herbs and pepper. Marinade the meat for 2 hours, then drain it well. Heat the oil in a flameproof casserole and brown the meat on all sides. Add about half the marinade liquor, the mustard and the tomato sauce, and cook for 1 hour. When the meat is well cooked, remove it and keep it hot. Add the blended flour to the gravy and boil for a few minutes, then remove the pan from heat and add the cream; strain over the hare.

BROWN CASSEROLE OF RABBIT

A rabbit, jointed
2 oz. seasoned flour
2 oz. dripping
1 onion or leek, sliced
1 meat cube or 2 tsps.
  meat extract
1 pint stock or water

2 carrots, peeled and diced
1 stalk of celery, cut up
A bouquet garni
1 tbsp. tomato ketchup
A pinch of ground nutmeg
Forcemeat balls or fried
  croûtons to garnish

Oven temperature: moderate (350°F., mark 4)

Wash and joint the rabbit and soak in cold salted water to remove the blood. Dry the pieces and toss in seasoned flour, then fry, several joints at a time, until lightly browned. Remove from the pan, add the onion or leek and fry gently for a few minutes; add the remaining flour and fry until lightly browned. Add the meat cube or extract with the liquid and stir until boiling. Put the rabbit and the vegetables into an ovenproof casserole and pour the sauce over. Add the bouquet garni, ketchup and nutmeg, cover and cook in the centre of the oven for about 2 hours. Remove the herbs and serve the casserole garnished with forcemeat balls or croûtons.

RABBIT HOTPOT

1 lb. rabbit
½ lb. carrots, peeled

1 lb. potatoes, peeled
1 pkt. of onion soup

Oven temperature: moderate (350°F., mark 4)

Cut up the rabbit into suitable-sized joints and wash well. Blanch by putting into a saucepan, covering with water and bringing to the boil. Remove the rabbit from the pan and place in an ovenproof dish; over the top arrange the thinly sliced carrots and the potatoes, cut into chunky pieces. Make up the soup with 1 pint water and pour over the top. Cook in the centre of the oven for 2 hours. (Serves 3–4.)

RABBIT MARENGO

A rabbit
2 oz. dripping
2 onions, skinned and cut into rings
1½ oz. flour
½ pint tomato juice
½ pint stock

Salt and pepper
10 mushrooms, washed and peeled
A bunch of herbs
Croûtons of fried bread and gherkins to garnish

Oven temperature: slow (300°F., mark 1)

Divide the rabbit into portions and soak for 1 hour in cold water. Melt the dripping, fry the onions until they are golden brown, then remove them to a casserole. Dip the pieces of rabbit into the flour and fry them slightly on all sides, then place them in the casserole. Add the rest of the flour to the fat in the pan and make a roux, gradually add the tomato juice and stock to make a sauce, season well and pour over the rabbit. Quarter the mushrooms and put them in the casserole with the herbs, tied in muslin. Cook towards the bottom of the oven for 2–2½ hours. Serve with croûtons and gherkins.

FRICASSEE OF RABBIT

A rabbit, jointed
1 large onion, skinned and stuck with 3 cloves
¼ lb. bacon, rinded and chopped
A bouquet garni
1 pint stock
1 oz. butter

3 level tbsps. flour
2 onions, skinned and sliced
1 glass white wine
2 egg yolks
Salt and pepper
Grated nutmeg
Sliced lemon and toast squares to garnish

Place the rabbit joints in a saucepan with the large onion, bacon and bouquet garni; add the stock and simmer for about 45 minutes. Melt the butter, add the flour and cook for 2–3 minutes. Strain the stock from the rabbit and stir gradually in to the flour; bring to the boil and continue to stir till it thickens. Add the rabbit, bacon and sliced onions and simmer until the onions are soft – about 30 minutes. Blend the wine and egg yolks together to a smooth cream, add a little of the sauce and return the blended mixture to the pan; add salt, pepper and a little grated nutmeg and allow to heat through, but do not boil. Place the rabbit joints on a serving dish and pour the sauce over them. Garnish with lemon slices and small squares of toast, or border with rice.

RABBIT STEW (SWEDISH)

2–3 lb. rabbit, jointed
2 level tsps. salt
1 level tsp. pepper
2 oz. butter or margarine
1 onion, skinned and sliced
½ pint chicken stock
¼ pint white wine
An 8-oz. can of tomato purée
1 level tsp. sugar
2 level tbsps. flour
2 tbsps. chopped parsley

Season the rabbit pieces with some of the salt and pepper and brown in the butter. Add the onion, stock, wine and remaining seasoning and simmer, covered, for ¾-hour. Remove the rabbit pieces and onion and keep hot. Stir the tomato purée and sugar into the liquid. Blend the flour with 2 tbsps. cold water, add to the mixture and cook till thickened. Replace the rabbit and onion and add the parsley, cover and simmer till heated through. Arrange on a large hot dish and sprinkle with more parsley, if desired.

STEWED VENISON

1 lb. meat from shoulder of venison, cut into ½-inch cubes
3 level tbsps. seasoned flour
1 oz. dripping or lard
2 onions, skinned and chopped
2 carrots, peeled and sliced
1 pint stock
Salt and pepper
A bouquet garni
2 tsps. vinegar

Oven temperature: warm (325°F., mark 3)

Toss the meat in the seasoned flour and fry it in the fat for 8–10 minutes, until well browned; remove from the pan, draining well, and put into a casserole. Fry the vegetables in the fat for about 5 minutes, until golden brown, remove from the pan, again draining well, and put into the casserole. Stir the rest of the seasoned flour into the fat remaining in the pan and cook slowly until brown. Remove the pan from the heat and gradually stir in the stock; bring to the boil and continue stirring until it thickens. Pour the sauce over the venison, season and add the bouquet garni and vinegar. Cover and cook in the centre of the oven for 2–2½ hours, until the meat is tender. Remove the bouquet garni before serving the venison.

CHAPTER 4

Fried and grilled poultry and game

Most food which is to be fried needs some form of coating before it is cooked. These are the chief ones which are suitable for poultry and game:

SEASONED FLOUR
Mix about 2 level tbsps. flour with about 1 level tsp. salt and a good sprinkling of pepper. Either pat it on to the portion of food or dip the pieces in the flour and shake them gently before cooking.

EGG AND CRUMBS
Have a beaten egg on a plate and some fresh white or dry bread-crumbs on a piece of kitchen paper. Dip the piece of poultry or game in egg and lift it out, letting it drain for a second or two. Transfer it to the crumbs and tip the paper until the food is well covered. Press in the crumbs with a palette knife or something similar, then shake the food to remove any surplus crumbs.

OTHER COATINGS
Crushed potato crisps may be used instead of seasoned flour. The seasoned flour may be flavoured with curry powder or other spices. Finely grated Parmesan cheese may be combined with flour to make a savoury coating.

Sometimes more than one coating is used – for instance:

Seasoned flour, then beaten egg and bread-crumbs

Evaporated milk, then seasoned flour

Seasoned flour, then beaten egg and equal parts of flour and grated Parmesan cheese

COATING BATTER

We give two recipes – the first the standard, simple one, the second a slightly richer batter which gives a lighter, crisper result. Batter is used chiefly when the food is to be deep-fried.

4 oz. plain flour	¼ pint milk or milk and water
A pinch of salt	(approx.)
1 egg, beaten	

Mix the flour, salt, egg and sufficient liquid to give a stiff batter which will coat the back of the spoon. Beat well until smooth. Dip the food into the batter, holding the pieces on a skewer or fork, and drain them slightly before lowering them into the hot fat.

4 oz. plain flour	1 egg, separated
A pinch of salt	2–3 tbsps. water or milk
1 tbsp. oil	and water

Mix the flour, salt, oil and egg yolk with sufficient liquid to give a stiff batter which will coat the back of the spoon; beat until smooth. Just before using, whisk the egg white stiffly and fold it into the batter. Dip the portions of food into seasoned flour before coating them as above with this batter.

FRIED CHICKEN

Allow a joint of chicken for each person and coat in one of the ways suggested above. Heat enough lard, cooking oil or butter in a frying-pan or skillet to give a depth of about ½ inch – you will need 4 oz. or so of fat. Place the chicken pieces skin side down and brown them quickly. Turn them over and brown the other side. Lower the heat and cook for about 15 minutes on each side, or until tender. Serve with potatoes and green peas or a green vegetable such as broccoli.

For a change, garnish the fried chicken with fried parsley and serve with a tomato sauce or gravy. (See chapter 10, page 139.) Alternatively, pile the pieces in a napkin-lined basket and garnish with rings of raw onion or green pepper.

FRIED CHICKEN WITH PINEAPPLE
(see colour picture No. 3)

4 frozen chicken joints, thawed	A 15-oz. can of pineapple rings, drained
Seasoned flour	Parsley to garnish
2 oz. butter	

Coat the chicken joints with seasoned flour and fry gently in the hot butter until brown and firm; keep them warm. Fry the well-drained pineapple slices on both sides until lightly browned. Dish up the chicken and pineapple with potato chips and green peas, or as desired.

Note: in the meal shown in the colour picture the chicken is preceded by jellied consommé (canned), which should be served with thin toast; to follow there is a simple summer sweet made of ice cream mounted on prepared melon slices and flanked by raspberries which have been well dredged with sugar.

FRENCH-FRIED CHICKEN

A chicken	1 egg, beaten
4 oz. plain flour	½ oz. butter, melted
¼ pint milk	Fat for frying

Cut the chicken into pieces. Make a batter with the flour, milk, egg and melted butter, beating it well. Dip each piece of chicken into the batter and fry in the hot fat until golden-brown. Finish cooking in the centre of a moderate oven (350°F., mark 4) until the chicken is tender – about 30 minutes. Serve with a good tomato sauce.

MATABELE FRIED CHICKEN

A chicken	4 rashers of bacon, rinded
Olive oil	8 oz. long-grain rice
Salt and pepper	Chicken stock
1 red pepper, seeded	2 rounds of pineapple, diced
1 green pepper, seeded	Chopped chives
1 large onion, skinned	

Divide the chicken into tidy joints and soak in the seasoned olive oil for about 30 minutes. Boil the remaining carcase to make stock for the rice. Cut up the peppers, the onion and the bacon. Heat 2 tbsps. oil in a frying-pan and fry the bacon, onions and peppers, then add the rice and fry till it becomes opaque. Add enough chicken stock to cover the rice, then pour in one-and-a-half times as much again. Season well, and simmer gently until all the liquid is absorbed and the rice is tender. Add the diced pineapple 5 minutes before the rice finishes cooking. Meanwhile fry the chicken in hot oil until tender and golden brown. Serve it on the rice, sprinkled with chopped chives.

SOUTHERN-STYLE FRIED CHICKEN

A chicken	1½ gills (approx. ¼ pint) milk or
Seasoned flour	single cream
Fat for frying	1½ gills (approx. ¼ pint)
Cooked peas to garnish	stock
the chicken	Sliced mushrooms (optional)
1 level tbsp. flour	Salt and pepper

Cut the broiler into 4 pieces, dip quickly in and out of cold water and drain. Dip each piece into the seasoned flour until thoroughly coated. Fry the chicken in hot fat until each piece is tender and brown on both sides. Arrange on a hot dish, garnish with the peas and keep hot while you make the gravy. Put 2 tbsps. fat into a saucepan, add the flour to make a roux and stir in the milk or cream and the giblet stock; if desired, add a few sliced mushrooms and allow to cook for a minute or two. Season well and serve.

VIENNESE CHICKEN

A chicken	Bread-crumbs
Juice of 2 lemons	Fat for frying
Olive oil	1 egg yolk
A bay leaf	$\frac{1}{4}$ pint milk
Thyme	$\frac{1}{4}$ lb. small mushrooms
Parsley	Salt and pepper
1 egg, beaten	Parsley to garnish

Joint the chicken and marinade for about 2 hours in the juice of 1 lemon and some olive oil, with the bay leaf, thyme and parsley. Drain the chicken, dip in beaten egg, coat with bread-crumbs and fry in hot fat until golden brown and tender. Meanwhile mix the egg yolk with the milk, mushrooms, salt and pepper and cook until thick. At the last minute pour in the remaining lemon juice and pour the sauce around the fried chicken. Garnish with chopped parsley.

SUPRÊMES OF CHICKEN

4 suprêmes (chicken breasts)	1 tbsp. oil
2 level tbsps. seasoned flour	$\frac{1}{2}$ pint well-flavoured white sauce (see chapter 10, p. 139)
1 egg, beaten	A squeeze of lemon juice
2 oz. fresh white bread-crumbs	1 egg yolk
1 oz. butter	1 tbsp. cream

Trim the suprêmes and coat with seasoned flour; dip in the beaten egg and then in bread-crumbs. Fry best side first in the butter and oil, turn them once and cook for about 20 minutes altogether. Remove them from the pan, drain on crumpled kitchen paper and keep hot. Mix the sauce, lemon juice, egg yolk and cream and re-heat without boiling, re-season if necessary and pour over the chicken.

Suprêmes are also excellent served cold with a salad and are ideal for a packed meal.

FRIED POUSSINS WITH GRAPES

2 poussins	3–4 oz. fat for frying
1 egg, beaten	6 oz. grapes, peeled
Bread-crumbs to coat	Melted butter

A simple but delicious way of serving plump, tender young birds for a special occasion.

Truss a couple of poussins and egg-and-crumb them. Heat the fat until it is smoking hot and fry the poussins until they are golden brown on one side (about 10 minutes), then cook them on the other side; drain them well. Meanwhile toss the peeled grapes in some melted butter. Dish up the poussins and garnish with grapes and with chipped potatoes. (Serves 2–4.)

CHICKEN À LA KIEV

4 oz. softened butter	1 egg, beaten
1 tbsp. chopped parsley	4 oz. fresh bread-crumbs
4 chicken breasts, boned	Fat for deep frying

Beat the softened butter and chopped parsley together, form into a roll and chill. Beat the boned chicken with a rolling pin until very thin. Divide the butter into 4, place a piece on each of the chicken breasts, wrap the chicken round the butter like a parcel and tie with cotton. Dip each parcel in beaten egg and coat with bread-crumbs. Heat the fat or oil until a 1-inch cube of bread will brown in 60–70 seconds, then fry the chicken for 5 minutes. Remove from the fat, drain on crumpled kitchen paper and remove the cottons before serving.

CHICKEN MARYLAND

A 2½–3-lb. chicken, jointed	1–2 tbsps. oil
3 level tbsps. seasoned flour	4 bananas
	Sweet corn fritters
1 egg, beaten	4 bacon rolls (see
Dry bread-crumbs	chapter 10, p. 139)
2 oz. butter	

Divide the chicken into fairly small portions, coat with seasoned flour, dip in beaten egg and coat with bread-crumbs. Fry the chicken in the butter and oil in a large frying-pan until lightly browned. Continue frying gently, turning the pieces once, for about 20 minutes, or until tender. Alternatively, fry them in deep fat for 5–10 minutes. (The fat should be hot enough to brown a 1-inch cube of bread in 60–70 seconds.) Serve the chicken with fried bananas, corn fritters and bacon rolls. (Serves 5–7.)

FRIED BANANAS

Peel and slice the bananas lengthways and fry gently for about 3 minutes in a little hot butter or lard, until lightly browned.

CORN FRITTERS

Make up Coating Batter 1 (see beginning of chapter). Fold in 1 small packet of frozen corn kernels (thawed). Fry in spoonfuls in a little hot fat until crisp and golden, turning them once. Drain well on crumpled kitchen paper.

CHINESE FRIED CHICKEN

4 chicken joints
6 tbsps. soy sauce
6 tbsps. sherry
1 level tsp. sugar

2 spring onions, skinned and chopped
3 level tbsps. flour
Deep fat for frying

Soak the chicken joints in the mixed soy sauce, sherry, sugar and onions for about an hour. Drain the chicken and dip each piece in flour. Heat some deep fat until it will brown a 1-inch cube of bread in 60 seconds. Fry the chicken for about 8–10 minutes, until golden brown. Serve with plain boiled rice to which has been added a little of the soy sauce and sherry. (Any soy sauce and sherry that is left over can be used for flavouring other sauces or soups.)

Instead of deep-frying the chicken joints, you can fry them for about 20 minutes in 2 oz. butter and 1 tbsp. oil in a frying-pan covered with a lid.

DEEP-FRIED SPRING CHICKEN (CHINESE)

1 large spring chicken
1 onion, skinned and chopped
2 tbsps. sesame oil
6 tbsps. soy sauce
6 tbsps. sherry

A little salt
1 level tsp. sugar
Flour
Lard for deep frying

Joint the chicken and cut it into about a dozen pieces. Mix the onion, oil, soy sauce, sherry, a little salt and sugar together and pour over the chicken; let it stand for about an hour. Remove the chicken, dip the pieces in flour and fry in the hot lard for 5–6 minutes, until golden brown.

Serve with a sauce made with stock flavoured with fried spring onions, garlic and chillies and thickened with corn-flour. Noodles make a good accompaniment. (Serves 2–3.)

PAPER-WRAPPED CHICKEN (CHINESE)

A 3-lb. chicken
2 tbsps. soy sauce
1 tbsp. sherry
1 level tsp. chopped fresh ginger
1 level tsp. salt

$\frac{1}{4}$ level tsp. pepper
$\frac{1}{2}$ level tsp. sugar
2 scallion stalks or spring onions, cut into 1-inch pieces
20 pieces of waxed paper, 4 inches square

Bone the chicken, remove and discard the skin and cut the flesh into slices about $1\frac{1}{2}$ inches long. Mix together the soy sauce, sherry, ginger, salt, pepper and sugar and soak the sliced chicken in this mixture for 30 minutes. Put 2 pieces of chicken and a piece of scallion on each square of waxed paper and wrap it up, folding the paper envelope fashion and bringing the last corner right over to hold the package securely. Heat the oil in a pan and when it is very hot, fry the chicken packages for about 2½ minutes. Drain well and serve very hot. Each person unwraps his chicken packets himself at table. (Serves 4–5.)

GRILLED CHICKEN

Young and tender birds (such as poussins or small broilers) and chicken joints are suitable for grilling. Split a whole bird down the back, but without cutting through the skin of the breast; flatten out, removing the breast-bone and breaking the joints where necessary. Skewer the legs and wings closely to the body, keeping the bird flat.

A frozen bird should of course be allowed to thaw first.

Joints require no special preparation.

Brush the chicken over with olive oil or melted butter, sprinkle with salt and pepper and place on a greased grid, skin side up. Grill under a moderate heat for 15–20 minutes. Turn once. Serve with a thin gravy made from the giblets and garnish with watercress.

Alternatively, sprinkle the chicken with a mixture of finely chopped onion, parsley and bread-crumbs, after brushing it with oil or butter; when it is cooked, garnish it with watercress and serve with brown or tomato sauce. (See chapter 10, page 139, for recipes.)

GRILLED CHICKEN (INDONESIAN)

A young chicken
Salt
Black pepper

2 tsps. melted butter
6 tbsps. soy sauce
2 red peppers

Split open the chicken, flatten it and rub well with salt and pepper. Mix the melted butter with the soy sauce and chopped red peppers, then put the chicken under the grill and brush it continually with this mixture. Cook until the chicken is browned on both sides and tender when tested – 15–20 minutes. Soy sauce burns easily, so take care not to let the grill get too hot. (Serves 2.)

GRILLED POUSSINS IN A BASKET

4 poussins
4 oz. butter, melted
Salt and pepper

2 onions, skinned and sliced
Watercress

Split the birds down the back. Trim off the legs and the wings at the first joint, open out the birds and flatten as much as possible. Brush all over with melted butter and season lightly. Grill under a medium heat, turning once or twice, for about 20 minutes, or until the poussins are tender. Serve on a napkin in a basket, garnished with the thinly sliced raw onion rings and watercress.

DEVILLED POUSSINS

4 poussins
½ level tsp. black pepper
2–3 tsps. made mustard
3–4 tbsps. oil

A little Cayenne pepper
2–3 tsps. Worcestershire
  sauce
2–3 tsps. vinegar

Split the birds down the back and open out. Blend all the remaining ingredients and when smooth spread the mixture on the poussins. Place them under a medium heat and grill, turning them once or twice, for about 20 minutes, until tender.

ITALIAN DEVILLED CHICKEN

A spring chicken
Olive oil
Salt and pepper
Ground ginger

1 onion, sliced and finely
  chopped
Chopped parsley

Cut a young spring chicken in half, or split, flatten out and skewer to keep in shape. Prepare a mixture of the olive oil, seasoning, ginger, onion and parsley. Turn the chicken in this mixture, leaving it in for at least 1 hour. (Cuts may be made in the flesh to let the seasonings penetrate.) Grill until golden brown and serve at once, with skinned boiled tomatoes.

TEXAS BARBECUED CHICKEN

4 oz. butter or margarine
2 oz. granulated sugar
¼ level tsp. Cayenne pepper
½ level tsp. prepared
  mustard
⅓ pint salad oil
A 14-oz. bottle of ketchup
3 tbsps. Worcestershire
  sauce

2 cloves of garlic, skinned
  and minced
2 oz. onion, minced
2 tbsps. lemon juice
¼ tsp. Tabasco sauce
2 ready-to-cook chicken,
  about 2 lb. each
Salt and pepper

Early in the day, make the barbecue sauce. Melt the butter in a small saucepan, stir in the sugar, then the rest of the ingredients (adding no salt or pepper). Simmer, uncovered, stirring occasionally, for 20 minutes.

About 2½ hours before the meal, start the barbecue fire. When the charcoal is glowing, rub the whole chicken with salt and pepper; then mount the chicken on the spit and cook for about 1 hour, or until tender, basting them frequently with the sauce and turning them now and then (if the spit is not of the revolving type). Serve half a chicken per person, handing

(Cont'd page 65)

Illustrations

1. Roast Turkey
2. Roast Wild Duck
3. Fried Chicken with Pineapple

4. Chicken in Orange Sauce;
   Mexican style Chicken with
   Wine

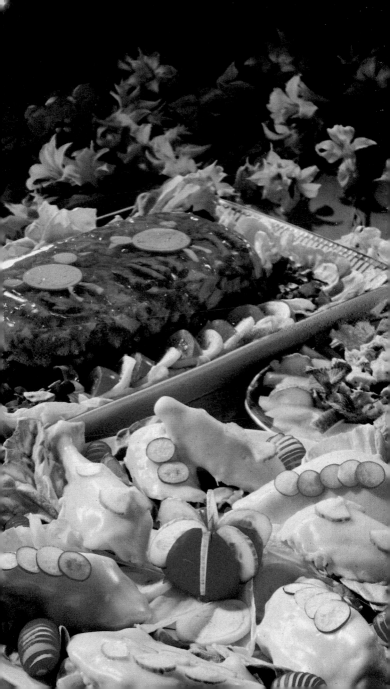

the rest of the hot sauce separately. Salad is the best accompaniment.

The chicken can of course be cooked on a rôtisserie unit.

PHEASANT À L'AMÉRICAINE

A young pheasant
2 oz. butter, melted
Salt and pepper
4 oz. fresh bread-crumbs
Cayenne pepper
4 thin rashers of bacon

4 tomatoes, halved
¼ lb. button mushrooms, washed
A bunch of watercress, trimmed and washed

Slit the pheasant down the back and flatten; brush it with melted butter and dust with salt and pepper. Grill lightly for 5 minutes under a medium heat, sprinkle with the bread-crumbs and dust with cayenne. Continue to grill for about 20 minutes, turning the bird frequently. Rind and roll up the rashers of bacon and grill them, with the tomatoes and button mushrooms, for 3–5 minutes, until cooked. Serve the pheasant with the bacon rolls, tomatoes, mushrooms and watercress arranged around it. (Serves 2–3.)

FILLETS OF HARE WITH CHERRIES

A young hare
½ oz. butter
4 rashers of streaky bacon
Salt and pepper
1 medium-sized onion, skinned and finely chopped

¼ pint Espagnole sauce (see chapter 10, p. 139)
½ pint port wine
1 tsp. tarragon vinegar
1 oz. glacé cherries, halved
Fried croûtons

Clean and skin the hare. Using a sharp knife, cut away the fillet or breast portion from either side of the breastbone. Bone also the shoulders and legs and shape the meat into fillets. Heat the butter in a pan and lightly fry the rashers. Remove the bacon, then fry the hare fillets until brown and tender (10–15 minutes). Season and add the onion, then fry for 1 minute. Pour off the fat and add the sauce, wine and vinegar; bring to the boil and add the halved glacé cherries. Serve the fillets hot, garnished with the croûtons.

Illustrations

5. Curry of cold Roast Chicken
6. Duckling with Grapes

7. Chicken in Aspic
8. Salmi of Poultry or Game

CHAPTER 5

Pies, patties and savouries

This chapter opens with a group of recipes for pies, flans, small pies and pasties and raised pies, all with a filling of poultry or game; the necessary pastry recipes are given at the end of the section (see pp. 72 to 74). The second part of the chapter is devoted to various savouries and snacks, some suitable as a light meal, some intended for use as after-dinner savouries.

CHICKEN PIE

12 oz. cooked chicken
½ pint thick white sauce
Salt and pepper
2 tsps. finely chopped onion

A small pkt. of mixed frozen
  vegetables, thawed
8 oz. shortcrust pastry

Oven temperature: fairly hot (400°F., mark 6)

Cut the chicken meat into fairly small pieces. Prepare the white sauce (using 1½ oz. butter, 1½ oz. flour and ½ pint milk – see pp. 139–140); season well. Stir in the chicken, onion and vegetables.

Leave on one side to cool slightly. Meanwhile prepare the pastry and divide into two. Roll out one half to line a 7-inch pie plate. Add the filling and smooth it flat. Roll out the second piece of pastry to form the lid. Damp the edges of the pastry, place the pastry lid in position. Seal the edges well, trim and "knock up". Bake towards the top of the oven until the pastry is crisp and brown, about 30–35 minutes.

CHICKEN AND LEEK PIE

A chicken
Stock or water
1 lb. leeks

Salt and pepper
8 oz. flaky pastry
Egg to glaze

Oven temperature: hot (425°F., mark 7)

Joint the chicken and simmer gently in stock or water for 30 minutes. Thoroughly wash the leeks, cut in half lengthways and

66

then cut into 2-inch pieces, tie together and cook for 15 minutes with the chicken. Remove the chicken flesh from the bones, put it with the leeks in a pie dish and season well, add some stock and cover with the pastry. Decorate the sides and top of the pie, and glaze with a little egg. Cook towards the top of the oven for 10 minutes, then reduce the heat to fairly hot (375°F., mark 6) and cook for a further 15–25 minutes.

CHICKEN AND MUSHROOM PIE

8 oz. flaky or rough puff pastry
A chicken
Flour
4 oz. mushrooms, washed and cut up
2 onions, skinned and chopped

4 oz. bacon, rinded and chopped
A little dripping
½ pint giblet stock
Salt and pepper
Egg to glaze

Oven temperature: hot (425°F., mark 7)

Make the pastry. Joint the chicken and flour the pieces. Fry the mushrooms, onions and bacon in the dripping until just beginning to colour, then remove from the fat. Fry the chicken joints and put them in the pie dish with the fried ingredients. Add 2 level tsps. flour to the fat, then gradually add the stock and bring to the boil; season well and pour over the ingredients in the pie dish. Cover with the pastry, brush with egg and cook in the centre of the oven for 45 minutes, reducing the temperature to moderate (350°F., mark 4) after 20 minutes. Serve hot.

BOER CHICKEN PIE (S. African)

A 3-lb. chicken
1½ pints water
1 level tbsp. salt
1 tsp. whole allspice
1 tsp. whole peppercorns
2 bay leaves
3 carrots, peeled and sliced
2 onions, skinned and quartered
2 sticks of celery, sliced
5 sprigs of parsley
2 oz. thinly sliced ham

2 hard-boiled eggs, sliced
1 oz. butter
1 oz. flour
2–3 tbsps. sherry
1 tbsp. lemon juice
1 level tsp. sugar
A pinch of ground mace
A pinch of pepper
1 egg yolk
8 oz. shortcrust pastry
Egg to glaze

Oven temperature: hot (425°F., mark 7)

This delicious pie can be prepared early in the day, kept in a cool place and baked just before it is required.

Quarter the chicken, put it in a large pan with the water, salt, allspice, peppercorns, bay leaves, vegetables and parsley sprigs (tied together). Cover and simmer for 30 minutes, or until the vegetables are tender but not over-done. Take out the

67

vegetables and chicken and strain the stock. Cut the vegetables up small; cut the meat from the chicken bones in large chunks. Put into a large pie dish alternate layers of chicken, vegetables, quarter-slices of ham, folded over, and hard-boiled egg. Melt the butter and gradually stir in the flour, ½ pint of the chicken stock, the sherry, lemon juice, sugar, mace and pepper. Cook until the sauce is thick and smooth. Beat the egg yolk well, stir slowly into the sauce and heat gently, stirring, till thick, but don't boil. Pour this sauce over the chicken and vegetables. Cover the pie with pastry, then, using a sharp knife, cut a short line from the centre towards each of the four corners and fold each pastry triangle back, leaving an open square. Brush the pastry over with beaten egg to glaze and bake towards the top of the oven for 25 minutes.

CHICKEN, CHEESE AND CELERY FLAN

4 oz. shortcrust pastry	½ pint milk or celery stock
1 onion, skinned and sliced	Salt and pepper
2 oz. margarine	4 oz. cooked chicken, chopped
1 small can of celery	1½ oz. cheese, grated
1 oz. flour	

Oven temperature: hot (425°F., mark 7)

Line a flan ring with the pastry. Cut out a round of greased greaseproof paper slightly larger than the pastry case and fit this, greased side down, inside the pastry. Half-fill the paper with uncooked haricot beans or rice or with stale bread crusts. Bake at the top of the oven for 10–15 minutes, until it has set. Remove the paper and baking beans from the pastry case, and return to a moderate oven (350°F., mark 4) for a further 5 minutes to dry out. Fry the onion in 1 oz. of the margarine until golden brown. Drain and cut up the celery and add to the onion. Make a white sauce with the remaining fat, the flour and the liquid; bring to the boil and pour on to the vegetables, season and add the chicken and half the cheese. Fill the flan case with this mixture, cover with the remaining cheese and brown under a red-hot grill. Serve hot or cold.

CHICKEN VOL-AU-VENT

8 oz. puff pastry	½ pint thick white sauce
6 oz. cooked chicken	Salt and pepper
3 oz. cooked ham	

Oven temperature: very hot (450°F., mark 8)

Roll the pastry out ½ inch thick and cut into an oval, using a cutter or a knife; mark a lid also, brush the top with egg, and bake in the centre of the oven for about 25 minutes. Remove the lid, take out any damp pastry that is inside and put the case back in the oven for a minute or two to dry.

To make the filling, cut the chicken and ham into pieces and mix with the sauce and seasoning; heat in a saucepan, and when you are ready to serve the vol-au-vent, pour the mixture into the case and put on the lid.

INDIVIDUAL CHICKEN POT PIES

A chicken	1½ oz. butter
5 small onions, skinned	1 level tbsp. flour
4 oz. mushrooms	Milk
2–3 tbsps. sherry	10 oz. shortcrust pastry
20 small potatoes, peeled	Egg to glaze

Oven temperature: hot (425°F., mark 7)

Steam the chicken with the onions. When it is cooked, remove the flesh and divide into convenient pieces. Cut up the mushrooms, add the sherry and cook with enough water to cover for about 5 minutes. Boil and drain the potatoes. Make a white sauce using the butter, flour and the liquor in which the mushrooms were cooked, made up to 1 pint with milk. Divide all these ingredients equally into 5 small soufflé dishes (3½ inches in diameter). Divide the pastry into 5 portions and roll each one to fit a dish. Cover the pies, taking great care not to stretch the pastry, and push the edges in before cutting off any excess. Using a pointed knife, outline a simple chicken shape on top of the pies. Brush with egg and bake in the centre of the oven for 20 minutes. (Serves 5.)

CHICKEN PUFFS

Oven temperature: hot (425°F., mark 7)

Leftovers of cold boiled fowl can be used to make these very delicious puffs. Mince the meat or chop it finely and blend it with a little white sauce. (You will probably have some of this left over – it is, of course, best if made from the chicken liquor.) Season with salt and pepper. Roll out some flaky or shortcrust pastry thinly and cut into squares or stamp into rounds. Place a spoonful of mixture on each piece of pastry, moisten the edges and fold in half to form triangles or half-circles. Brush the tops with a little beaten egg, make a small hole in the top with a skewer and bake towards the top of the oven for about 15 minutes. Serve hot or cold.

CHICKEN BOUCHÉES

8 oz. puff pastry	4 oz. cooked chicken, chopped
Beaten egg	1 tsp. lemon juice
2 oz. mushrooms	2 tsps. chopped parsley
A little milk or butter to cook mushrooms	¼ pint thick white sauce

Oven temperature: very hot (450°F., mark 8)

Roll out the pastry $\frac{1}{2}$ inch thick and cut out a number of bouchée cases, marking the tops with a smaller cutter so that they can be easily removed after baking. Brush with egg and bake in the centre of the oven for 15 minutes. Cut out the tops, scoop the uncooked part from inside the patties and put them back in the oven for a few minutes to dry the inside. Meanwhile cook the mushrooms in a little milk or butter, chop and allow to cool, then mix with the remaining ingredients. When the cases are cold, fill them with the chicken and mushroom mixture and put on the lids.

CHICKEN PICNIC PASTIES

1 onion, skinned and chopped	$\frac{1}{2}$ oz. seasoned flour
2 rashers of bacon, rinded and chopped	$\frac{1}{4}$ pint stock
	Salt and pepper
$\frac{1}{2}$ oz. butter	8 oz. bought puff pastry
$\frac{1}{2}$ lb. cooked chicken, minced	Egg to glaze

Oven temperature: hot (425°F., mark 7)

Fry the onion and bacon in the butter; add the chicken, the flour and the stock, season well and allow to cook for a few minutes, then cool. Roll out the pastry and cut into large rounds. Divide the filling between them, damp the edges of the pastry, fold over and seal well. Brush with egg and bake towards the top of the oven for 20–25 minutes.

RAISED GAME PIE

12 oz. hot-water crust pastry	The meat of 1 cooked pheasant or 2 pigeons, cut into small pieces
12 oz. sausage-meat	
4 oz. lean ham, cut into small cubes	
	Salt and pepper
6 oz. lean chuck steak, cut into small cubes	Beaten egg
	$\frac{1}{4}$–$\frac{1}{2}$ pint jellied stock

Oven temperature: hot (425°F., mark 7)

Make the pastry and cover it with a basin or a cloth to prevent a skin forming on it. Cut off a quarter of the pastry and keep it covered. Mould the remaining paste into a hollowed-out shell to form the bottom and sides of the pie. Fasten 3–4 folds of greased greaseproof paper round it to hold its shape. (The pastry will be soft at first, but will soon stiffen to hold this raised shape.) Line the base and sides of the pie with sausage-meat, to hold the pastry in a good shape. Mix the ham, steak and pheasant or pigeon meat, season well and fill the pie with the mixture. Damp the inner top edge of the pie wall and press into place a lid made from the remaining paste; press the edges together to form a rim. Cut the rim at $\frac{1}{2}$-inch intervals with scissors and fold down alternate "tabs". Make a small hole in the centre of the lid. A few leaves cut from any trimmings of pastry may be used as decoration.

70

Put the pie on a baking sheet and bake in the centre of the oven for 15–20 minutes; reduce the oven temperature to moderate (350°F., mark 4) and bake for a further 1½ hours, or until the meat is tender when tested with a skewer. If the top of the pie appears to be over-browning, cover it with a piece of greaseproof paper. Remove the pie from the oven and cool. Pour the jellied stock through the hole in the top and leave the pie to get cold. Top up with more stock if necessary.

If you have a 7-inch cake tin with a loose base, the pie may be baked in this. Grease the tin, line it with three-quarters of the pastry rolled out ¼ inch thick, fill as above and put on the lid. When the pie has cooked for 1½ hours, remove it from the tin and brush the top and sides with beaten egg. Put it on a baking tray and cook for a further 30 minutes, until golden brown. (Serves 6–8.)

RABBIT PIE

A small rabbit	2 tbsps. chopped parsley
A piece of fat bacon	¼ level tsp. mixed herbs
2–3 potatoes, peeled and sliced	1 bay leaf
1 onion, skinned and sliced	Stock or water
	8 oz. shortcrust pastry
Salt and pepper	Egg to glaze

Oven temperature: hot (425°F., mark 7)

Wash the rabbit thoroughly and cut into neat joints, putting aside the head and thin pieces of ribs for stock. Fill a pie dish with alternate layers of rabbit, bacon and vegetables, sprinkling each layer with seasoning and herbs. Put in the kidneys and heart of the rabbit, the bay leaf and sufficient liquid to come half-way up the dish. Roll out the pastry and cover the pie, brush with beaten egg and bake in the centre of the oven for 15 minutes or so, until the pastry is set and beginning to brown, then lower the heat to warm (325°F., mark 3) and cook for about 1½ hours in all.

RABBIT AND BACON TURNOVERS

12 oz. flaky pastry	Salt and pepper
8 oz. cooked rabbit	A little gravy or
4 oz. cooked bacon, chopped	stock
1 hard-boiled egg, chopped	Egg to glaze

Oven temperature: hot (425°F., mark 7)

Make the pastry and set aside to get very cold. Meanwhile prepare the filling for the turnovers. Cut up the rabbit into small pieces and mix with the bacon and egg. Season and moisten with a little gravy or stock. Roll out the pastry and cut into rounds, using a small plate as guide. Place some of the

71

filling on one half of each round, damp the edges and fold the pastry over to form a crescent shape; press the edges together and flake them. Place the turnovers on a baking tin, make some slits in the top and brush over with a little beaten egg or egg and milk. Bake towards the top of the oven for about 20–25 minutes.

SHORTCRUST PASTRY

4 oz. plain flour	1 oz. margarine
A pinch of salt	4 tsps. water (approx.)
1 oz. lard	

Mix the flour and salt together. Cut the fats into small knobs and add it. Using both hands, rub the fat into the flour between finger and thumb tips. After 2–3 minutes there will be no lumps of fat left and the mixture will look like fresh breadcrumbs. Add the water a little at a time, stirring with a round-bladed knife until the mixture begins to stick together. With one hand, collect it together and knead lightly for a few seconds, to give a firm, smooth dough. The pastry can be used straight away, but it is better allowed to "rest" for 15 minutes. It can also be wrapped in polythene and kept in the refrigerator for a day or two.

When the pastry is required, sprinkle a very little flour on a board or table and roll out the dough evenly, turning it occasionally. The usual thickness is about $\frac{1}{8}$ inch; don't pull or stretch it. Use as required.

The usual oven temperature for shortcrust pastry is hot (425°F., mark 7).

FLAKY PASTRY

8 oz. plain flour	8 tbsps. cold water to
A pinch of salt	mix (approx.)
6 oz. butter or a mixture	A squeeze of lemon juice
of butter and lard	Beaten egg to glaze

Mix together the flour and salt. Soften the fat by "working" it with a knife on a plate; divide it into 4 equal portions. Rub one quarter of the softened fat into the flour and mix to a soft, elastic dough with the water and lemon juice. On a floured board, roll the pastry into oblong 3 times as long as it is wide. Put another quarter of the fat over the top two-thirds of the pastry in flakes, so that it looks like buttons on a card. Fold the bottom third up and the top third of the pastry down and give it a half turn, so that the folds are not at the sides. Seal the edges of the pastry by pressing with the rolling pin. Re-roll as before and continue until all the fat is used up.

Wrap the pastry loosely in greaseproof paper and leave it to "rest" in the refrigerator or cool place for at least 30 minutes before using. This makes the handling and shaping of the pastry easier and gives a more evenly flaked texture.

Sprinkle a board or table with a very little flour. Roll out the pastry ⅛ inch thick and use as required. Brush with beaten egg before baking, to give the characteristic glaze.

The usual oven for cooking flaky pastry is hot (425°F., mark 7).

PUFF PASTRY

8 oz. plain flour	8 tbsps. cold water to
A pinch of salt	mix (approx.)
8 oz. butter	A squeeze of lemon juice
(preferably unsalted)	Beaten egg to glaze

Mix the flour and salt. "Work" the butter with a knife on a plate until it is soft, then rub about ½ oz. of it into the flour. Mix to a fairly soft, elastic dough with the water and lemon juice and knead lightly on a floured board until smooth. Form the rest of the butter into an oblong and roll the pastry out into a square. Place the fat on one half of the pastry and enclose it by folding the remaining pastry over and sealing the edges with a rolling pin. Turn the pastry so that the fold is to the side, then roll out into a strip 3 times as long as it is wide. Fold the bottom third up and the top third down and seal the edges by pressing lightly with the rolling pin. Cover the pastry with waxed or greaseproof paper and leave to "rest" in a cool place or in the refrigerator for about 20 minutes. Turn the pastry so that the folds are to the sides, and continue rolling, folding and resting until the sequence has been completed 6 times altogether.

After the final resting, shape the pastry as required. Always brush the top surfaces with beaten egg before cooking, to give the characteristic glaze of puff pastry.

The usual oven for cooking puff pastry is very hot (450°F., mark 8).

ROUGH PUFF PASTRY

8 oz. plain flour	8 tbsps. cold water to mix
A pinch of salt	(approx.)
6 oz. fat (butter or	A squeeze of lemon juice
margarine and lard	Beaten egg to glaze
mixed)	

Mix the flour and salt. Cut the fat (which should be quite firm) into cubes about ¾ inch across. Stir the fat into the flour without breaking up the pieces and mix to a fairly stiff dough with the water and lemon juice. Turn it on to a floured board and roll into a strip 3 times as long as it is wide. Fold the bottom third up and the top third down, then give the pastry

73

half a turn so that the folds are at the sides. Seal the edges of the pastry by pressing lightly with a rolling pin. Continue to roll and fold in this way, 4 times altogether.

Leave to "rest" wrapped in greaseproof paper for about ½ hour before using. Roll out and use as for flaky pastry. Glaze with egg before baking.

The usual oven for cooking this pastry is hot (425°F., mark 7).

HOT-WATER CRUST PASTRY

1 lb. plain flour
2 level tsps. salt
4 oz. lard

¼ pint plus 3 tbsps. milk or milk and water

Mix the flour and salt. Melt the lard in the liquid, then bring to the boil and pour into a well made in the dry ingredients. Working quickly, beat with a wooden spoon to form a fairly soft dough. Turn it out on to a lightly floured board and knead until smooth. Use as required. Keep the part of the dough that is not actually being used covered with a cloth or an up-turned basin, to prevent it hardening before you can use it.

The usual oven is hot (425°F., mark 7), reducing to moderate (350°F., mark 4) after about 15 minutes.

Savouries Made with Poultry and Game

CHICKEN À LA KING

2 oz. butter
4 oz. mushrooms, sliced
½ a green pepper, seeded and finely chopped (or 1 small canned pimiento, chopped)
1½ oz. flour

¾ pint milk or milk and chicken stock, mixed
8–12 oz. cooked chicken, diced
Salt, pepper and paprika or ground nutmeg
1–2 tbsps. sherry (optional)

Melt the butter and fry the mushrooms and pepper until soft. Stir in the flour, cook for 2–3 minutes, remove from the heat and stir in the liquid gradually. Bring to the boil and continue to stir until it thickens. Add the chicken, season to taste and add the sherry, if used. Serve with boiled rice or buttered noodles or as a snack with toast or crisp rolls.

Chicken à la King can be bought in cans and kept as a standby for a quick meal; serve as suggested above.

74

CHICKEN AU GRATIN WITH BROCCOLI

A 10-oz. pkt. of frozen broccoli
½ lb. cooked chicken, diced
1½ oz. butter or margarine
4 level tbsps. flour
½ level tsp. salt
½ pint chicken stock
½ pint evaporated milk, less 3 tbsps.
2 oz. Cheddar or Cheshire cheese, grated
2 oz. bread-crumbs
1 oz. butter for topping

Oven temperature: fairly hot (375°F., mark 5)

Cook the broccoli according to the directions on the packet and drain it. Place the chicken in an ovenproof dish and put the broccoli in a layer on top. Melt the butter or margarine in a saucepan and work in the flour and salt. Gradually stir in the combined chicken stock and evaporated milk; bring to the boil, stirring. Remove from the heat and add the cheese, then pour over the chicken and broccoli. Sprinkle with the bread-crumbs and dot with flakes of butter. Bake towards the top of the oven for about 20 minutes.

CHICKEN RAMEKINS

½ oz. butter
4 oz. cooked chicken, minced
2 mushrooms, chopped
2 eggs, separated
2 tbsps. single cream
Salt and pepper

Oven temperature: moderate (350°F., mark 4)

Grease 4 ramekins with the butter. Mix the chicken and mushrooms and bind with the egg yolks and cream; season to taste with salt and pepper. Whisk the egg whites stiffly and fold into the chicken mixture. Divide this mixture between the ramekins, place the ramekins on a baking tray and cook in the centre of the oven for 15–20 minutes. Serve at once.

The chicken mixture need not be cooked in separate dishes, but can be put into a greased 1-pint soufflé dish, baked just above the centre of a fairly hot oven (400°F., mark 6) for 25–30 minutes and served as a savoury.

CHICKEN-STUFFED AUBERGINES

2 even-sized aubergines
½ lb. cold cooked chicken, chopped
1 onion, skinned and chopped
¼ lb. tomatoes, skinned and chopped
Olive oil
Salt and pepper
A little chopped parsley

Oven temperature: fairly hot (400°F., mark 6)

Put the aubergines in a bowl, pour on some boiling water and leave them for about 10 minutes, then remove them and dry them well. Cut each aubergine in half and take out the flesh, leaving the shell unbroken. Cook the chicken, onion and tomatoes together in a little olive oil, season with salt and pepper, and add the chopped parsley, then add the flesh of the aubergines and mix well. Fill the halved aubergines with this savoury mixture, put them in a greased ovenproof dish and bake towards the top of the oven for 15–20 minutes, until the top is nicely browned.

CHICKEN-STUFFED TOMATOES

8 large tomatoes	4 oz. cooked peas
6 oz. cooked chicken, diced	Mayonnaise
1 small green or red pepper, seeded and chopped	Lettuce

Cut the tops off the tomatoes, scoop out the centres and mix them with the chicken, pepper, peas and a little mayonnaise. Fill the tomatoes with the mixture and put back the tops. Arrange on a bed of lettuce.

CHICKEN TERRAPIN

1 cold roasted chicken	Salt and pepper
⅛ pint sherry	6 oz. cooked rice
¼ pint double cream	

Cut the chicken flesh into cubes, place in a thick-based pan and add the sherry. Heat gently, turning the pieces the whole time. When the chicken is heated through, pour a little of the sherry into the cream, blend and season. Return this mixture carefully to the pan and heat gently, but do not boil. Serve the chicken with the rice. (This chicken mixture may also be served on toast or accompanied by toast fingers.)

CREAMED CHICKEN WITH MUSHROOM SAUCE

4 frozen chicken joints	3 tbsps. water
2 oz. butter	3 tbsps. sherry
Salt and pepper	Chopped parsley and
A 10-oz. can of condensed mushroom soup	chopped chives to garnish

Thaw the chicken. Melt the butter in a frying-pan and brown the joints evenly. Add the other ingredients, cover and cook gently for 30–45 minutes.

Garnish with chopped parsley and chives in equal proportions and serve with fingers of toast or boiled rice.

CREAMED CANNED CHICKEN

2 pints milk	A 12-oz. can of boned
2 oz. fat	chicken
2 oz. plain flour	1 onion, skinned and diced
1 chicken bouillon cube	1 pimiento, seeded and
½ level tsp. salt	diced
¼ level tsp. pepper	2 oz. blanched almonds
½ level tsp. curry powder	6 slices of buttered toast

76

Heat the milk. Melt the fat in a large saucepan, add the flour, crumbled bouillon cube and seasonings and cook for a few minutes to form a roux. Gradually pour in the heated milk, stirring, until the mixture thickens. Add the chicken, onion and pimiento and heat for 10–15 minutes. Toast the almonds under the grill and chop roughly. Pour the creamed mixture on to the toast and top with the almonds. (Serves 6.)

CROUSTADES OF CHICKEN

1 stale loaf	6 oz. cold chicken, chopped
1 oz. butter	2 oz. cooked mushrooms,
1 oz. flour	chopped
½–¾ pint milk	Deep fat for frying
Salt and pepper	

Cut the loaf into 3-inch cubes and scoop out the centre of each. Meanwhile make a sauce with the fat, flour, milk and seasoning and heat the chicken and mushrooms in it. Heat the fat until smoking hot, fry the croustades golden brown, drain well, then fill them immediately with the chicken mixture.

Other savoury fillings may also be used with these croustades.

DEVILLED CHICKEN

Joints of cold chicken	A pinch of pepper
1 level tsp. made mustard	A pinch of Cayenne pepper
¼ level tsp. salt	Olive oil or melted butter

Divide the chicken into neat pieces if necessary. Mix the seasonings to a smooth paste with the oil or butter. Make some slits across the chicken joints and fill these with the paste, then brush more paste over the flesh. Brown on all sides under a very hot grill and serve with potato crisps and watercress.

Other poultry and game can be treated in the same way.

FRIED SLICED CHICKEN (CHINESE)

½ lb. raw white chicken meat	1 clove of garlic, skinned
Salad oil	Fat or oil for frying
¼ lb. French beans, peppers or	Salt and pepper
other green vegetables	A little cooking sherry
¼ lb. mushrooms, peeled	Sugar
1 onion, skinned	

Slice the chicken thinly and coat the pieces with oil to prevent their sticking together. Slit each bean lengthwise and cut into 1-inch pieces. Cut the mushrooms and onion into small slices. Boil the beans till almost cooked, drain, cool by rinsing in cold water and drain. Rub the inside of the frying-pan with the garlic and heat the fat. Fry the onion till just cooked, seasoning to taste; remove and keep hot. Wipe the pan with a clean cloth and shallow-fry the chicken slices over a brisk heat until almost tender. Add the vegetables, sherry and a little sugar and stir well before serving.

PILAU OF CHICKEN LIVERS

5–6 chicken livers	6 oz. long-grain rice
2 oz. butter	Powdered mace
¾ pint chicken broth or water	½ level tsp. curry powder
	A pinch of saffron
Pepper and salt	(optional)
1 medium-sized onion, skinned and chopped	1 level tbsp. sultanas
	Paprika pepper

Wash the chicken livers well, cut them into small pieces and fry in a little of the butter until well browned. Cover with the broth, season well and simmer until tender. Meanwhile put the remainder of the fat into a saucepan, add the onion and fry until golden brown. Add the washed and well-drained rice and the seasonings and cook slowly until the grains are very lightly browned; if necessary add a little more fat. Add the chicken liver stock and cook until the rice has absorbed the liquid, but do not over-cook it – the rice grains should remain separate. Add the chicken livers and sultanas and blend well. Serve on a hot dish, garnished with a little paprika.

SPEEDY CHOP SUEY

A 10-oz. jar of chicken fillets in jelly	1 level tbsp. cornflour
	1 tsp. soy sauce
A 1-lb. can of chop suey vegetables	Gravy browning
	Boiled rice

Lift the chicken meat from the jelly and slice thinly, then heat gently in the jelly. Drain the liquid from the chop suey vegetables and heat it. Blend the cornflour to a smooth cream with a little cold water, gradually stir in the hot vegetable liquid and bring the mixture to the boil; boil for 1 minute, stirring. Add the vegetables, stir in the soy sauce, carefully fold in the chicken slices, with their liquid, and colour with a few drops of gravy browning. Heat through and serve with plain boiled rice.

CHICKEN LIVER CROÛTES

3–4 chicken livers	Croûtes of fried bread
1 oz. melted butter	2 hard-boiled eggs
A little lemon juice	Chopped parsley
Cayenne pepper and salt	

Fry the chicken livers in half the butter for about 10 minutes, then pound them to a paste and add the remaining butter, lemon juice and seasonings. Spread thickly on the fried croûtes and top each with a quarter of egg. Sprinkle with parsley and salt. (Serves 2.)

CHICKEN LIVER SAVOURIES

1 chicken liver
4 rashers of bacon, rinded
4 mushrooms
Salt and pepper

1 oz. butter
4 small pieces of toast
Watercress to
  garnish

Prepare the chicken liver and divide into 4 pieces. Roll up each piece of liver in a rasher of bacon; skewer together and grill under a moderate grill till cooked through. Prepare the mushrooms and cook in the butter, with seasoning and 1 tbsp. water. Put the mushrooms on to the buttered toast and pour their liquor over them. Put a bacon roll on each piece of toast and serve at once, garnished with watercress.

CHICKEN SMÖRREBRÖD
(see colour picture No. 10)

These Scandinavian open sandwiches are made from a very wide variety of ingredients, attractively arranged and garnished. Cold chicken makes a very good main component for smörrebröd.

For the base use brown or white bread, plain cheese biscuits, etc., and spread generously with butter or a mild cream cheese.

Suggested mixtures are:

1. Cold chicken, tomato and lettuce.
2. Cold chicken and endive, garnished with carrot.
3. Chopped chicken mixed with mayonnaise and garnished with radishes, tomato, lettuce, parsley, etc.
4. Salami slices, covered with chopped chicken mixed with mayonnaise.
5. Ham slices, with chopped chicken and hard-boiled egg.

TOASTED CHICKEN SANDWICHES

Mix some diced chicken with a little white sauce. Toast some slices of white bread on one side only and butter the untoasted side. Spread the chicken mixture generously on to the buttered side, sandwich together, cut into triangles and serve at once.

DEVILLED TURKEY DRUMSTICKS

Cut the drumsticks from a cooked turkey. (Other fair-sized portions can be used in the same way.) Score the flesh with a sharp knife, then brush over with melted butter.

To prepare the devilled mixture, mix on a plate 1 level tsp. each of French and English mustard, 2 level tsps. finely chopped chutney, a pinch of ground ginger and a little pepper, salt and Cayenne. Spread this mixture over and into the cuts

79

and leave the turkey legs for 1 hour or longer. Grill them on a greased grid under a medium heat until crisp and brown, turning them regularly to ensure even cooking. Serve garnished with watercress. (Serves 2.)

STUFFED TURKEY DRUMSTICKS
Oven temperature: fairly hot (375°F., mark 5)
Remove the bones and tendons from the drumsticks without breaking the skin, then fill the cavity in each with forcemeat or sausage-meat, keeping the original shape of the drumstick. Close the opening with a small skewer, cocktail stick or some string. Put the drumsticks in a greased ovenproof dish, add enough stock to come half-way up, and bake in the centre of the oven for about 1 hour, or until they are quite tender. (Serves 2.)

FRIED TURKEY
About ½ lb. turkey breast	2 tsps. tomato paste
2 small onions, skinned and chopped	Salt and pepper
	Sugar
2 oz. bacon, rinded and chopped	Beaten egg
	Bread-crumbs
½ oz. dripping	Deep fat for frying
1 oz. flour	Mashed potato
½ pint stock	

Cut some good slices of cooked turkey breast. Fry the onions and bacon in the melted dripping; when golden brown, add the flour, then gradually add the stock. Bring to the boil, add the tomato paste, with salt, pepper and sugar to taste, and simmer gently for about 15 minutes. Coat the turkey slices with egg and bread-crumbs, fry in deep fat and serve on a bed of mashed potato, surrounded by the sauce. (Serves 2–3.)

SAVOURY TURKEY BORDER
½ lb. cooked turkey	1 onion, skinned, finely chopped and fried
Salt and pepper	
1 oz. butter	1 green pepper, seeded and sliced
1 oz. flour	
1 rasher of bacon, rinded and chopped	Lemon juice
	1 egg yolk
3 olives, chopped	Mashed potato

Cut the turkey meat into small pieces and season it. Melt the butter in a pan, add the flour and cook for a few minutes. Add the bacon, olives, onion and the thin slices of green pepper. Cook over a low heat, then add the turkey and a little lemon juice and heat thoroughly. Re-season if necessary and finally bind the mixture with the egg yolk. Serve in a piped border of creamy mashed potatoes. (Serves 2–3.)

80

TURKEY AND EGG BRIDGE ROLLS

Small bridge rolls
Cold turkey (or
  chicken)
1–2 hard-boiled eggs

A little white sauce
Salt and pepper
Asparagus tips or
  watercress to garnish

Take the top off the rolls and scoop out the bread from the lower half. Cut up the turkey and eggs, bind together with the sauce and season well. Fill the empty bridge rolls with the mixture and garnish with asparagus tips or watercress.

TURKEY CIGARS

1 oz. butter
1 oz. flour
¼ pint stock
Salt and pepper
Lemon juice
4 oz. turkey, minced

2 oz. ham, minced
1 oz. mushrooms, minced
1 tbsp. top of the milk
Beaten egg and fine
  bread-crumbs to coat
Fat for frying

Melt the butter, stir in the flour and gradually add the stock; bring to the boil, season and add a few drops of lemon juice. Add the turkey, ham, mushrooms and milk and let the mixture cool. Form into cigar shapes, brush with beaten egg, coat with bread-crumbs and fry in really hot fat until golden brown. Serve hot with a good sauce, or cold with salad. (Makes about 4 "cigars".)

CURRIED CANNED TURKEY

1 small onion, skinned and
  chopped
1 oz. fat
2 oz. bacon, rinded and
  chopped
1 level tbsp. curry
  powder

3 level tbsps. flour
¼ pint stock, made from
  a cube
A 15-oz. can of minced
  turkey
Salt and pepper

Fry the onion lightly in the fat until soft. Add the bacon and fry for a further 1–2 minutes. Stir in the curry powder and flour and cook for 2–3 minutes, until browned. Remove the pan from the heat and gradually stir in the stock. Bring to the boil and continue to stir until the mixture thickens. Add the turkey and re-heat. Season to taste and serve with rice or creamed potatoes.

GAME CROQUETTES

¾ lb. cold cooked game
¾ lb. creamed potatoes
Salt and pepper

Beaten egg
Bread-crumbs
Fat for frying

Remove any bones or pieces of skin from the cold game and mince the flesh finely. Place it in a bowl with the creamed potatoes and seasoning and mix well. Form the mixture into croquettes, coat them with beaten egg and roll them in bread-crumbs. Heat the fat in a pan until smoking hot, then fry the croquettes until they are golden brown, turning them gently to avoid breaking. Drain the croquettes thoroughly and serve at once in a hot dish, accompanied by mushrooms and game chips and garnished with watercress. (Serves 4–5.)

MOCK SALMI OF WILD DUCK

This is a good way of using up any leftover pieces of these birds. Cut the meat into neat pieces and sprinkle with mixed salt and Cayenne pepper. Put the meat in a pan with a wine-glassful of olive oil, a glassful of claret and the juice of 2 Seville oranges. Shake the pan well over the heat until the duck pieces are very hot; serve with triangles of toast.

CHAPTER 6

Salads and cold dishes

CHICKEN SALAD

Roast the chicken the day before it is to be used and let it get cold without carving it. Slice the flesh neatly, cutting it from the bones wherever possible, and arrange it on a flat dish. Garnish with sprigs of watercress, parsley or small cress. Slice the stuffing with the flesh; if the bird has not been stuffed, small fried or baked forcemeat balls can be served with the chicken meat.

CHICKEN AND ALMOND SALAD

2–4 oz. raisins, stoned
12 oz. cooked chicken meat
2 oz. almonds, blanched
A small piece of raw onion, skinned (optional)
2–3 tbsps. mayonnaise or salad cream
2–3 tbsps. single cream
Salt and pepper
A squeeze of lemon juice
1 tbsp. chopped parsley
Lettuce or watercress, washed and trimmed

Cover the raisins with boiling water, leave for 5 minutes and drain. Cut the chicken meat into chunks. Roughly chop the almonds and brown lightly under the grill. Grate the onion. Mix the mayonnaise, cream, seasoning, lemon juice and parsley and combine with the raisins, chicken, almonds and onion in a bowl. Serve on a bed of lettuce or watercress.

CHICKEN AND CELERY SALAD

1 cooked chicken
2–3 sticks of celery, chopped
1 green pepper, seeded and minced
1 level tsp. grated onion
¼ pint mayonnaise
¼ pint single cream
1 tsp. lemon juice
Salt and pepper
Lettuce leaves
Pineapple chunks and asparagus tips

Cut the chicken into pieces, and mix with the celery, pepper,

83

onion, mayonnaise, cream and lemon juice; season well. Pile on to a bed of lettuce leaves and surround with pineapple and asparagus.

CHICKEN AND HAM SALAD

4 oz. boned cooked chicken, diced

6 oz. cooked ham or tongue, diced

A small can of pineapple chunks, drained, or ¼ of a melon, peeled and chopped

2 red-skinned eating apples, diced

6 oz. long-grain rice, cooked
Salad cream
Juice and grated rind of ½ a lemon
Lettuce or watercress and tomato

Mix the chicken, ham, and pineapple or melon, apple and rice. Blend the salad cream with the lemon juice and rind and fold into the other ingredients. Serve on a bed of lettuce or watercress and garnish with wedges of tomato.

CHICKEN AND GRAPE SALAD

1–2 lettuces
1 cold chicken, jointed and boned
1 lemon
2 hard-boiled eggs, chopped

6 small onions, skinned and chopped
1 tsp. chopped parsley
French dressing
¼ lb. green grapes

Shred the lettuces and arrange them on a dish. Dice the chicken, keeping the white meat separate from the brown meat. Peel the lemon, remove the pith and pips and dice the flesh. Arrange the chicken meat on the lettuce and scatter with the lemon, eggs, onions and parsley. Cover with French dressing and decorate with the grapes.

VIRGINIAN CHICKEN APPLE SALAD

8 oz. red-skinned eating apples, diced but unpeeled
4 tbsps. lemon juice
1¼ lb. cooked chicken meat, diced
8 oz. celery, sliced
2 oz. almonds, blanched and slivered

4 oz. stuffed olives, sliced
4 tbsps. salad cream
⅛ pint double cream, whipped
2 level tsps. salt
1 lettuce
Endive or chicory
1 red-skinned apple to garnish

Toss the apple in half the lemon juice. Combine the chicken, apple, celery, nuts and olives. Blend the salad cream, whipped cream and salt, add the chicken mixture and mix all lightly together. Place in the refrigerator to chill. To serve, heap the salad on a bed of lettuce and endive or chicory. Core the apple, slice into rings, without peeling, dip them in the remaining lemon juice and arrange round the salad, with some endive or chicory tucked in the centre of each ring. (Serves 4–6.)

CHICKEN AND RICE SALAD

1 apple
Lemon juice
½ lb. cold cooked chicken
4 tbsps. dry cooked rice
1 celery heart, chopped
1 hard-boiled egg, chopped

1–2 oz. stoned raisins
  or dates
Mayonnaise
Salt and pepper
Chicory, radishes, etc.

Dice the apple without peeling it and marinade it in the lemon juice. Cut up the chicken into small pieces and mix with the rice, celery and apple. Add the egg and the raisins or chopped dates, mix with the mayonnaise, add a little seasoning and serve in a large bowl or in individual portions on crisp lettuce leaves, with other salad vegetables if desired.

CURRIED CHICKEN SALAD

6 oz. long-grain rice
½ a cooked chicken
1 small cauliflower, washed and
  trimmed
3 tbsps. French dressing
¼ pint mayonnaise
2 tbsps. milk or single cream
3 level tsps. curry powder

Salt and pepper
1 small green pepper,
  seeded and cut into strips
2 sticks of celery, chopped
1–2 small onions, skinned and
  finely sliced
1 lettuce, washed

Cook the rice in the usual way and leave to cool. Cut the chicken meat into chunks. Divide the cauliflower into small sprigs and toss with the rice in the French dressing. Combine the mayonnaise, milk or cream, curry powder, and seasoning in a large bowl, add the chicken and toss together. Add the rice mixture, the green pepper, the celery and the onions and serve on a bed of lettuce.

Flaked coconut, salted peanuts, pineapple cubes, tomato wedges and red-currant jelly, served in small dishes, make good accompaniments.

CALYPSO CHICKEN SALAD

1 fresh pineapple (about 2 lb.)
2½ lb. cooked chicken
4 oz. long-grain rice, cooked
8 oz. cooked peas
4 sticks of celery, sliced
9 tbsps. French dressing

½–1 level tsp. curry powder
1½ level tsps. salt
A little fresh lime juice
1 lime, cut in wedges
  (optional)
Lettuce

Remove the pineapple core and cut the flesh into 1-inch chunks. Cut the chicken flesh into 1-inch pieces. Put all the ingredients apart from the lime wedges into a large bowl, toss lightly, then put into the refrigerator or in a cold place. Serve on individual beds of crisp lettuce leaves, garnished with the lime. (Serves 6.)

For a party-piece, you might buy 2 pineapples (keeping the flesh of one for use at a later meal) and use "bowls" made from the shells of both as individual containers for the salad. To make the "bowls", cut each pineapple lengthwise into 3 wedge-shaped pieces and take out the flesh, being careful not to damage the shell or the green top.

CHICKEN AND PINEAPPLE SALAD
(see colour picture No. 7)
Dice some cold cooked chicken and cucumber and mix them together; add a little chopped mint and arrange on a dish. Surround with sliced pineapple and cucumber, garnish with mint leaves and serve very cold.

CHICKEN CHAUDFROID
¼ pint aspic jelly
A cooked chicken (about 3 lb. before cooking)
¼ pint Béchamel sauce (see chapter 10, p. 139)

Cucumber, pickled walnuts, radish and strips of lemon rind to garnish the chaudfroid

Make up the aspic as directed on the packet and leave it until it has almost reached setting point. Place the chicken on a cooling rack over a tray or large plate. Add half the aspic to the Béchamel sauce, stir in lightly and allow to thicken but not set. (Keep the remaining aspic in a basin which is standing in a bowl of warm water.) Coat the chicken by pouring the sauce steadily over it to give a smooth, even surface; allow the excess to run off and collect in the tray. Decorate the chicken with strips of cucumber skin, pieces of pickled walnut, slices of radish and strips of lemon rind, then carefully spoon over it the remaining aspic (which should be at setting point), so that the coated bird is completely covered but the decoration is not disturbed. (Serves 4–5.)

CHAUDFROID OF CHICKEN PIECES
(see colour picture No. 7)
A chicken (2½–3 lb.)
1 calf's foot
2 carrots, peeled and sliced
Thyme and marjoram
Salt and pepper
1½ oz. butter

1½ oz. flour
2 tbsps. single cream
2 egg yolks
Cucumber, radish or cress leaves to garnish chicken
Lettuce, tomatoes, etc.

Cook the chicken with the calf's foot, the carrots, thyme, marjoram, salt and pepper and water to cover; simmer gently for 45–50 minutes, then remove the chicken and allow to cool. Boil the stock to reduce it slightly. Make a roux with the butter and flour, add ¾ pint of the stock and allow to cook and thicken, stirring all the time. Add the cream, beat in the egg yolks and allow to cool. Cut the chicken into pieces, dip each piece twice into the tepid sauce and leave to drain on a rack.

86

Arrange on a lettuce-lined dish and decorate with cucumber, radish or cress leaves. Garnish the dish with tomato, cucumber and hard-boiled egg and add some cut radishes. (Serves 6–7.)

CHICKEN MOUSSE

¼ pint aspic jelly
Slices of cucumber and thin strips of tomato and lemon rind to garnish
12 oz. cooked chicken, minced

¼ pint Béchamel sauce (see chapter 10, p. 139)
2–3 tbsps. mayonnaise
½ pint double cream, whipped

Line a 1½-pint mould or some individual moulds with a little aspic jelly and allow to set. Decorate with a few slices of cucumber and strips of tomato and lemon rind, spoon a little more jelly over and allow to set. Mix the chicken, Béchamel sauce and mayonnaise and add the remainder of the aspic jelly. When the mixture is on the point of setting, fold in the whipped cream. Turn the mixture into the mould or moulds and leave to set. When it is cold and firm, turn out and garnish with sliced cucumber, etc.

MOUSSE MARGUERITE

8 oz. cooked chicken, minced
2 level tsps. salt
Pepper
3 tbsps. lemon juice
1 level tsp. ground celery seed

¼ pint mayonnaise
¾ oz. gelatine
1½ gills stock
¼ pint double cream or evaporated milk, whipped
Chopped aspic to decorate

Blend the chicken, salt, pepper, strained lemon juice, celery seed and mayonnaise together. Dissolve the gelatine in the stock and allow to cool before adding it to the chicken mixture. When it is on the point of setting, fold in the whipped cream. Pour quickly into a wetted mould and leave in a cool place. When the mousse is required for serving, turn it out on to a bed of chopped aspic.

To prepare chopped aspic, dissolve 1 oz. gelatine in prepared aspic jelly, set it and chop it on wet greaseproof paper with a wet knife.

CHICKEN AND HAM MOUSSE

¼ pint aspic jelly
Hard-boiled egg, peas, etc. to garnish
½ lb. cooked chicken
2 oz. cooked ham
2 oz. mushrooms
¾ pint milk

1 oz. butter
1 oz. flour
Salt and pepper
½ oz. gelatine
2 egg whites
Watercress or lettuce to decorate

Line a mould with aspic jelly (made up as directed on packet) and decorate with sliced hard-boiled egg, peas, olives, mushrooms or radishes, arranged in an attractive pattern. Cover with more aspic and allow to set. Meanwhile mince the chicken and ham very finely. Wash and cut up the mushrooms and cook in some of the milk; strain the liquid, make it up to $\frac{1}{2}$ pint with the remaining milk and with it make a white sauce, using the butter and flour. Add the chicken and ham and the remaining aspic and season well. Dissolve the gelatine in a little hot water and add this to the mixture. Finally whisk the egg whites till stiff and fold them in. Pour the mixture into the mould and leave to set. Turn it out and decorate.

CHICKEN AND HAM SLICES

1 pint aspic jelly
6 oz. cooked ham, minced
6 oz. cooked chicken, minced
2 hard-boiled eggs, chopped
Salad

Make up the aspic as directed on the packet. Divide it into three portions and mix one with the ham, one with the chicken and one with the chopped eggs. Set the ham mixture in the bottom of a loaf tin; when it is quite firm, set the egg mixture on this, then add the chicken jelly. Leave to set quite firmly, then turn out and serve with salad.

CHICKEN AND MUSHROOM DARIOLES

$\frac{1}{2}$ pint liquid aspic
  jelly (made up as directed
  on packet)
$\frac{1}{2}$ a cucumber, cubed
4 oz. mushrooms
A little milk
$\frac{1}{4}$ pint white sauce
$\frac{1}{2}$ lb. cooked chicken, cut up
Salt and pepper
Lettuce and salad plants

Pour a little of the aspic into each dariole mould, decorate with cubed cucumber and allow to set. Chop the mushrooms and cook in a little milk; mix them with the remaining aspic, the sauce and the chicken. Season well, pour into the dariole moulds and leave to set, then turn out on to a bed of lettuce. Decorate with other salad vegetables.

CHICKEN AND TONGUE LOAF

$\frac{1}{2}$ lb. cooked chicken
$\frac{1}{2}$ lb. tongue
1 green pepper
1 red pepper
6 olives
$\frac{1}{4}$ oz. gelatine
$\frac{1}{2}$ pint good chicken stock
Salt and pepper
Peaches to garnish

Cut up the chicken and tongue; seed the peppers and chop them and the olives finely, then mix with the meats. Dissolve the gelatine in some of the stock, add the rest, season well and add to the mixture. Set in a loaf tin and serve sliced, garnished with peaches (or as desired).

88

CHICKEN LOAVES

Leftovers take on a new dignity when served in this way; it is also a good idea for using one or two pieces of cut raw chicken.

Prepare ½ pint white sauce and add ¼ lb. minced chicken meat and 2 beaten eggs. Mix well, season, place in some well-greased individual loaf tins and cover each with greased paper. Steam for 30 minutes, or until well set. Turn the loaves out and allow to cool. Serve on a bed of lettuce and decorate with slices of carrot and sprigs of parsley.

CHICKEN IN ASPIC
(see colour picture No. 7)

A medium-sized cooked
  chicken
1 pint aspic
Hard-boiled egg, sliced

Asparagus tips
1 small pkt. of frozen
  peas

Cut up the chicken into small pieces. Make up the aspic and when it is cold, pour a little in an oblong mould; when this sets decorate with hard-boiled eggs and asparagus. Pour a little more aspic over the decoration and allow to set in the refrigerator. Mix the chicken with most of the aspic, just keeping enough back to mix with the peas, and pour in; put the mould in a cold place to set. Meanwhile cook the peas and when they are cold, mix with the remaining aspic and pour into the mould. Leave to set and turn out when required. Serve with salad. (Serves 4–6).

CHICKEN IN CURRY MAYONNAISE

8 oz. (approx.) cooked chicken
  or turkey diced
1–2 red apples, peeled and
  diced
3–4 sticks celery, diced
1 tbsp. mixed herbs (optional)

2–3 tsps. curry powder
1 tbsp. lemon juice
¼ pint salad cream
¼ pint single cream (or a small
  can of cream)
Lettuce

Mix together the chicken, apple, celery and herbs in a salad bowl. Blend the curry powder with the lemon juice and add to the salad cream. Fold in the cream. Pour the curry mayonnaise over the salad, then toss lightly. Serve on a bed of lettuce, or with cold cooked rice.

COLD CHICKEN SOUFFLÉS

½ oz. gelatine
¼ pint liquid aspic jelly
½ pint white sauce
8 oz. minced chicken
Salt and pepper

1 small can of evaporated
  milk
2 egg whites
Salad garnish

Dissolve the gelatine in the aspic jelly, mix with the sauce and

89

chicken, season and leave till nearly set. Whip up the evaporated milk, and when it is stiff, fold it into the mixture; lastly add the stiffly beaten egg whites; pour quickly into prepared soufflé dishes and leave in a cold place to set. When firm, remove the papers carefully with the help of a hot wetted knife and decorate with radish or cucumber and parsley sprigs. Serve with lettuce.

GALANTINE OF CHICKEN

A boiling chicken	2 oz. cooked ham, chopped
Salt and pepper	2 oz. cooked tongue, chopped
12 oz. sausage-meat	$\frac{1}{2}$–$\frac{1}{2}$ pint aspic jelly
2 hard-boiled eggs, sliced	Sliced cucumber, olives, egg, etc., to garnish

Bone the bird as described in the Supplement, p. 165.

When all the bones are removed, spread out the bird and sprinkle the flesh with salt and pepper. Cover the body of the bird with the sausage-meat, pushing it inside the wings and legs so that they regain their original shape. Arrange the sliced eggs, ham and tongue over the sausage-meat and season again. Wrap the cut ends of the skin over one another to make a neat shape, as like that of the original bird as possible. Using a large bodkin or trussing needle and a piece of string, sew the skin in place.

Wrap the bird in a clean cloth, tie firmly, put in a large pan and cover with salted water. Put on the lid and simmer for about 2 hours or until tender. When the chicken is cooked, remove from the pan and re-shape. When it is cold, remove the cloth, coat with aspic jelly (made according to the manufacturer's instructions), decorate with slices of cucumber, stuffed olives, hard-boiled egg, etc., and cover with more aspic jelly; leave to set. Serve the galantine sliced, accompanied by a salad.

JELLIED CHICKEN SALAD

$\frac{3}{4}$ pint chicken stock	2 tbsps. chopped pickle (optional)
Salt and pepper	8 oz. cooked peas
$\frac{1}{2}$ oz. gelatine	Lettuce, cucumber and
$\frac{1}{2}$ lb. diced chicken	radishes to garnish
$\frac{1}{4}$ pint mayonnaise	

Skim any fat from the chicken stock and season it well. Dissolve the gelatine in a little stock over hot water and mix with all the ingredients (except the lettuce, etc.); pour into a wetted mould and leave to set. Place lettuce leaves on a dish and arrange the sliced chicken mould on them. Garnish with cucumber and radishes.

Other poultry (or game) leftovers may be used in this way, the vegetable or salad garnish being varied accordingly.

JELLIED CHICKEN AND HAM

½ pint aspic jelly	Radish
½ lb. chicken pieces	Hard-boiled egg
¼ lb. ham pieces	Lettuce
6 olives, chopped	

Pour some of the aspic into a wetted loaf tin and leave to set. Mince the chicken and ham very finely and mix with the rest of the aspic and the olives; pour into the loaf tin and leave to set. Turn out and decorate with sliced radish and hard-boiled egg and lettuce.

PIQUANT CHICKEN MOULD

½ pint chicken stock	2–3 sticks of celery, chopped
1 tbsp. gelatine	1 small green pepper, seeded
¼ tsp. Tabasco sauce	and diced
2–3 tbsps. lemon juice	1 red-skinned eating apple,
5 tbsps. mayonnaise	diced
2 tsps. very finely chopped	8–12 oz. cooked chicken, diced
onion	Lettuce

Place the chicken stock in a saucepan, sprinkle the gelatine over the surface and dissolve over a low heat, but do not boil. Add the Tabasco sauce and lemon juice; leave to cool. Gradually whisk in the mayonnaise. When beginning to set, fold in the onion, celery, pepper, apple and finally the chicken. Turn into a dampened mould and leave to set. Unmould on to lettuce leaves or other green salad.

COLD CHICKEN CURRY – 1

10 oz. long-grain rice	½ pint mayonnaise
A medium-sized cooked	1 small head of celery,
chicken	chopped
1 small cauliflower	1 lettuce
2 level tbsps. curry powder	½ lb. tomatoes, skinned and
Salt and pepper	sliced
2 tbsps. single cream or	2 onions, skinned and cut
top of the milk	into rings

Cook the rice (see p. 150). Cut the chicken into small pieces. Wash the cauliflower and cut the flower into small pieces. Fold the curry powder, salt, pepper and cream into the mayonnaise. When the rice is cooked, add the chicken, cauliflower and celery, then fold in the mayonnaise mixture; chill thoroughly. Just before serving, arrange on lettuce leaves in a large dish and decorate with tomato slices and onion rings. (Serves 4–5.)

Another cold chicken curry recipe is given overleaf. For either recipe you could buy pieces of cooked chicken instead of a whole bird.

COLD CHICKEN CURRY – 2

A chicken
2 oz. butter
2 large onions, skinned
  and sliced
1 level tbsp. curry powder
2 level tbsps. flour
¾ pint stock

1 apple
Salt to taste
1 level tsp. sugar
Lemon juice
¼ pint single cream
Banana and parsley to
  garnish

Cut the chicken into pieces. Melt the butter and fry the chicken until golden brown; remove it, and fry the onions. Add the curry powder and flour, fry for a minute and gradually add the stock. Put the chicken into the sauce, also the cut-up apple, salt, sugar and a little lemon juice. Simmer gently for about 1 hour, add the cream and leave to cool. Remove the surface skin, garnish with banana and parsley and serve with boiled rice, tomato salad and chutney. (Serves 4–5.)

DUCK AND TANGERINE SALAD

2 lettuce hearts
¾ lb. cold cooked duck
6 tangerines
1 bunch of watercress

½ lb. cooked peas
2 tbsps. French dressing
Parsley and tangerine sections
  to garnish

Arrange the lettuce heart on a flat dish. Slice the cooked duck and arrange the pieces neatly on the lettuce. Peel the tangerines, removing any white pith, and divide 2 of them into sections. Push a small bunch of watercress into the top of each of the whole tangerines and put these on the dish with the sliced duck. Toss the cooked green peas in the French dressing and arrange them round the duck. Garnish with parsley and the tangerine sections.

Cooked goose may be served in the same way.

CHAUDFROID OF PHEASANT

1 pheasant
Minced pheasant, chicken
  or other game or poultry
  for filling
A piece of ham (about ¾ lb.)
Stock
Carrot, onion and turnip,
  peeled

Peppercorns
A bouquet garni
Brown chaudfroid sauce
  (see chapter 10, p. 139)
Aspic jelly
Cooked vegetables for
  garnish

Bone the pheasant as described in the Suppplement, p.165. and stuff the wings and legs with the minced filling. Cut the piece of ham into a wedge shape to represent the breast bone, put it in place and stuff the bird with the rest of the filling. Sew up the ends, press the bird into shape and tie the legs as if it were trussed for roasting. Put it in a pudding cloth and sew tightly to keep it a good shape, tucking the ends underneath and sewing them down. Re-shape the bird and simmer it gently for 1½ hours in a pan of stock with the flavouring vegetables, peppercorns and bouquet garni. When the pheasant is cooked, take it out, tighten the cloth and leave to cool. When it is quite cold, skin it and put it on a wire rack. Meanwhile prepare a chaudfroid sauce and when this is on the point of setting, pour it over the bird and leave to set. Coat with aspic and when this sets, decorate with the cooked vegetable garnish. Cover again with aspic jelly and leave to set. Serve the pheasant on a dish of salad.

TERRINE OF HARE, RABBIT OR GAME

½ lb. calves' liver	1 hare, or rabbit, or
¼ lb. fat bacon, rinded	equivalent in game
Salt and pepper	2 level tsps. mixed herbs
1 onion, skinned and finely chopped	A little butter

Oven temperature: fairly hot (375°F., mark 5)

Soak the liver in cold water for ½ hour, then dry it in a cloth. Cut the liver and the bacon into small dice and fry them together until cooked, adding a little more fat if necessary. Season well and sprinkle in the onion. Now drain off the fat and put the mixture through a mincing machine. Mince the rabbit or hare liver and any trimmings and add these to the mixture.

Wash the rabbit or hare and cut it in small joints, or better still, in small pieces free from bone. Season with pepper, salt and finely powdered herbs, then fry the pieces for a few minutes in the fat left over from frying the liver. Grease a strong terrine or ovenproof dish and put in a layer of the liver mixture. On this put a layer of rabbit or hare; continue putting in alternate layers until the dish is full, making the last layer one of liver mixture. Smooth over the top with a knife, cover with greased paper, stand the terrine in a tin with hot water coming half-way up the sides and cook in the centre of the oven for 1½ hours. Run a little liquid butter over the top. Serve the terrine cold, with a crisp green salad. (Serves 5–6.)

CHAPTER 7

Poultry and game soups

The basis of most of these soups is of course a stock made from chicken, turkey, etc. We also include a few soups featuring eggs.

CHICKEN, TURKEY OR GAME STOCK

A carcase of chicken, turkey or game bird	1 onion, skinned and sliced
Cleaned feet of the bird	1 carrot, peeled and sliced
Giblets	Outside sticks of celery, scrubbed and sliced
½ level tbsp. salt	A bouquet garni (see p. 24)
Cold water to cover	

Place all the ingredients in a large pan, bring to the boil, skim, cover and simmer for 3–4 hours. Strain and when cold remove all trace of fat. Store in a cool place; if not in a refrigerator, boil up daily.

CHICKEN BROTH

1 small boiling chicken	2 oz. each carrot and celery, diced
Cold water (3–4 pints)	
2 level tsps. salt	1 heaped tbsp. long-grain rice
¼ level tsp. pepper	
1 onion, skinned and halved	Chopped parsley

Ask the butcher to pluck and draw the chicken and remove the head and feet. Wash the bird, cut it in half, put into a large pan, cover with water and add the seasoning and vegetables. Bring to the boil and simmer for 3–3½ hours, adding more water if necessary. Strain, then remove any grease from the top of the broth with a metal spoon or by drawing a piece of kitchen paper across the surface of the liquid. Return the broth to the pan, bring to the boil, sprinkle in the rice and simmer for 15–20 minutes, until the rice is soft. Serve sprinkled with chopped parsley.

Some of the meat can be finely chopped and added to the broth, the rest being used in made-up dishes (e.g. fricassee).

The broth can also be made with a chicken carcase instead of a whole chicken, when it will need to be simmered for 1–1½ hours only.

RICH CREAM OF CHICKEN

1 onion, skinned and finely chopped	½ pint milk
½ a green pepper, seeded and finely chopped	2 oz. mushrooms, sliced
	4 oz. peas
2 oz. butter	Chunks of chicken
2 oz. plain flour	1 bay leaf
1 pint chicken stock	Salt and pepper
	Toast croûtons

Sauté the onion and pepper for 5 minutes in the butter. Add the flour and stir until cooked but not brown, then mix in the stock and milk gradually. Add the mushrooms, peas, chicken, bay leaf and seasoning and bring to the boil, stirring all the time. Simmer gently for 1 hour. Serve with croûtons of toast.

CHICKEN AND RICE SOUP

2 oz. instant rice	2 egg yolks
2 pints chicken stock (made from 2 bouillon cubes)	Juice of 1 lemon

Cook the rice in the stock for 10 minutes, remove from the heat and cool slightly. Pour on to the egg yolk, gently whisking all the time. Finally add the lemon juice and serve at once.

ALMOND CHICKEN SOUP

2 tbsps. olive oil	1 tsp. chopped parsley
4 oz. almonds, finely chopped	1 oz. bread-crumbs
	2 pints chicken stock
1 tbsp. chopped onion	Salt and pepper
½ tsp. chopped garlic	

Heat the olive oil and slowly cook in it the chopped almonds, onion, garlic and parsley, stirring all the time: the mixture should be well cooked, but not browned. Add the bread-crumbs and cook very slowly for a further 3 minutes. Pour on the stock, season well and simmer for 15 minutes.

CHICKEN SOUP WITH POACHED EGGS

2 pints chicken broth	Butter or margarine
A 10-oz. can of consommé (undiluted)	4 eggs
	Grated Parmesan or Cheddar cheese
8 1-inch slices of long Continental bread	

Heat the broth and consommé in a saucepan and bring to the

boil; meanwhile sauté the bread in hot butter in a large frying-pan until browned on both sides. Poach the eggs in the hot (not boiling) soup in the usual way, then place one egg in each soup plate. Pour some broth over the eggs (strain it if desired). Sprinkle the sautéed bread with cheese, place 2 slices beside each egg and serve with additional cheese.

COCK-A-LEEKIE

1 boiling fowl (about 2½ lb.)	Salt and pepper
2 pints stock or water	6 prunes (optional)
4 leeks, cleaned and sliced	

Cover the fowl with stock or water and add the leeks and seasoning. Bring to the boil and simmer gently for 3½ hours, until tender. Remove the chicken from the stock, carve off the meat and cut into fairly large pieces. Serve the soup with the chicken pieces in it, or serve the soup on its own, with the chicken as a main course.

If prunes are used, soak them overnight in cold water, halve and stone them and add to the stock 30 minutes before the end of the cooking.

MULLIGATAWNY SOUP

1 onion, skinned and finely chopped	1 oz. butter
1 carrot, peeled and finely chopped	1¾ pints brown stock
	1–2 tbsps. curry powder
½ lb. tomatoes, skinned and chopped	2 cloves
	1 tbsp. chopped parsley
½ a green pepper, seeded and chopped	Sugar, salt and pepper
	3 level tbsps. flour or cornflour
2 sticks of celery, scrubbed and finely chopped	¼ pint milk
	Leftovers of cold cooked chicken meat, cut small
1 apple, peeled and finely chopped	1 oz. cooked rice

Cook the vegetables and apple in the butter for 5 minutes. Add the stock, flavourings and seasonings, cover and simmer for 2–2½ hours. Sieve the soup, return it to the pan and re-heat. Blend the flour and milk to a smooth cream, stir in a little of the hot soup and return the mixture to the pan. Add the chicken meat and the rice, bring to the boil, stirring until the soup thickens, and cook for a further 2–3 minutes. Re-season if necessary before serving.

CHINESE CHICKEN NOODLE SOUP

3 oz. raw chicken meat	1 oz. egg noodles
2 oz. bamboo shoots	Salt to taste
3 oz. ham	1 tbsp. vesop
2 pints chicken stock	1 tbsp. sherry

96

Slice the chicken, bamboo shoots and ham into matchstick strips, then simmer in the stock for 10 minutes. Add the noodles and salt and simmer for 5 minutes. Stir in the vesop and sherry and cook for 3 minutes.

CHINESE EGG FLOWER SOUP

2 pints chicken stock	½ level tsp. salt
6 eggs	2 scallions or spring onions,
2 tbsps. soy sauce	finely chopped
1 tsp. vinegar	

Heat the stock in a saucepan. Meanwhile beat the eggs well, then pour in a thin stream into the soup, stirring. Add the soy sauce, vinegar and salt and simmer for 1 minute. Garnish with scallions.

EGG AND TOMATO SOUP

2 lb. tomatoes	Salt
1 large onion	Pepper
A little oil or butter	½ level tsp. sugar
2 pints water	A knob of butter
A little finely chopped parsley	2 hard-boiled eggs, sliced

Slice the tomatoes without peeling them and skin and slice the onion. Put these into a pan with some oil or butter and cook for 10 minutes, crushing the tomatoes to release the juice. Add the water and parsley, cover, simmer for 1 hour, then sieve; add the salt, pepper and sugar. Stir in a knob of butter just before serving, then pour the soup into a hot tureen containing the sliced hard-boiled eggs.

GIBLET SOUP

Giblets from 2 chickens	A bouquet garni
3 pints stock or stock and water	Salt and pepper
	1 oz. butter
A few chicken bones	1 oz. flour
1 onion, skinned and cut up	1 small glass of port
1 carrot, peeled and cut up	(optional)

Wash the giblets thoroughly, put them into a pan with the stock and add the bones, vegetables, herbs and seasoning. Cover and simmer gently until the giblets are tender – about 2 hours. Strain off the liquor; cut up the edible parts of the giblets and reserve them. Melt the butter in a pan, add the flour to make a roux and add the giblet stock gradually, stirring well to keep it smooth. Cook for about 5 minutes, then add the giblet meat and seasoning to taste; if port is included, stir it in just before serving the soup.

The giblets and carcase of a turkey (or other poultry) may also be used in this way.

GAME SOUP WITH SAVOURY DUMPLINGS

½ a 4-oz. pkt. of unsweetened
suet pudding mix
½ level tsp. mixed dried
herbs

A can of game soup plus
½ canful water
Salt and pepper if required

Empty the suet pudding mix into a basin, stir in the herbs and make up as directed. Divide the mixture into 16 pieces and make into small dumplings. Bring the soup and water to the boil, drop in the dumplings and when they rise to the top, lower the heat, cover the pan and simmer for 15 minutes. Check the seasoning. (These dumplings may also be served with home-made game soup of course.)

HOLLANDAISE SOUP

1 tsp. each carrot and
cucumber "peas" and green
peas to garnish
1 oz. butter
1 oz. flour

1 pint white stock
Salt and pepper
¼ pint milk
1 egg yolk
2–3 tbsps. single cream

First make the garnish; Cut pea-sized balls from pieces of carrot and cucumber, then cook separately in boiling salted water, drain and rinse. Melt the butter in a thick pan, remove from the heat, add the flour and mix in carefully. Return the pan to the heat and cook the mixture without browning. Slowly add the seasoned stock, stirring constantly, and bring to the boil; add half the milk. Blend the egg yolk, cream and remaining milk. Add the vegetable garnish to the soup, then strain in the egg and cream mixture and cook gently, without boiling, until the egg yolk thickens. (Serves 3–4.)

HARE OR RABBIT SOUP

½ a hare or rabbit
2 oz. butter or dripping
1 onion, skinned and sliced
2 oz. lean ham or bacon,
diced
A stick of celery, scrubbed and
sliced
1 carrot and 1 turnip, peeled
and chopped

A bouquet garni
Salt and pepper
3 pints beef stock
3 level tbsps. flour
1 glass port
2 tsps. red currant jelly
A squeeze of lemon juice
Forcement balls (optional)

The tougher parts of a hare or rabbit (legs, head) may be used for making soup. Cut them into pieces and break or chop the bones. Fry the meat and bones in the fat with the onion and the ham or bacon for 5–10 minutes, until well browned. Add the other vegetables, bouquet garni, seasoning and stock, mix well, cover and simmer gently for 3–4 hours. When the meat and vegetables are soft, strain off the liquid through a sieve and rub some of the meat through. Allow the soup to become cold, skim off any fatty layer and return it to a saucepan to re-heat. Blend the flour with the wine to a smooth cream. Stir in a little of the hot soup and return the mixture to the pan with the red currant jelly. Bring to the boil, stirring until the soup thickens, then cook for a further 5 minutes and add the lemon juice and more seasoning if necessary. If the blood from the hare has been kept, stir it into the soup, but don't boil again, or the soup will curdle.

A garnish of forcemeat balls may be served with this soup.

HARE GIBLET SOUP

2 sets of hare giblets	1½ pints stock
1 large carrot, peeled	1 oz. dripping
1 onion, skinned	1 oz. flour
1 small turnip, peeled	Salt and pepper
A piece of celery, scrubbed	¼ pint port wine
1 rasher of bacon, rinded	

Wash the giblets and cut them up. Slice the vegetables and cut up the bacon and simmer them with the giblets and stock for 2 hours. In another pan make a brown roux with the fat and flour and strain the soup into it. Either chop the vegetables and giblets finely, or sieve them, and add them to the soup. Cook for a further 10 minutes, season to taste and just before serving, add the port wine.

CHINESE BIRDS' NEST SOUP

3 oz. dried birds' nest	2 egg whites
1 tbsp. sherry	1 level tbsp. cornflour
2 pints chicken stock	1 level tsp. Ac'cent
4 oz. cooked chicken meat, shredded	1 oz. chopped ham to garnish

Soak the birds' nest in boiling water for 6 hours. Drain, add the sherry, ½ pint hot water and the stock to the birds' nest and simmer for ¾ hour. Add the chicken meat. Whisk the egg whites slightly and add to the boiling soup, whisking all the time. Blend the cornflour to a smooth cream with a little water, add the Ac'cent and stir into the soup. Simmer for a further 10–15 minutes. Serve garnished with the ham.

Note: Birds' nest is sold at certain shops specialising in Eastern foodstuffs. Ac'cent is a monosodium glutamate preparation which replaces seasonings used in the East to enhance the flavour of the food.

FIFTEEN-MINUTE HEARTY SOUPS
A very quick meal can be made by using canned or packet soups as a basis. Add any of the following to give "body":

99

diced fresh vegetables, frozen vegetables, fried chopped bacon, diced ham, sliced frankfurters or grilled chipolatas, small herb dumplings, pasta or rice. Grated cheese can be served with any of these soups.

Try the following combinations:

Mix 1 can of chicken noodle soup with 1 of cream of mushroom and heat. Garnish with watercress.

Fry 1 tbsp. mixed red and green peppers in $\frac{1}{4}$ oz. butter. Combine with 1 can of cream of chicken soup and simmer for 10 minutes before serving.

Fry 1 tbsp. each finely chopped onion, parsley and almonds in 1 tbsp. oil for 5 minutes. Add 1 can of cream of chicken soup and simmer for 10 minutes.

CHAPTER 8

Cooking with eggs

Eggs are invaluable for a multitude of quick snacks, for they are available all the year round and remain cheap compared with other protein foods such as meat and fish. They are indispensable in most cakes and in many other dishes, from sauces to hot and cold puddings.

We give here recipes for the best-known savoury egg dishes. Many others using eggs are of course included in other books in this series, especially those dealing with puddings, cakes and savouries. Several of the recipes in the Cheese chapter of this book (p. 120) also include eggs.

Buying and Storing Eggs
Eggs are usually sold in the following grades: large, standard and medium. The standard and medium sizes are perfectly suitable for most ordinary cooking, but when using medium eggs for such things as rich cakes and meringues, you may need to add an extra egg or egg white to make up the necessary volume.

A number of shops sell eggs obtained direct from the producers, and these are usually marked "Farm" or "Free Range" eggs.

The colour of the eggshell varies according to the breed of chicken and does not affect the egg's flavour or food value.

Store eggs in a cool place; if they are put in the refrigerator, keep them well away from the ice-box and take them out some time before using, to give them time to reach room temperature, otherwise they crack when being boiled and are also difficult to whisk. Use the refrigerator racks or boxes provided, as these are designed to protect the eggs. Don't store eggs next to cheese, fish or onions, as they absorb strong flavours.

As eggs are nowadays plentiful and relatively cheap all the

year, it is not worth preserving them unless you keep your own hens and have a sudden glut of eggs. They can be preserved in waterglass, according to the instructions on the container.

There is always a small air space inside an egg and this increases as the egg ages. The fresher the egg, therefore, the fuller it is, and that is the basis of the following test. Place the egg in a tumbler of cold water. If fresh and full, it lies flat at the bottom of the glass. If the egg tilts slightly, it is probably not fresh enough to boil, but will fry or scramble satisfactorily; if it floats, it is very likely to be quite bad.

FRESH STALE BAD

USING EGGS IN COOKERY

Apart from their uses as a main dish, eggs have three main functions in cookery:

1. EMULSIFYING: The yolk only is used as an emulsifying agent in such mixtures as mayonnaise.
2. THICKENING AND BINDING: Beaten eggs are used to thicken sauces and in custards, for binding such things as fish cakes and for coating foods which are likely to disintegrate during the cooking, such as fried fillets of fish, fritters and croquettes, etc.
3. RAISING: Eggs are used as a raising agent for batters and for many cakes. Where an extra light mixture is required, the egg whites are whisked separately before being added. Whisked egg whites are also used for making meringues, soufflé omelettes, soufflés and various light, foamy sweets and icings.

COOKING EGGS

Except in the case of hard-boiled eggs, the more lightly egg dishes are cooked, the better. This applies particularly to fried and baked egg dishes and to omelettes, where too long cooking makes the eggs tough. Cook custards and similar egg dishes very slowly over a low heat, or stand them in a water bath or double saucepan.

TO SEPARATE AN EGG

There are special gadgets for doing this, but failing a separator, this is the method.

102

Give the egg a sharp knock against the side of a basin or cup and break the shell in half – tapping it lightly two or three times is liable to crush the shell instead of breaking it cleanly and may cause the yolk to mix into the white. Having broken the shell, pass the yolk back and forth from one half of the shell to the other, letting the white drop into the basin. Put the yolk into another basin. If you are separating more than one egg, use a third basin for cracking the eggs (so that if any of the yolks should break, only the one white will be spoilt); put the second yolk in with the first one and tip the white in with the first white. Continue in this way.

DUCK'S EGGS
Ducks' eggs are larger and richer than hens' eggs. They need to be thoroughly cooked to be safe, at least 10 minutes being allowed for boiling. They can be included in cakes (except sponge mixtures) and puddings, but they should not be used for making meringues or any sweet which is cooked for only a short time, or at a low temperature, nor should they be preserved or stored.

TURKEY AND GOOSE EGGS
These are as delicate in flavour as hens' eggs, but they are, of course, much larger. They can be cooked by any of the methods given for hens' eggs and can be used for all cakes and puddings. Allow a longer time for boiling – for soft-boiled eggs allow about 7 minutes. One goose egg will make sufficient scrambled egg for 4 people.

GULL, PHEASANT AND GUINEA-FOWL EGGS
These are usually sold hard-boiled and served as an hors d'oeuvre. Cook them for 10–15 minutes. Plovers' eggs (the taking of which is now prohibited) used to be eaten in the same way.

BOILED EGGS
Eggs should be simmered rather than boiled. Put them into boiling water, using a spoon, lower the heat and cook for 3 minutes for a light set and up to 4½ minutes for a firmer set. Alternatively, put them in cold water and bring slowly to the boil – they will then be lightly set. The water in each case should be just sufficient to cover the eggs.

Fresh eggs tend to take a little longer to cook than those which are a few days old.

HARD-BOILED EGGS
Put the eggs into boiling water, bring back to the boil and

cook for 10–12 minutes. Hard-boiled eggs should be placed at once under running cold water and left until they are cold; this prevents a discoloured rim forming round the outside of the yolk and enables the shell to be easily removed. Crack the shell all round by tapping on a firm surface, then peel it off.

CODDLED EGGS
Place the eggs in boiling water, cover, remove from the heat and keep in a warm place for 8–10 minutes; they will then be lightly set.

POACHED EGGS
The eggs may be cooked in a special poaching pan or in a frying-pan with the aid of round pastry cutters. To use an egg poacher, half-fill the lower container with water, place a small piece of butter in each cup and put over the heat; when the water boils, break the eggs into the cups, season lightly and cover the pan with the lid. Simmer gently until the eggs are set and loosen them with a knife before turning out. To use a frying-pan, half-fill it with water, adding a pinch of salt or a few drops of vinegar to help the eggs keep their shape and give added flavour. Grease the required number of plain pastry cutters. Bring the water to the boil, put in the cutters and break an egg into each; cook gently until lightly set and lift out with a slotted spoon or fish slice. Drain the eggs before serving.

CHEESY EGGS
(see colour picture No. 9)

4 eggs	A little made mustard
1 oz. butter	A 10½-oz. can of asparagus
1 oz. flour	tips
½ pint milk	8 slices of white bread
3 oz. cheese, grated	Fat for frying
Pepper and salt	Paprika pepper

Poach the eggs. Meanwhile, melt the butter, work in the flour and very gradually stir in the milk to make a white sauce; cook for 5 minutes. Add the grated cheese; when this has just melted, season to taste with pepper, salt and a little made mustard. Add the drained asparagus tips (reserving a few for garnish). Either cut 8 rounds of bread 3 inches across or, using 4 slices only of bread, cut 8 triangles. Fry the bread pieces until golden brown and drain them. Arrange 4 rounds or triangles on a hot plate and top each with a poached egg; coat with the cheese sauce. Garnish with the remaining fried bread, the asparagus tips and a dusting of paprika pepper.

104

FRIED EGGS

Melt a little dripping or lard in a frying-pan. Break each egg separately into a cup and drop carefully into the hot fat. Cook gently and use a spoon to baste with the fat, so that the eggs cook evenly on top and underneath. When they are just set, remove them from the pan with a fish slice or broad palette knife. If the eggs are to be served with fried bacon, cook this first, then remove the rashers and keep them hot while frying the eggs in the hot bacon fat.

SCRAMBLED EGGS

Melt ½ oz. butter in a strong pan. Whisk 2 eggs with 2 tbsps. milk or water and some salt and pepper. Pour into the saucepan and stir slowly over a gentle heat until the mixture begins to thicken. Remove from the heat and stir until creamy. Pile on to hot buttered toast and serve immediately. (1–2 servings.)

Scrambled Egg Variations

Add to a 4-egg mixture one of the following ingredients:
2 oz. lightly fried sliced mushrooms
2 tomatoes, skinned, chopped and lightly fried
  with a diced rasher of bacon
2 oz. chopped ham, tongue or other cooked meat
2 oz. sliced cooked pork sausages
2 oz. Finnan haddock (or other smoked fish), cooked, freed
  of bones and skin and flaked
2 oz. picked shrimps
2–3 oz. grated cheese
2 level tsp. dried herbs or 1 level tbsp. finely chopped
  mixed fresh herbs
3–4 tbsps. well-drained canned sweet corn

SCRAMBLED EGGS PLUS

Pile some plain scrambled egg on to one half of a slice of buttered toast and on the other half pile hot cooked mushrooms, tomatoes, green peppers or flaked boned fish.

SCRAMBLED EGGS WITH
SHRIMPS AND MUSHROOMS

4 eggs	½ lb. shrimps, shelled
Salt and pepper	¼ lb. mushrooms, chopped
3 tbsps. sherry	3 tbsps. lard
1 onion, skinned and	Scallop shells for serving, if
chopped	available

Beat the eggs, season, add the sherry and mix well. Fry the chopped onion, shrimps and mushrooms in the hot lard, then pour in the egg mixture. Cook for a few minutes, stirring, until set. Serve in scallop shells. (3–4 servings.)

105

BAKED EGGS
Oven temperature: moderate (350°F., mark 4)
Place the required number of individual ovenproof dishes or cocottes on a baking sheet, with a knob of butter in each dish. Put them in the oven for 1–2 minutes, until the butter has melted. Break an egg into each dish, sprinkle with a little salt and pepper, place in the centre of the oven and leave until the eggs are just set – about 5–8 minutes. Garnish if desired and serve at once – for breakfast or (accompanied by vegetables) as a snack.

EGGS BAKED IN CREAM
Oven temperature: moderate (350°F., mark 4)
Butter as many small ovenproof dishes or cocottes as required. Put 1 tsp. cream in the bottom of each and add a light sprinkling of salt and pepper. Break 1 egg into each, sprinkle more salt and pepper on top, and cover with more cream. Place the dishes in a meat tin containing sufficient water to come halfway up the sides and cook in the centre of the oven until the eggs are just set – about 15 minutes. Serve at once.

EGGS WITH BACON EN COCOTTE
2 rashers of bacon, rinded and chopped	Pepper and salt Butter
2 eggs	

Oven temperature: Moderate (350°F., mark 4)
Divide the bacon between 4 cocotte dishes and bake towards the top of the oven for about 10 minutes, or until lightly cooked. Break an egg into each dish, sprinkle with pepper and a little salt, put in a few dots of butter on each and bake just above the centre of the oven, until the eggs are lightly set – 7–10 minutes. Serve hot.

Omelettes

With care anyone can master the art of omelette making. Delicate handling is needed, but a little practice perfects the knack – don't be discouraged if your first two or three omelettes are not successful.

Two points about omelettes that make them particularly convenient are the short time they take to make and the way they enable one to use up odds and ends – such as cooked meat, fish or vegetables – either in the omelette itself, as a filling or as an accompaniment.

Have everything ready before beginning to make an omelette, including a hot plate on which to serve it – an omelette must never wait, but rather be waited for.

106

The Pan

Special little omelette pans are obtainable and should be kept for omelettes only. If you have not got such a pan, however, a thick-based frying-pan can equally well be used. Whether of cast iron, copper, enamelled iron or aluminium, the pan should be thick, so that it will hold sufficient heat to cook the egg mixture as soon as this is put in. Thus the omelette can be in and out of the pan in about 2 minutes – one of the essentials for success; slow cooking and over-cooking both make an omelette tough.

To season a new omelette pan, put in a knob of butter and heat it slowly, then rub the butter well in with a piece of kitchen paper.

To clean an omelette pan after use, don't wash it, but rub it over first with some kitchen paper, then with a clean cloth. If it is still not clean, put it over a gentle heat, sprinkle in a little salt, rub round vigorously with a small pad of kitchen paper and dust it out with a clean cloth. The salt, being gritty, ensures that the surface of the pan is perfectly clean and smooth.

A few minutes before you want to cook an omelette, place the pan on a very gentle heat, to ensure that it is heated evenly right to the edges – a fierce heat would cause the pan to heat unevenly. When the pan is ready for the mixture it will feel comfortably hot if you hold the back of your hand about an inch away from the surface.

Fat for Greasing Omelette Pans: Undoubtedly butter gives the best flavour, but unsalted margarine can be used as a substitute. Bacon fat can also be used.

Types of Omelette: Basically, there are only two different kinds of omelette – the plain and the soufflé, in which the egg whites are whisked separately and folded into the yolk mixture, giving it a fluffy texture. Plain omelettes are almost invariably savoury, and soufflé omelettes are most commonly served as a sweet. There are, of course, many different omelette variations, achieved by the different ingredients added to the eggs or used in the filling. In this chapter we concentrate on savoury omelettes – sweet ones will be found in the book on sweets and puddings in this series.

PLAIN OMELETTE

Allow 2 eggs per person. Whisk them lightly, season with salt and pepper and add 1 tbsp. water. Place the pan over a gently heat and when it is hot add a knob of butter to grease it lightly. Pour the beaten eggs into the hot fat. Stir gently with the back of the prongs of a fork, drawing the mixture from the sides to the centre as it sets and letting the liquid egg from the centre run to the sides. When the egg has set, stop stirring and cook for another minute until it is golden underneath. Tilt the pan away from you slightly and use a palette knife to fold over a third of the omelette to the centre, then fold over the opposite third. Turn the omelette out on to the warmed plate, with the folded sides underneath, and serve at once. Don't overcook or the omelette will be tough.

SOUFFLÉ OMELETTE

2 eggs	2 tbsps. water
Salt and pepper to taste	½ oz. butter

Separate the yolks from the whites of the eggs, putting them in different bowls. Whisk the yolks until creamy. Add the seasoning and the water and beat again. Whisk the egg whites as stiffly as possible. At this point place the pan containing the butter over a low heat and let the butter melt without browning. Turn the egg whites into the yolk mixture and fold in carefully, using a spoon, but don't over-mix. Grease the sides of the pan with the butter by tilting it in all directions and then pour in the egg mixture. Cook over a moderate heat until the omelette is golden-brown on the underside. Now place the pan under the grill or in a moderate oven (350°F., mark 4) until the omelette is browned on the top. Remove at once when it is ready, as over-cooking tends to make it tough. Run a spatula gently round the edge and underneath the omelette to loosen it and make a mark across the middle at right angles to the pan handle; add any required filling – see suggestions given for plain omelettes – and double the omelette over. Turn it gently on to a hot plate and serve at once. (1 serving.)

A recipe for a cold soufflé omelette is given at the end of the omelette recipes, p. 111.

CHICKEN AND MUSHROOM OMELETTES (ITALIAN)

4 oz. mushrooms, sliced	4 eggs
1 oz. butter	Salt and pepper
4 oz. cooked chicken, diced	1 level tbsp. grated Parmesan
¾ pint seasoned white sauce	or Provoloni Cheese

Oven temperature: hot (425°F., mark 7)

Cook the mushrooms in the butter for 5 minutes, add the chicken and half the sauce, mix well and cook for 2–3 minutes longer, stirring all the time. Make as many small omelettes as possible, using 2 tbsps. of mixture to each omelette. Avoid cooking them more than absolutely necessary. Spread some of the filling on each omelette and roll up. Place the omelettes in a shallow buttered casserole, add the rest of the sauce and sprinkle with cheese. Bake towards the top of the oven for 10–15 minutes and garnish as desired. (2 servings.)

GRUYÈRE OMELETTE

6 eggs
2 level tsps. finely
  chopped fresh herbs (or 1
  level tsp. dried herbs)
Salt and pepper

4 oz. Gruyère cheese, cut in
  wafer-thin slices
¼ pint double cream
6 rashers of lean bacon,
  rinded

Mix the eggs with a fork, add the herbs, seasoning and the sliced cheese. Stir in the cream. Put the bacon into a saucepan of boiling water, blanch for 1–2 minutes, remove, drain and dry carefully. Put the rashers side by side in the omelette pan and fry gently until they are lightly cooked but not crisp. Take out and keep hot. While the fat from the bacon is still hot, pour in the omelette mixture; lay the bacon across the top and cook until the omelette is set but not firm. Do not fold over. (3–4 servings.)

OMELETTE CARDINAL

4 eggs
Salt and pepper
1 oz. butter
1 orange, washed

6 oz. prawns, shelled
1 tbsp. single cream
¼ pint white sauce

Mix the eggs with a fork and add the seasoning. Heat the butter in a frying-pan, pour in the egg mixture and cook in the usual way. Peel the orange very thinly and carefully, in order to obtain only the outer rind. Cut into very thin Julienne strips the length of a matchstick. Complete the peeling of the orange, remove the pith and then slice. Just before folding the omelette, fill it with half the Julienne strips and half the prawns, mixed with the cream. Fold the omelette and slide it on to a hot serving dish. Make an incision lengthwise down the centre of the omelette and fill with the rest of the prawns. Pour the sauce over either end. Arrange the orange slices round the dish and sprinkle the rest of the Julienne strips on top. (2–3 servings.)

OVEN OMELETTE

4 rashers of streaky bacon,
  rinded and chopped
½ an onion, skinned and
  chopped
2 level tsps. seasoned flour

1 tbsp. chopped parsley
4 eggs
¼ pint milk
4 oz. cheese, grated

Oven temperature: moderate (350°F., mark 4)

Fry the bacon and drain it with a slotted spoon, leaving the fat in the frying-pan. Put the bacon into a lightly greased deep pie plate. Add the onion to the bacon fat in the pan and fry until golden; add the flour and stir. Spread this mixture over the bacon and sprinkle with the chopped parsley. Whisk together the eggs and milk, pour them over the onion mixture and sprinkle the cheese on top. Bake in the centre of the oven for 30 minutes, until firm. (3–4 servings.)

SCANDINAVIAN OVEN OMELETTE

2 oz. bacon, diced	½ pint milk
2 eggs	Salt to season

Oven temperature: moderate (350°F., mark 4)

Butter a small pie dish and put in the bacon. Beat up the eggs with the milk, season with a little salt and pour the mixture over the bacon. Bake in the centre of the oven till quite set – 30 minutes. (2 servings.)

This dish may also be made with smoked salmon or anchovies instead of bacon.

SPANISH OMELETTE – 1

1 small onion, skinned and chopped	2 tbsps. cooked peas
Olive oil	2 cooked potatoes, diced
1 tomato, skinned and chopped	2 canned pimientos, chopped
	4 eggs
	Salt and pepper

Fry the onion lightly in a little oil, add all the other vegetables and cook for a few minutes, stirring. Whisk the eggs, season well and pour over the vegetables in the pan. Cook slowly, shaking the pan occasionally. When one side is lightly and evenly browned, turn the omelette over and cook the other side. Do not fold it. Serve hot, accompanied by a green salad. (2–3 servings.)

As the omelette is so thick, it may be easier to use a plate to turn it. When the first side is browned, cover the omelette with a plate and turn the pan, omelette and plate over together, so that the omelette falls on to the plate; turn the pan right way up and slide the omelette back into it, browned side uppermost. Alternatively, brown the second side of the omelette under the grill.

SPANISH OMELETTE – 2

4 medium-sized potatoes, peeled and thinly sliced	4 oz. garlic sausage, finely diced
3 tbsps. cooking oil	Salt and pepper
3 eggs	Butter

Fry the potatoes in the oil for about 5 minutes, or until soft, stirring occasionally, but taking care not to break them up; drain on absorbent kitchen paper. Beat the eggs in a large bowl and add the potatoes, sausage, salt and pepper. Melt a little butter in a 7-inch frying pan, add the egg mixture and press down well. Cook gently until the top is just set, brown under a grill and invert the omelette on to a serving dish. Serve hot or cold, cut into wedges. (2–3 servings.)

VEAL AND HAM OMELETTE

1 clove of garlic, skinned
2 tbsps. thick brown
  or tomato sauce
2 oz. cold cooked veal,
  minced

2 oz. ham, minced
Salt and pepper
1 oz. butter
2 eggs
1 tbsp. milk

Wipe a frying pan round with a piece of cut garlic and re-heat the sauce in it, then add the minced meats and re-heat gently; add more seasoning if necessary. Melt the fat in an omelette pan and meanwhile beat the eggs and add the milk and seasoning. Make a plain omelette, put the hot filling into it just before folding it up and serve immediately. (1–2 servings.)

COLD ASPARAGUS OMELETTE

4 eggs
Salt and pepper
½ oz. butter

Asparagus tips
¼ pint thick white sauce
¼ pint double cream

Separate the eggs; beat the yolks and whip the whites to a stiff froth. Fold them together and add 1 tsp. cold water and some seasoning. Melt the butter in a heated omelette pan and cook the omelette. Mix the asparagus tips with ⅛ pint of the sauce, place this mixture on the omelette, and fold it over; put the omelette on a dish and leave it to get quite cold. Cool the remainder of the white sauce, sieve it and then whisk in the whipped cream. Pour this sauce over the omelette and serve cold. (2 servings.)

EGGS À LA FLORENTINE

1 lb. spinach
½ oz butter
Salt and pepper
2 oz cooking cheese, grated

4 eggs
2–3 tbsps. cream
Grated Parmesan cheese
Parsley to garnish

Oven temperature: moderate (350°F., mark 4),
Wash the spinach well, put in a pan with a little salt and just the water that clings to the leaves and cook for 10–15 minutes, until tender. Drain well, chop roughly and mix with the butter and seasoning. Put into an ovenproof dish and cover with grated cheese. Break the eggs on to a saucer and slide side by side on to the cheese; bake in the centre of the oven for 10 minutes. Remove from the oven, spoon the cream over and sprinkle with Parmesan cheese. Return the dish to the oven and bake for a further 10–15 minutes, until the eggs are firm. Serve garnished with parsley.

111

EGGS À LA MORNAY
(see colour picture No. 11)

1½ oz. butter
1 oz. flour
½ pint milk
Salt and pepper

2 oz. cheese, grated
4 eggs, hard-boiled and
   sliced
Parsley to garnish

Melt 1 oz. butter, stir in the flour and cook for 2–3 minutes.
Remove the pan from the heat and gradually stir in the milk,
bring to the boil and continue to stir until the sauce thickens.
Season well and stir in 1 oz. of the cheese. Lay the eggs in
an ovenproof dish. Pour the sauce over them, sprinkle the
remaining cheese over the top, dot with shavings of butter and
brown under a hot grill for a few minutes. Garnish with
parsley sprigs.

EGGS AU GRATIN

½ pint white sauce
4 eggs
2 oz. cheese, grated

3 tbsps. bread-crumbs
Salt and pepper
1 oz. butter

Make the white sauce. Grease an ovenproof dish large enough
to hold the eggs; poach these and transfer them to the dish.
Sprinkle with half the grated cheese, then cover with the
sauce. Cover with the remaining grated cheese and the bread-
crumbs, seasoned with salt and pepper. Dot the butter over the
top and brown under the grill.

EGG FRICASSEE

4 hard-boiled eggs, shelled
½ pint Béchamel sauce (see
   chapter 10, p. 139)

1 tsp. chopped parsley
Boiled rice or toast
   fingers

Cut the eggs into quarters and heat thoroughly in the sauce.
Arrange on a hot dish, sprinkle with parsley and serve with
boiled rice or fingers of toast.

EGG AND SPAGHETTI CASSEROLE
(see colour picture No. 11)

6 oz. spaghetti
Salt and pepper
2 oz. butter or margarine
1½ oz. flour
1 pint milk
1 small onion, skinned and
   finely minced

A little made mustard
4 oz. cheese, grated
1 lb. runner beans, prepared
   and cooked
4 eggs
A little melted butter

Oven temperature: moderate (350°F., mark 4)
Cook the spaghetti in salted water until just tender and drain
well. Melt the butter or margarine and stir in the flour. Add the
milk gradually and stir until it boils. Add the onion, season-

ings and half the cheese. Put half the spaghetti into a greased casserole, place some of the runner beans on top and then half the sauce. Repeat, finishing with a sprinkling of cheese and reserving a few beans for garnish. Bake in the centre of the oven for about ½ hour. Meanwhile boil the eggs for 5 minutes, until set but not hard-boiled; shell, halve and arrange over the spaghetti, with some beans tossed in butter. (Serves 4–5.)

EGG RISOTTO

4 eggs	Salt and pepper
6 oz. rice	3 oz. grated Gruyère and
¼ pint stock	Parmesan cheese, mixed

Soft-boil the eggs and put them into cold water, then remove the shells. Boil the rice for 10 minutes, drain well, then cook in the stock, simmering slowly for 15 minutes, or until all the stock has been absorbed: season well. Grease a large shallow ovenproof dish and put the rice into it. Cut each egg in half; with the back of a tablespoon make 8 depressions in the rice to hold the half-eggs and put them in these "nests". Season the eggs and sprinkle with the grated cheese, putting a double layer over each egg. Put the dish under a very hot grill for 3 minutes, to brown well.

CURRIED EGGS – 1

5 eggs, hard-boiled	1 oz. flour
2 small onions, skinned	½ pint stock
A small piece of apple, peeled	Salt
2 oz. butter	2 tsps. lemon juice
1 level tsp. curry powder	Boiled rice
	Stuffed olives to garnish

Slice 3 of the eggs. Chop the onions and apple finely. Melt the butter, fry the onion lightly, add the apple, curry powder and flour and cook for a few minutes. Gradually add the stock, salt and lemon juice, boil up and skim, then simmer for about ¼ hour. Heat the sliced eggs in this sauce, then turn the mixture into a hot dish and surround with boiled rice. Decorate with olives and the remaining eggs, cut in wedges. Serve this mild curry with lemon, preserved ginger and coconut.

CURRIED EGGS – 2

2 oz. butter	½ pint stock or water
1 onion, skinned and finely chopped	Salt
½ an apple, peeled and finely chopped	2 tsps. lemon juice
2 level tsps. curry powder	4 eggs
3 level tbsps. flour	Boiled rice
	Chopped parsley
	Paprika pepper

113

Melt the butter in a saucepan and lightly fry the onion until golden. Add the apple, curry powder and flour and cook for a few minutes, stirring occasionally. Add the stock gradually and season with salt and lemon juice. Bring to the boil, stirring all the time, cover and simmer for about 30 minutes. Hard-boil the eggs during the last 10 minutes of the time, shell and halve them. Place them in a hot dish and pour the sauce over. Surround with the rice and garnish with parsley and paprika.

EGG AND MUSHROOM CURRY (INDIAN)

4 eggs	2 level tsps. garam-masala
1 medium-sized onion, skinned and chopped	½ level tsp. chilli powder
¼ oz. preserved ginger, chopped	3 medium-sized tomatoes, sliced
1 tbsp. fat	2 tbsps. milk
½ level tsp. turmeric	½ lb. mushrooms, sliced
½ level tbsp. dried herbs	Salt
	2 tsps. lemon juice

Hard-boil the eggs. Fry the onion and ginger in the fat, and stir in the turmeric, herbs, garam-masala and chilli powder. Add the tomatoes, milk, mushrooms and some salt, fry lightly, cover the saucepan and continue to cook for 30 minutes. Put in the halved eggs, then simmer for a further 20 minutes and add the lemon juice. Serve with boiled rice.

Note: Garam Masala is a flavouring made by mixing 1 level tsp. each of ground cloves, ground cinnamon, ground black pepper, cumin seeds and ground cardamom seeds. It may be bought at shops specialising in Eastern foods, etc.

HOT STUFFED EGGS – 1

4 eggs, hard-boiled	A ½-pint can of tomato juice
2 oz. mushrooms, chopped	
1 onion, skinned and chopped	1 level tsp. sugar
1½ oz. margarine	Salt and pepper
	2 level tsps. cornflour

Cut the eggs in half lengthways and remove the yolks. Lightly fry the mushrooms and onion in the hot fat for 5 minutes, until golden brown; put half the mixture in a basin. Add the tomato juice, sugar and seasoning to the remaining mixture in the pan and cook for 5 minutes. Blend the cornflour to a smooth cream with a little water, stir in a little of the hot tomato juice and return it to the pan. Bring to the boil, stirring until it thickens, and continue cooking for 1–2 minutes. Keep this tomato sauce hot. Meanwhile mix the egg yolks with the remaining onion and mushroom mixture in the basin and use to stuff the eggs. Place on a dish and pour the tomato sauce round it.

114

HOT STUFFED EGGS – 2

2 hard-boiled eggs
½ oz. butter
½ oz. flour
2–3 tbsps. milk
¾ oz. grated cheese
Salt and pepper

Beaten egg and
  bread-crumbs to coat
Deep fat for frying
Fried parsley for garnish
Cheese sauce
  (see chapter 10, p. 139)

Split the eggs in half lengthways, remove the yolks and sieve them. Melt the butter, stir in the flour and milk and cook, stirring, until the mixture leaves the sides of the pan. Add the cheese, seasoning and sieved egg yolks, mix well and fill the egg-white cases with this mixture. Coat with egg and bread-crumbs and fry in hot fat until golden brown. Garnish with fried parsley and serve with cheese sauce. (Serves 2.)

COLD STUFFED EGGS

4 eggs, hard-boiled
1 oz. butter
1 tbsp. mayonnaise

Salt and pepper
Parsley

Cut the eggs in half lengthwise; remove the yolks, put in a basin, mash with a fork and mix in the butter, mayonnaise and seasoning. Mix until smooth, put into a forcing bag with a ½-inch star pipe and pipe back into the egg whites. Garnish with sprigs of parsley.

Variations
1. Add 1 tsp. anchovy essence to the yolk mixture.
2. Add a little minced tongue or ham to the yolk mixture.
3. Add a pinch of curry powder to the yolk mixture.
4. Place the egg white cups on rounds of buttered bread and garnish with sliced stuffed olives.
5. Combine the sieved egg yolks with 2 oz. finely grated cheese (or cream cheese) a little whipped double cream and some seasoning. Place the stuffed egg halves on small plain biscuits that have been spread with anchovy butter. Garnish with a little finely grated cheese, red pepper or chopped parsley.

SCOTCH EGGS

4 eggs, hard-boiled
2 level tsps. seasoned flour
Worcestershire sauce
½ lb. sausage-meat or
  skinless sausages

1 egg, beaten
Dry bread-crumbs
Deep fat
Parsley

Dust the eggs with the seasoned flour. Add a few drops of Worcestershire sauce to the sausage-meat and divide it into 4 equal portions. Form each quarter into a flat cake and work it round an egg, making it as even as possible, to keep the egg a

115

good shape, and making sure there are no cracks in the sausage-meat. Brush with beaten egg and toss in bread-crumbs. Heat the fat until it will brown a cube of bread in 40–50 seconds. (As the sausage-meat is raw, it is essential that the frying should not be hurried unduly, so the fat must not be too hot.) Fry the eggs for about 7–8 minutes. When they are golden brown on the outside, remove them from the fat and drain on crumpled kitchen paper.

Cut the eggs in half lengthways, garnish each half with a small piece of parsley and serve either hot with tomato sauce (see chapter 10, p. 139) or cold with a green salad.

EGG MAYONNAISE

4 hard-boiled eggs
A few lettuce leaves
¼ pint mayonnaise
Chopped parsley or paprika

Cut the eggs lengthways into halves or quarters. Wash and drain the lettuce and put on a shallow dish. Serve the eggs on the lettuce, cut side down; coat with the mayonnaise and garnish with parsley or paprika.

PICKLED EGGS

For every 6 hard-boiled eggs allow:

1 pint white wine or cider vinegar
6 cloves of garlic, skinned
1 oz. pickling spice
A small piece of orange peel
A piece of mace

Boil all the ingredients (except the eggs) for 10 minutes in a heavy pan with a well-fitting lid. When the mixture is cool, strain it into a wide-mouthed glass jar with a screw-lid or a tight cork. Put in the eggs (shelled but whole) and leave for at least 6 weeks before eating.

More hard-boiled eggs can be added as convenient, but they must always be covered by the liquid.

Serve as a snack or buffet dish or with salad.

Soufflés

Eggs are an indispensable ingredient in all soufflés, and it is the stiffly whisked whites which give the characteristic light, airy texture.

In this book we confine ourselves to savoury soufflés, but sweet ones (hot and cold) will be found in the companion volume on *Sweets, Puddings and Desserts*.

Hot soufflés are traditionally made in a special soufflé dish, fairly shallow in depth (usually 2–3 inches), straight-sided, smooth inside and fluted on the outside. They are generally of plain white ovenproof china, but are also obtainable in coloured chinaware and in ovenproof glass. A straight-sides casserole-type dish may also be used.

It used to be the fashion to tie a paper band round the dish, arranging it to come 3 inches above the top, so that when you peeled off the paper after cooking the soufflé, it stood much higher than the dish. However, this step is often omitted nowadays. Simply butter the dish and if you wish dust it with fine bread-crumbs or grated Parmesan cheese, though some people find that the soufflé "climbs up" better in an un-greased dish.

In all soufflés, it is essential to separate the eggs carefully, leaving not a speck of yolk in the whites. The whites must be beaten until stiff but *not* dry. They must be folded gently and evenly through the mixture – don't beat or stir rapidly.

The foundation soufflé mixture, or panada, consists of flour, butter and milk, in the proportions shown below; its prepara-tion is important, for unless it is smoothly blended and thoroughly amalgamated with the egg yolks, the soufflé may be leathery. When making it, use a rather large saucepan – big enough not only to beat in the egg yolks, but also to fold in the whites.

BASIC SOUFFLÉ MIXTURE

1½ oz. butter
1 oz. flour
½ pint milk
4 large eggs, separated

Salt and pepper
Filling or flavouring
(see below)

Oven temperature: moderate (350°F., mark 4)
Grease a 7-inch soufflé dish (2-pint capacity). Melt the butter and stir in the flour. Cook slowly for 2–3 minutes. Gradually stir in the milk and beat the mixture until smooth. Cook for a further 3–4 minutes. Beat in the egg yolks and add the season-ing and filling or flavouring. Fold in the stiffly whisked egg whites until evenly distributed. Turn the mixture into the prepared dish and bake in the centre of the oven for about 45 minutes, until well risen and golden brown. Serve at once.

SOUFFLÉ FILLINGS AND FLAVOURINGS
Ham: Add 4–6 oz. cooked ham, finely chopped.
Fish: Add 4–6 oz. cooked smoked haddock, finely flaked and with all skin and bone removed.
Mushroom: Add 4–6 oz. mushrooms, chopped and cooked in butter until tender.
Crab: Add 4 oz. canned crabmeat, finely flaked, and include a few drops of Tabasco sauce and a little paprika pepper.
Lobster: Add 4 oz. cooked lobster meat, finely chopped; season the mixture well.

117

CHICKEN SOUFFLÉ

1½ oz. butter
1 oz. flour
½ pint milk
4 large eggs,
  separated

8 oz. cooked chicken, freed
  of all skin, bone, etc., and
  minced
1 tbsp. lemon juice
Salt and pepper

Oven temperature: moderate (350°F., mark 4)
Grease a 7-inch soufflé dish (2-pint capacity). Melt the butter, stir in the flour and cook for 2–3 minutes. Gradually stir in the milk and cook for a further 3–4 minutes. Beat the egg yolks in, then stir in the chicken and lemon juice, with the seasoning. Fold in the stiffly whisked egg whites until evenly distributed. Turn the mixture into the dish and bake in the centre of the oven for about 45 minutes, until well risen and golden brown. Serve at once, with fingers of toast.

ASPARAGUS SOUFFLÉ

A 10½-oz. can of cut asparagus
  tips, drained
5 eggs, separated

Freshly ground pepper
A 10½-oz. can of condensed
  asparagus soup

Oven temperature: fairly hot (375°F., mark 5)
Grease a 7-inch soufflé dish (2-pint capacity). Put half the asparagus in a layer at the bottom of the dish. Stir the beaten egg yolks and pepper into the soup. Fold in the stiffly whisked egg whites until evenly distributed. Turn half this mixture into the dish, add the rest of the asparagus, and then the remaining soufflé mixture. Bake in the centre of the oven for 30–40 minutes, until well risen and golden brown. Serve at once.
Note: Condensed mushroom, chicken or celery soup can be used in the same way, with or without the addition of 4 oz. grated cheese.

CHEESE SOUFFLÉ: See Cheese chapter, p. 120.

COLD SAVOURY SOUFFLÉS

These are set with gelatine and contain cream (or evaporated milk). Since the mixture does not rise as with a hot soufflé, the effect is simulated by putting a paper collar round the dish and filling the dish above the level of its actual rim, so that when the paper is removed, the soufflé appears to have risen.

For a good result, use a soufflé dish with straight sides and a thin rim. Cut a piece of double greaseproof or better still, non-stick (silicone) paper long enough to encircle the dish, with a slight overlap, and deep enough to come 1½–2 inches above the rim. Secure it in place with string, an elastic band, sticky tape or pins. Place the prepared case on a flat tray or plate for easy handling. To remove the paper when the soufflé is set, ease it away with a warm knife.

COLD HAM SOUFFLÉ

½ pint Béchamel sauce (see p. 140)
4 large eggs, separated
4 level tsps. gelatine
4 tbsps. water

8 oz. ham, finely minced
½ level tsp. chopped tarragon
¼ pint single cream
Mustard and cress to garnish

Prepare a 5-inch soufflé dish (1¼-pint capacity). Make the Béchamel sauce and beat in the egg yolks one at a time. Dissolve the gelatine in the water as follows: place the water in a small basin or cup, sprinkle the gelatine over and dissolve by standing the basin in a pan of hot water. Add to the egg mixture and leave in a cold place, stirring occasionally, until beginning to set. Stir the minced ham into the egg mixture, with the tarragon and the cream. Check the seasoning. Fold in the stiffly whisked egg whites, turn the mixture into the prepared dish and leave in a cold place to set. Remove the paper collar and garnish the soufflé with mustard and cress.

COLD CHICKEN SOUFFLÉS: See Chapter 6, p. 83.

CHAPTER 9

Cheese and cheese cookery

All cheese is made from milk curd, separated from the whey – usually by the action of rennet – and suitably ripened.

The quality and the source of the milk (whether cow's, goat's or ewe's) and the particular processes used in the making, give rise to the almost endless variety of cheeses. Local conditions of climate and vegetation and of course seasonal changes also influence the finished product. This explains why some cheeses are essentially local and cannot be produced in large quantities or under factory conditions. These lists may guide you when you are trying different home-produced and imported varieties.

British Cheeses

Blue Vinney (Blue Dorset)
A hard cheese made in Dorsetshire from skimmed cows' milk. It is white in colour, with a blue vein, hard in texture and of a rather strong flavour.

Caerphilly
Originally a Welsh cheese, this is now made also in Somerset, Wiltshire, Devon and Dorset. It is a whole milk cheese pressed only lightly and eaten in its "green" state, when about ten days old. Caerphilly is soft and white with a creamy mild flavour, and is best served uncooked.

Cheddar
Cheddar is perhaps the best-known and most widely used of the English cheeses and one of the oldest. Made originally in Somerset – where the finest Cheddar cheese is still to be obtained – it is now produced in various other parts of the country and also in Scotland, Canada, Australia and New Zealand. In fact the name "Cheddar" is given to any cheese which undergoes the "cheddaring" process, regardless of

where it is made, but the original farmhouse Cheddar is still considered the best. It is a hard, yellow, slightly salty cheese, varying in flavour from mild to quite strong, and is equally good cooked or uncooked.

Cheshire

Said to be the oldest English cheese, Cheshire is another very well-known type. Like Cheddar, it is a hard cheese, but rather more crumbly in texture, with a mild yet mellow flavour. There are two varieties – the red, which is artificially coloured, and the white; the red is usually rather milder than the white. Occasionally, more by accident than design, a red Cheshire cheese will turn blue, that is to say, it develops a system of blue veins which spread all over the cheese and give it a very fine, rich texture and flavour. In all its forms Cheshire cheese is equally good cooked or uncooked.

Derby

A hard, close-textured white cheese, mild in flavour when young, but developing a full flavour as it matures.

Sage Derby, which is layered with sage leaves to give green bands through the cheese, is a very good variant, but is unfortunately not widely available.

Double Gloucester

An orange-yellow, hard cheese with a close, crumbly texture and a good rich flavour, rather similar to that of a mature Cheddar.

Dunlop

A Scottish cheese made originally in Dunlop, Ayrshire, but now fairly general throughout Scotland. It is not unlike Cheddar, but moister and of a closer texture.

Lancashire

A fairly hard cheese, crumbly in texture when cut. When new it has a mild, tangy flavour, which develops considerably as it matures. It can be eaten uncooked, but is an excellent cooking cheese.

Leicester

A hard cheese with a mild, slightly sweet flavour and orange-red colour.

Stilton

The town of Stilton is in Huntingdonshire, but genuine Stilton cheese is made also in Leicestershire and Rutland. Stilton is probably the most renowned English cheese. It is a white double-cream cheese that is produced from the richest milk (to which the cream of other milk may also be added) and it is made only from May to September.

121

Stilton is semi-hard and has a blue veining, caused by a mould which is inoculated into the cheese; the veins of blue mould should be evenly distributed throughout. The rind, of a dull, drab colour, should be well crinkled and regular and free from cracks. The cheese is at its best when fully ripe, that is 6–9 months after it has been made. A good Stilton needs no port or anything else added to it; only if it has gone dry through exposure to air should this be necessary.

Wensleydale
Made in the valley of Wensleydale in Yorkshire. Originally it was a double-cream cheese, cylindrical in shape, which was matured until it became blue – in this form it was considered one of the best English blue cheeses, next only to Stilton. Latterly it has been sold white and unripe, and in this form it is a mild, creamy-coloured cheese with a rather flaky texture.

Soft Cheeses

The soft cheese made in England are of the "unripened" type. At one time there were various regional ones, known by such names as Cambridge, Slipcote, Smearcase and York. Nowadays, they are usually known simply as cream cheese and cottage (or curd) cheese, though the old names persist in some localities.

1. *Cream Cheese* denotes cheese made from the cream of the milk, and there are two kinds; Double Cream Cheese is made from creamy milk with a high fat content (45–50 per cent) which is warmed, then left to sour naturally or soured by adding a "starter". It is then put to drain in muslin and when solid is seasoned or flavoured and shaped into cakes. Single Cream Cheese is produced from creamy milk with a 25–30 per cent fat content. It is made by a similar method to that used for the double type, but a cheese-making rennet is usually used to aid souring and obtain a good curd – this gives a more "cheesy" flavour. It is produced especially in Cornwall and Devon, but also in other farming areas. These single cream cheeses are made in small quantities, as they only keep for 2–3 days.

2. *Cottage or Curd Cheese* is made from skimmed milk, by a similar method to that used for cream cheese.

Commercially-produced Soft Cheeses are mainly sold pre-packed in packets and cartons, under the brand names of the large dairy concerns through some are sold loose, by weight. One of the chief producers of such cheeses labels them as follows:

"Cream Crest" a true cream cheese made from cream with a

minimum fat content of 45 per cent. (Another true cream cheese is produced by St. Ivel.)

"Superb Creamery" a soft curd cheese, enriched with cream and having a butter content of 35 per cent. (A similar cheese produced by another manufacturer is known as "Philadelphia".)

"Supreme Farmer" an enriched curd cheese, but with a slightly lower fat content. (The French Demi-Sel – see Continental Cheeses – is similar.)

"Cottage" cheese, made from milk with a low fat content.

"Curd" cheese, made from natural whole milk.

Processed Cheeses

1. *Firm Types:* These are usually made from such cheeses as Cheddar, Cheshire and Gruyère, which are broken down, mixed with any off-cuts of the same cheese and with emulsifying salts and then formed into blocks; these are sold (whole or sliced) in hermetically sealed plastic packs or in foil.

2. *Creamy Types:* Made in a similar way to the firm cheeses, but with the addition of butter as well as emulsifying salts. The finished cheese is of a soft creamy texture and pale in colour, it often has an added flavouring such as chopped ham, shrimps, celery, herbs, garlic, etc., and it is usually sold in small foil-wrapped portions (often individual size) or in little plastic containers.

Foreign Cheeses

Supplies available in this country vary from time to time, and from one locality to another; only the very largest shops can afford to stock a really comprehensive range, but the following cheeses can all be obtained in one or other of the better grocers, provision shops, delicatessens and supermarkets.

Alpestra (Alpin): Hard, dry cheese made in the French Alps.

Austrian Smoked Cheese: Cylindrical, with "sausage skin" covering; close-textured (like Edam or Gouda) and with distinctive smoky flavour; good with wine.

Bel Paese: Italian; soft, creamy and rich, very mild in flavour; texture slightly rubbery, but nonetheless agreeable. Good for cooking certain Italian dishes.

Bondon: Small, cylindrical, whole-milk cheese from Normandy. When ripe has a fairly pungent flavour.

Bresse Bleu: French imitation of Gorgonzola; creamy-textured and strong-flavoured.

Brick: American; usually made in shape of a brick; semi-soft, with small holes; rather less sharp in flavour than Cheddar.

Brie: French: Soft, with a crust rather than a rind; when in good condition, it is runny in texture, but a poor Brie is dry and chalky; well-flavoured.

Cacciocavallo: Italian: name due to the fact that the roundish cheeses are strung together in pairs and dried suspended over a pole, as though astride a horse. If eaten fresh, the cheese has a tangy taste and firm, yet soft texture; if kept, it becomes hard and is then grated and used in cooking.

Camembert: French; soft, and with a distinctive flavour that strengthens as it ripens.

Danish Blue: Soft and white, with blue veins, sharp and rather salty in taste.

Demi-Sel: French; a soft, mild cream cheese.

Edam: Dutch; bright red outside, yellow inside; mild in flavour, close and fairly soft in texture.

Emmenthal: Swiss; hard, pitted with numerous fairly large irregular holes; like Gruyère, which it resembles, it has a distinctive flavour. Used in cooking, especially for cheese fondues.

Danish Emmenthal is a good copy of the Swiss product.

Fontainebleau: French; creamy cheese, which is sometimes eaten with strawberries.

Fromage de Monsieur: French; soft and slightly like Camembert, but milder.

Gervais: French; cream cheese, sold packed in boxes of 6 small portions.

Gorgonzola: Italian; semi-hard, with a creamy texture. It is blue-veined and normally has a strong flavour. However, there are mild varieties of Gorgonzola, the Dolcelatte, made from a sweet milk, being much milder in flavour than the ordinary type; between the two comes the kind known as creamy Gorgonzola.

Gouda: Dutch; similar in taste and texture to Edam, but larger and flatter, and without the red outside coat.

Gruyère: Swiss; hard, honeycombed with holes which are smaller and fewer than in Emmenthal; the cheese has a more creamy texture, and a distinctive, slightly acidulous flavour. Used in cooking, particularly for cheese fondues.

French Gruyère is also available.

Havarti: Danish; foil-wrapped; semi-firm texture, rather open; good full flavour.

Kümmelkäse: German; caraway-flavoured; good with cocktails, etc.

Limburger: Belgian or German; strong, "ripe" flavour and smell.

Marc de Raisin: French; semi-hard, with a "crust" of grape-

124

skins and pips replacing the usual rind. A rather tasteless cheese.

Mozzarella: Italian; round, soft cheese, originally made from buffaloes' milk, but now also made from cows' milk. Should be used fresh. Eaten by itself it is somewhat tasteless, and it is more useful in making Italian dishes such as pizza.

Munster: Alsatian; semi-hard cheese, which is good for both cooking and table use; not unlike Pont l'Éveque in flavour.

Mycella: Danish; soft-textured, creamy with green veins; slightly aromatic flavour.

Mysöst (Gietöst): Norwegian; whey cheese, principally made from goats' milk. Hard and dark brown, with a sweetish flavour.

Neufchâtel: French; whole-milk cheese; soft, dark yellow and with a flavour similar to that of Bondon.

Parmesan: Italian; very hard, ideal for cooking and for grating to serve with pasta, etc.

Petit Suisse: French; soft, creamy and unsalted cheese, made into little cylindrical shapes. Often eaten with strawberries or other fruit, accompanied by caster sugar.

Pommel: French; a brand of double-cream cheese, similar to Petit Suisse.

Pont l'Évêque: French; semi-hard cheese, sold in small square boxes; delicious mild flavour, somewhere between that of a Brie and a Camembert.

Port du Salut: French; semi-hard, with very good mild flavour.

Roquefort: French; made of ewes' milk; white with blue veins, has a sharp, distinctive flavour; rather salty; creamy and rather crumbly in texture, somewhat like a Stilton.

Samsoe: Danish; firm-textured, with regular holes, golden in colour; mild and sweet in flavour. *Danbo* is a small, square-shaped version; *Fynbo*, *Elbo* and *Tybo* are other variants, fairly similar in type; *Molbo* has a richer, more fruity flavour; *Maribo* is also more full-flavoured.

THE CHEESE COURSE

A cheese board or platter is one of the best ways of finishing a meal and many people prefer it to a sweet.

A cheese board should offer a variety of colours and shapes of cheeses – for instance, white, deep yellow and blue; flat, rounded and in segments.

Buy only in small quantities, as this is more economical. Have a board large enough for easy cutting. With the cheese serve:

1. Biscuits (savoury or salty, plain or semi-sweet), rolls or bread (French, granary, wholemeal or rye, cut into chunks and put in a basket or on a plate).

125

2. Butter – in one slab or cut into small cubes for easy serving
3. Salad ingredients or crisp vegetables – lettuce, chunks of celery, leaves of chicory, wedges of tomatoes, small whole radishes, sprigs of watercress, sticks of carrot, trimmed spring onions.
4. A bowl of fresh fruit, when appropriate.

STORING AND COOKING CHEESE

Though cheese often requires months – sometimes years – to bring it to full maturity, once ripe it deteriorates comparatively rapidly. So buy only enough to last a few days to a week and store it in a cool place, such as a cold larder; cover it loosely to protect it from the air, but do not make it air-tight. If entirely exposed to the air, cheese will become hard and dry, and if tightly covered it is likely to mould. A cheese dish with a ventilated cover is good for the purpose; failing this, cover it with an upturned bowl. A refrigerator is not ideal for storing cheese, but if it must be used, the cheese should first be wrapped in waxed paper, polythene or foil or be tightly covered, otherwise it dries too rapidly.

If you want cheese to become hard and dry, leave it exposed to the air in a dry though cool place. It is best to hang it in a muslin bag, as then the air can circulate completely. If the cheese is left on a plate or board too dry, stand it on its rind; cheese that has no rind should be turned occasionally, otherwise the underside will remain soft and will very likely mould. Cheese that has formed mould on the surface is not necessarily spoiled – the mould should be scraped off and the cheese either used up quickly or dried for grating.

Hard cheese can be grated for cooking (use a fine grater), but a soft processed cheese should be shredded rather than grated. Very soft cheeses can be sliced and added to sauces and so on without shredding or grating.

The less cooking cheese has, the better. Over-heating tends to make it tough, so when making a dish such as Welsh Rarebit or cheese sauce, heat the cheese very gently and do not cook the mixture more than is absolutely necessary once the cheese has been added.

We give a selection of typical cheese recipes here; more will be found in the book on Savouries in this series. The Eggs chapter in this book contains various recipes which combine eggs and cheese.

CHEESE ON TOAST

8 oz. firm cheese, grated
½–1 tsp. Worcestershire
   sauce
1 level tsp. dry mustard

Salt and pepper
Milk to mix
Buttered toast

126

Mix the cheese and seasonings and bind to a paste with milk. Spread on the toast and cook under a hot grill until golden and bubbling.

WELSH RAREBIT

8 oz. Cheddar cheese, grated	Salt and pepper
1 oz. butter	3–4 tbsps. brown ale
1 level tsp. dry mustard	Buttered toast

Place all the ingredients in a thick-based pan and heat very gently until a creamy mixture is obtained. Pour over the toast and put under a hot grill until golden and bubbling.

BUCK RAREBIT

This is a Welsh Rarebit topped with a poached egg.

FRIED CHEESE SLICES

Allow 1 slice of bread per person; fry in about 1 oz. butter until the first side is golden. Turn the slices and cover with a slice of Gruyère, Port Salut or Bel Paese. Cover the frying-pan with a lid or large plate and cook gently until the cheese melts. Just before serving, crumble some crisply grilled bacon and sprinkle over the slices.

CHEESE DREAMS

Make some small cheese sandwiches in the usual way and cut off the crusts. Melt some butter in a frying pan and fry the sandwiches until golden and crisp on both sides. Serve at once.

CHEESE PASTRY

4 oz. plain flour	2 oz. Cheddar cheese, finely grated
A pinch of salt	
2 oz. butter or margarine and lard	A little beaten egg or water

Mix the flour and salt together and rub in the fat as for short-crust pastry, until the mixture resembles fine crumbs in texture. Mix in the cheese. Add the egg or water, stirring until the ingredients begin to stick together, then with one hand collect the dough together and knead very lightly to give a smooth dough. Roll out as for shortcrust pastry and use as required. The usual temperature for cooking cheese pastry is fairly hot (400°F., mark 6).

RICH CHEESE PASTRY

3 oz. butter or margarine and lard	4 oz. plain flour
	A pinch of salt
3 oz. Cheddar cheese, finely grated	A little Cayenne (optional)

Cream the fat and cheese together until soft, using a wooden spoon or a palette knife. Gradually work in the flour and salt (with the Cayenne if used), until the mixture sticks together. With one hand collect it together and knead very lightly until smooth. Cover with greaseproof or waxed paper and leave in a cool place.

Use as required: this rich pastry is good for small savouries, such as cocktail titbits, but the first one is better for pies, tarts, flans and so on, as it is easier to handle and less liable to crack when shaped. Use the same oven temperature as for ordinary Cheese Pastry.

CHEESE STRAWS

4 oz. plain flour	2 oz. strong Cheddar cheese,
Salt and Cayenne pepper	grated
2 oz. butter	1 egg yolk

Oven temperature: fairly hot (400°F., mark 6)

Season the flour with the salt and Cayenne. Rub in the butter to give the texture of fine bread-crumbs. Mix in the cheese and the egg yolk and enough cold water to give a stiff dough. Roll out the pastry thinly and trim into oblongs 8 inches long and 2½ inches wide. Put on to a greased baking tray and cut each into straws 2½ inches long and ¼ inch wide, separating them as you cut. Roll out the remaining pastry and cut rounds with a 2-inch plain cutter, then cut out the centre of the rounds with a 1½-inch plain cutter; put on to the baking tray. Bake towards the top of the oven for 10–15 minutes, until pale golden in colour. Remove from the oven and cool slightly on the tray before cooling completely on a wire rack. If you like dust the ends of the straws with paprika pepper and put a few into each ring before serving.

CHEESE BUTTERFLIES

2 oz. cheese pastry (see above)	Finely chopped parsley or
4 oz. cream cheese	paprika pepper
A little milk	

Oven temperature: fairly hot (400°F., mark 6)

Roll the pastry out thinly and cut into small rounds with a plain 1-inch cutter; cut half the rounds into two. Put on a baking tray and bake just above the centre of the oven for 10–15 minutes, until a light golden brown. Cool. Mix the cheese to a piping consistency with a little milk. Using a large star pipe, pipe a large star on each round. Set 2 half-biscuits in the

(Cont'd page 129)

cheese to form "wings" and decorate with chopped parsley or paprika pepper.

CREAM CHEESE BOATS

4 oz. cheese pastry (see above)   3–4 slices of
3 oz. cream cheese, flavoured   processed cheese
   to taste (see below)

Oven temperature: fairly hot (400°F., mark 6)

Line some boat-shaped moulds with the pastry. Prick the bottom and sides well and bake (empty) just above the centre of the oven for 10–15 minutes, until golden brown. When they are cool, pipe with the flavoured cheese and decorate with triangular "sails" cut from the sliced processed cheese.

Suitable flavouring ingredients for the cream cheese are finely minced ham, mashed tuna fish, chopped chives, sieved canned pimiento and so on.

CHEESE TARTLETS

4 oz. flaky or shortcrust   4 oz. Cheddar or Cheshire
   pastry (see p. 72)   cheese, grated
1 oz. butter   1 tbsp. fresh white
2 eggs, beaten   bread-crumbs
3 tbsps. single cream or   Salt and pepper
   milk   Slices of tomato

Oven temperature: fairly hot (400°F., mark 6)

Roll the pastry out thinly and line some patty tins with it. Melt the butter and add the beaten eggs, cream or milk, cheese, bread-crumbs and seasoning. Put a little of this mixture into each pastry case and place a slice of tomato on top of some of the tartlets. Bake just above the centre of the oven for a few minutes, until the filling is lightly set and golden brown – 15–20 minutes.

YORK CHEESE FINGERS

4 oz. flaky pastry (see p. 72)   Finely grated cheese
4 oz. Wensleydale or   for top of fingers
   processed cheese   2 oz. (approx.) minced ham
Beaten egg to glaze   A little horseradish sauce

Oven temperature: hot (425°F., mark 7)

Roll the pastry out thinly and cut the cheese into very thin slices (soft or processed cheese is best for this purpose). Put the cheese slices on one half of the pastry, fold the other half over and roll out again. Cut the pastry into fingers about 3 inches long and ½ inch wide. Brush them with egg and sprinkle with grated cheese. Bake on a greased baking sheet towards

---

Illustrations

13. Hot Cheese Soufflé   15. Cheese Cocktail Snacks
14. Cheese and Potato Pie   16. Fondue

the top of the oven for about 15 minutes, until the pastry is golden brown. Spread with the minced ham mixed with a little horseradish sauce. Cut into fingers to serve.

CHEESE DARTOIS

4 oz. flaky pastry (see chapter 5, p. 66)
1 egg
2 oz. Parmesan cheese, finely grated

Salt, pepper and Cayenne pepper
1 oz. butter or margarine

Oven temperature: hot (425°F., mark 7)

Roll out the pastry thinly and divide it into two portions. Beat the egg and add the cheese, seasonings and melted fat; spread the mixture over one-half of the pastry, damp the edges and place the other piece of pastry on top, press the edges well together and mark across in strips. Bake in the centre of the oven for about 15 minutes, until the pastry is golden-brown. Divide into fingers or small squares and serve either hot or cold.

CHEESE AIGRETTES

1½ oz. butter
¼ pint water
2½ oz. plain flour, sifted
2 eggs, beaten

2 oz. strong cheese, grated
Salt, pepper and Cayenne pepper
Fat for deep frying

Heat the butter and water in a saucepan until the fat dissolves and bring to the boil. Remove from the heat, add the flour all at once and beat well until the paste is smooth and leaves the sides of the pan. Allow to cool slightly, then beat in the eggs gradually. Add the cheese and season well. Heat the pan of fat and drop in teaspoonfuls of the mixture. Fry until golden, drain well on crumpled kitchen paper and serve hot.

CHEESE ÉCLAIRS

1½ oz. butter or margarine
¼ pint water
2½ oz. plain flour, sifted

2 eggs, lightly beaten
½ pint rich cheese sauce (see opposite)

Oven temperature: fairly hot (400°F., mark 6)

Melt the fat in the water and bring to the boil; remove from the heat and quickly tip in the flour all at once. Beat until the paste is smooth and forms a ball in the centre of the pan. (Take care not to over-beat, or the mixture becomes fatty.) Allow to cool slightly, then beat in the eggs gradually, adding just enough to give a smooth, glossy mixture, of piping consistency. Using a forcing bag with a ½-inch nozzle, pipe 2-inch lengths or small balls of the paste on to a baking tray and bake towards the top of the oven for about 30 minutes, until the éclairs are well risen, crisp and golden brown. Remove from the tray, slit down the sides with a sharp-pointed knife to allow the steam to escape and leave on a rack to cool. When they are cold, fill with the cold cheese sauce, or with softened cream cheese mixed with a little anchovy paste.

RICH CHEESE SAUCE FOR ECLAIRS

1 oz. butter
1 oz. flour
½ pint milk
Salt and pepper
A pinch of dry mustard

A pinch of Cayenne pepper (optional)
2–4 oz. strong cheese, grated
A little single cream (optional)

Melt the butter, add the flour and mix with a wooden spoon until smooth. Cook over a gentle heat for 2–3 minutes, stirring until the mixture begins to bubble. Remove it from the heat and add the liquid gradually, stirring after each addition to prevent lumps forming. Bring the sauce to the boil, stirring continuously, and when it has thickened, cook for a further 1–2 minutes. Add the seasonings and stir in the cheese and cream (if used). Don't re-boil, or the cheese will be overcooked.

CHEESE AND TOMATO FLAN
(see colour picture No. 11)

6 oz. cheese, grated
2 eggs
½ oz. flour
Salt and pepper
¼ pint milk (approx.)
A cooked flan case (see p. 68)

½ lb. tomatoes, skinned and sliced
A knob of butter
A few thin fillets of anchovy

Oven temperature: fairly hot (375°F., mark 5)

Mix the cheese, eggs, flour, seasoning and sufficient milk to make a soft paste; spread this over the base of the flan case. Lay the tomato slices over the top in 2 rows, season lightly and put some thin shavings of butter over them. Bake towards the top of the oven for 20–30 minutes. Garnish with thin strips of anchovy criss-crossed down the centre of the flan. (4–6 servings.)

FLUFFY CHEESE FLAN

1 oz. butter or margarine
1 oz. flour
½ pint milk
4 oz. cheese, grated

Salt and pepper
2 eggs, separated
A cooked flan case (see p. 68)

Oven temperature: hot (425°F., mark 7)

Melt the fat, stir in the flour and cook for 2–3 minutes. Remove the pan from the heat and gradually stir in the milk. Bring to the boil and continue to stir until the sauce thickens. Remove from the heat and stir in 3 oz. of the cheese, the seasoning and egg yolks; pour into the pastry case. Whisk the egg whites

131

stiffly, pile on top of the flan and sprinkle with the remaining cheese. Reduce the heat to moderate (350°F., mark 4) and return the flan to the oven for about 10 minutes, or until it is heated through and the meringue is golden.

Variation
Add 1 small skinned and chopped onion (lightly boiled); 2 oz. sliced mushrooms, lightly fried; or 2 skinned and chopped tomatoes to the sauce before putting it in the case.

QUICHE LORRAINE

4 oz. flaky pastry	2 eggs, beaten
3–4 oz. lean bacon, rinded and chopped	¼ pint single cream or creamy milk
3–4 oz. Gruyère cheese, thinly sliced	Salt and pepper

Oven temperature: fairly hot (400°F., mark 6)
Roll out the pastry and line a 7-inch plain flan ring or sandwich cake tin, making a double edge. Cover the bacon with boiling water and leave for 2–3 minutes, then drain well. Put into the pastry case, with the cheese; mix the eggs and cream, season well and pour into the case. Bake towards the top of the oven for about 30 minutes, until the filling and pastry are well risen and golden.

There are many variations on this traditional dish – it can be made with either bacon or cheese, or both as here. The cheese and bacon given above may be replaced by 3 oz. blue cheese mixed with 6 oz cream cheese In some recipes lightly boiled rings of onion or leek are used instead of, or as well as, the bacon Milk can be used instead of cream.

CHEESE AND POTATO PIE
(see colour picture No. 14)

1½ lb. potatoes	4–6 oz. Cheddar cheese, grated
1 level tsp. salt	Freshly ground pepper
1½ oz. butter	Sliced tomato and parsley to garnish
2 tbsps. single cream or top of the milk	

Oven temperature: hot (425°F., mark 7)
Peel the potatoes and cook them in boiling salted water, then drain thoroughly. Add the butter and cream and beat until light and fluffy. Stir in three-quarters of the grated cheese, check the seasoning and turn the mixture in to a buttered pie dish (1½–2 pint size). Skin and slice 1–2 tomatoes and arrange on top of the pie. Sprinkle the remaining cheese over the top and bake the pie in the centre of the oven for 20–30 minutes, until the cheese has melted and browned. Add the parsley garnish before serving. (Serves 4–5.)

132

MACARONI CHEESE

6 oz. macaroni
1½ oz. butter
1½ oz. flour
1 pint milk
Salt and pepper

A pinch of grated nutmeg or ½ level tsp. made mustard
6 oz. cheese, grated
2 tbsps. fresh white bread-crumbs (optional)

Oven temperature: very hot (450°F., mark 8)

Cook the macaroni in fast-boiling salted water for 15 minutes only and drain it well. Meanwhile melt the fat, stir in the flour and cook for 2–3 minutes. Remove the pan from the heat and gradually stir in the milk. Bring to the boil and continue to stir until the sauce thickens; remove from the heat and stir in the seasonings, 4 oz. of the cheese and the macaroni. Pour into an ovenproof dish and sprinkle with the bread-crumbs (if used) and the remaining cheese. Bake towards the top of the oven for about 10 minutes, or until golden and bubbling.

Quick macaroni can be used – cook it as directed on the packet.

Macaroni Cheese Variations

Add to the sauce any of the following:
1 small onion, skinned, chopped and boiled.
4 ozs. bacon or ham, chopped and lightly fried.
½–1 green pepper, seeded, chopped and blanched.
½–1 canned pimiento, chopped.
1 medium-sized can of salmon or tuna, drained and flaked.
2 oz. mushrooms, sliced and lightly fried.

RISOTTO ALLA MILANESE
(Cheese Risotto)

1 onion, skinned and finely chopped
3 oz. butter
8 oz. long-grain rice
¼ pint dry white wine

1½ pints boiling chicken stock (made from a cube)
Salt and pepper
2–3 level tbsps. grated Parmesan cheese

Fry the onion gently for about 5 minutes in 2 oz. of the butter, until it is soft and just beginning to turn golden. Add the rice and continue frying, stirring all the time, until the rice looks transparent. Pour in the wine and allow to bubble briskly until well reduced. Add about ½ pint of the stock and the seasoning and cook over a moderate heat in the open pan until the stock has been absorbed. Continue adding the stock until it is all used and the rice is just soft – 15–20 minutes. Add the remaining butter and stir in well. The cheese can also be stirred in until it melts, or if preferred it can be served separately.

Traditionally, 1–2 oz. of beef marrow is included, being fried after the onion is soft; the rice is coloured with saffron,

133

which is dissolved in a little of the stock and added towards the end of the cooking time. If these two ingredients are omitted, the risotto should strictly speaking be called a *Risotto bianco*.

CHEESE PUDDING

4–6 slices of white bread (4 oz.)	2 eggs, beaten
4 tbsps. dry white wine (optional)	½ pint milk
1 oz. butter, melted	Salt and pepper
	4 oz. cheese, grated

Oven temperature: fairly hot (375°F., mark 5)

Cut the bread into cubes and place in a 1½-pint greased oven-proof dish with the wine (if used) and the butter. Mix the eggs and milk, season well and pour over the bread mixture. Sprinkle with the cheese and bake towards the top of the oven for 30 minutes, until golden and well risen. Serve at once.

CHEESE SOUFFLÉ
(see colour picture No. 13)

1½ oz. butter	4 large eggs, separated
1 oz. flour	6 oz. Cheddar cheese, grated
¼ level tsp. dry mustard	Salt and pepper
½ pint milk	

Oven temperature: moderate (350°F., mark 4)

Grease a 7-inch soufflé dish (2-pint capacity). Melt the butter, stir in the flour and mustard and cook slowly for 2–3 minutes. Gradually stir in the milk and beat the mixture until smooth. Cook for a further 3–4 minutes. Beat the egg yolks into the mixture and stir in the cheese. Season with salt and pepper. Fold in the stiffly whisked egg whites, until evenly distributed. Turn the mixture into the prepared dish. Bake in the centre of the oven for about 45 minutes, until well risen and golden brown. Serve at once.

SIMPLE CHEESE SOUFFLÉ

1 pint milk and water	Salt and pepper
3 oz. bread-crumbs	Mustard
1 egg, separated	2–3 oz. cheese, grated

Oven temperature: fairly hot (400°F., mark 6)

Heat the liquid and pour it over the bread-crumbs; leave to soak for about 15 minutes, and then beat up well with a fork, adding the egg yolk, salt, pepper, mustard and cheese. Lastly, fold in lightly the very stiffly whisked egg white and pour the mixture into a greased pie dish. Bake in the centre of the oven for 30–40 minutes, until well risen and golden brown. Serve at once.

CHEESE RAMEKINS
(see colour picture No. 12)

¾ oz. fresh white
  bread-crumbs
2 tbsps. single cream
4 eggs, separated

4 oz. butter
4 oz. Cheddar cheese, finely
  grated
2 tbsps. sherry

Oven temperature: fairly hot (400°F., mark 6)

Heat the crumbs in the cream until soft, then beat with the egg yolks, butter and grated cheese. Add the sherry and mix to a smooth paste, then add the beaten egg whites. Pour the mixture into paper cases or small individual dishes and bake towards the top of the oven for about 20 minutes, until nicely browned. Serve hot.

COLD CHEESE SOUFFLÉ
(see colour picture No. 12)

½ pint Béchamel sauce
1 egg yolk
4 oz. Gruyère cheese,
  grated
Salt and pepper
Mustard
2 level tsps. gelatine

2 tbsps. stock or water
1 tsp. lemon juice
⅛ pint (2½ fl. oz.)
  double cream
2 egg whites
Cucumber to garnish

Make the Béchamel sauce (see chapter 10, p. 139) and allow to cool. Beat the cooled sauce, the egg yolk and the grated cheese together, then re-season to taste with salt, pepper and mustard. Dissolve the gelatine in the warm stock and add to the cheese mixture, with the lemon juice. Whisk the cream and the egg whites separately. Fold first the cream, then the egg whites, into the cold cheese mixture. Pour into a lightly oiled soufflé dish and leave overnight to set. Garnish with sliced cucumber and serve with a green salad.

BAKED CHEESE POTATOES

6 large potatoes
6 tbsps. hot milk
3 oz finely grated
  cheese
Salt and pepper

A little butter or
  margarine
Paprika
Parsley

Oven temperature: fairly hot (400°F., mark 6)

Wash and scrub the potatoes, prick them several times with a fork, and bake in the centre of the oven, until well cooked – about 1–1½ hours. Then cut the potatoes in halves lengthwise and scoop out the centre, being careful to keep the skins intact. Put the potato into a basin and mix it with a fork until free from lumps. Add the hot milk, most of the cheese and seasoning to taste. Stir until blended and then fill up the potato shells with the mixture. Sprinkle the rest of the cheese on the top, brush over lightly with a little melted butter and brown in the oven. Sprinkle with a little paprika before serving and garnish with parsley.

CHEESE AND POTATO CAKES

1 lb. potatoes, boiled and mashed	Salt and pepper
1 oz. butter	1–2 level tbsps. flour, if necessary
4 oz. cheese, grated	Beaten egg and dry bread-crumbs
1 level tbsp. chopped chives (or a little grated onion)	

Oven temperature: fairly hot (375°F., mark 5)

Mix the potatoes with the butter, cheese, chives (or onion) and seasoning and beat until smooth, adding a little flour if necessary to make a firm mixture. Turn on to a floured board and form into a roll. Cut into 1-inch slices and shape into round cakes. Coat with egg and dry bread-crumbs, place on a baking sheet and bake near the top of the oven for about 20 minutes; alternatively, fry the cakes.

These are good served with grilled bacon and tomatoes.

CHEESE PANCAKES

½ pint milk	4 mushrooms, washed, skinned and sliced
1 egg	
4 oz. flour	1 oz. butter
4 small tomatoes, skinned, seeded and sliced	½ pint good white sauce
	3 oz. grated cheese

Make the pancake batter in the usual way with the milk, egg and flour. Sauté the tomatoes and mushrooms in a little butter, then mix with a little sauce. Fry the pancakes and fill them with the hot savoury filling. If any sauce remains, pour it over the pancakes. Sprinkle with the grated cheese and grill till golden brown. Serve at once.

CHEESE COCKTAIL TITBITS
(See colour picture No. 15)

On a large platter arrange bite-sized sandwiches with cheese fillings of various kinds; small cheese pastries, cheese butterflies and so on. Place a tomato or red-skinned apple in the centre and on this mount cocktail sticks with an assortment of cheese and other titbits. Here are some suggestions:

A chunk of pineapple, a maraschino cherry and a piece of Cheddar cheese.

Strips of blanched green pepper interspersed with chunks of cheese.

A sausage, split in halves lengthwise, filled with a slice of cheese with a slice of cucumber wrapped round uncut end.

136

A ball cut from Cheddar cheese, with a maraschino cherry.

Chunks of cheese combined with a folded slice of ham or other meat, topped with a slice of stuffed olive.

Cheddar or other cheese with a chunk of celery and/or a cocktail onion.

A tiny cooked sausage, a piece of cheese and a cocktail onion.

CREAM CHEESE BALLS

12 oz. cream cheese	2 level tbsps. curry powder
4 oz. coarse-cut coconut	Parsley

Roll the cheese into small balls and chill them. Blend the coconut and curry powder, brown under a moderately hot grill and cool. Roll the balls in the coconut mixture and chill again before serving. Serve spiked on cocktail sticks or as desired. Sprinkle with chopped parsley.

CHEESE DIPS AND DUNKS

A dip is a soft, well-flavoured mixture, hot or cold, and a dunk is a bite-size portion of something firm or crisp which can be dipped into it.

A hot dip usually has a white sauce base to which various seasonings and flavourings can be added, while many of the cold ones are based on cream cheese.

To use as dunks you can buy small savoury biscuits, gristicks, potato crisps and so on, or you can cut French bread into small chunks or prepare raw carrot or celery sticks or radishes. For something a little more substantial, offer cooked chipolata sausages, fried scampi, tiny meat balls or cubes of grilled marinaded steak – fix them firmly on cocktail sticks so that they can be dipped into the savoury mixture.

CHIVE DIP

4 oz. cream cheese	1 tbsp. cream or top of the
2 tbsps. chopped chives	milk (if necessary)

Blend all the ingredients to a soft cream. Serve with chipolatas, cubed steak or French bread.

GARLIC DIP

4 oz. cream cheese	Salt and pepper
1 clove of garlic, skinned and crushed	1 tbsp cream or top of the milk (if necessary)

Blend the ingredients to a soft cream and season to taste. (Garlic salt may be used instead of crushed garlic.) Serve with sausage or meat titbits or French bread.

BLUE CHEESE DIP

4 oz. Danish Blue or
  Roquefort cheese, softened
3 oz. cream cheese, softened

1 tbsp. lemon juice
½ level tsp. salt

Blend all the ingredients to a smooth cream and serve with chunks of French bread.

PIMIENTO DIP

4 oz. cream cheese
1 tbsp. cream or top of the
  milk (if necessary)
Salt and pepper

½ a green pepper, finely
  chopped
½ a red pepper, finely
  chopped

Blend the cream cheese and cream or milk to a soft cream. Season to taste and stir in the green and red pepper. Serve with scampi, savoury biscuits or French bread.

FONDUE
(See colour picture No. 16)

1 clove of garlic, skinned
¼ pint dry white wine and a
  squeeze of lemon juice
8 oz. cheese, cut in thin strips
  (half Gruyère, half
  Emmenthal)

2 level tsps. cornflour
A little pepper and grated
  nutmeg
Salt and pepper to taste
1 liqueur glass of Kirsch

Rub the inside of a flameproof dish with the crushed garlic, place the dish over a gentle heat and warm the wine and lemon juice in it. Add the cheese and continue to heat gently, stirring well until the cheese has melted and begun to cook. Add the cornflour and seasonings, blended to a smooth cream with the Kirsch, and continue cooking for a further 2–3 minutes; when the mixture is of a thick creamy consistency, it is ready to serve.

Traditionally, fondue is served at the table in the dish in which it was cooked, kept warm over a small spirit lamp or dish-warmer. To eat it, provide cubes of crusty bread which are speared on a fork and dipped in the fondue. Pieces of celery, etc., may also be used.

An anglicised version of fondue can be made using a strong-flavoured Cheddar cheese, cider instead of white wine and brandy instead of Kirsch.

138

CHAPTER 10

Sauces, accompaniments, garnishes, stuffings

Sauces

THIN OR CLEAR GRAVY

Pour off all the fat from the roasting tin except 1 tbsp. Sprinkle in 4 level tbsps. flour and (in the case of poultry) stir in about $\frac{1}{2}$ pint giblet stock; failing this, use other stock as available, or water. Bring to the boil, stirring, season with salt and pepper and add a touch of gravy browning if necessary. In the case of chicken, the finely chopped liver may be included to give a richer flavour.

SIMPLE WHITE SAUCE – BLENDING METHOD

$\frac{1}{2}$ oz. (1$\frac{1}{2}$ level tbsps.) cornflour or flour	A knob of butter
$\frac{1}{2}$ pint milk	Salt and pepper

1 – *Pouring Consistency*

Put the cornflour or flour in a basin and blend with 1–2 tbsps. of the milk to a smooth cream. Heat the remaining milk with the butter until boiling; pour on to the blended mixture, stirring all the time to prevent lumps forming. Return the mixture to the pan and bring to the boil, stirring continuously with a wooden spoon. Cook for 1–2 minutes after the mixture has thickened, to make a white, glossy sauce. Add salt and pepper to taste before serving.

2 – *Coating Consistency*

Increase the quantity of cornflour to $\frac{3}{4}$ oz. (2 level tbsps.).

139

SIMPLE WHITE SAUCE – ROUX METHOD

1 – *Pouring Consistency*

¾ oz. butter
¾ oz. (2 level tbsps. approx.)
    flour

½ pint milk or milk and
    stock
Salt and pepper

Melt the fat, add the flour and stir with a wooden spoon until smooth. Cook over a gentle heat for 2–3 minutes, stirring until the mixture (called a roux) begins to bubble. Remove from the heat and add the liquid gradually, stirring after each addition to prevent lumps forming. Bring the sauce to the boil, stirring continuously, and when it has thickened, cook for a further 1–2 minutes. Add salt and pepper to taste.

Both this and the blended sauce overleaf may be flavoured as desired – see Cheese, Mushroom and Parsley Sauces.

2 – *Coating Consistency*

1 oz. butter
1 oz. (3 level tbsps.)
    flour

½ pint milk or milk and
    stock
Salt and pepper

Make the sauce as above.

For a thick coating sauce increase the quantities to 1½ oz. each of butter and flour.

3 – *Binding Consistency* (*Panada*)

2 oz. butter
2 oz. (6 level tbsps.)
    flour

½ pint milk or milk and
    stock
Salt and pepper

Melt the fat, add the flour and stir well. Cook gently for 2–3 minutes, stirring, until the roux begins to bubble and leave the sides of the pan. Add the liquid gradually, bring to the boil, stirring all the time, and cook for 1–2 minutes after it has thickened; add salt and pepper to taste.

This very thick sauce is used for binding mixtures such as croquettes.

BÉCHAMEL (RICH WHITE) SAUCE

½ pint milk
1 shallot, skinned and
    sliced (or a small piece of
    onion, skinned)
A small piece of carrot,
    peeled and cut up

½ a stick of celery, cut up
½ a bay leaf
3 peppercorns
1 oz. butter
1 oz. (3 level tbsps.) flour
Salt and pepper

Put the milk, vegetables and flavourings in a saucepan and bring slowly to the boil. Remove from the heat, cover and leave to infuse for about 15 minutes. Strain the liquid and use this with the butter and flour to make a roux sauce (see beginning of chapter). Season to taste before serving.

This classic sauce is the basis of many other sauces, and a few examples are given here.

140

ESPAGNOLE (RICH BROWN) SAUCE

1 oz. streaky bacon, chopped
1 oz. butter
1 shallot, skinned and
  chopped (or a small piece o
  onion, chopped)
1 oz. mushroom stalks, washed
  and chopped

1 small carrot, peeled and
  chopped
¾–1 oz. (2–3 level tbsps.) flour
½ pint beef stock
A bouquet garni
2 level tbsps. tomato paste
Salt and pepper

Fry the bacon in the butter for 2–3 minutes, add the vegetables and fry for a further 3–5 minutes, or until lightly browned. Stir in the flour, mix well and continue frying until it turns brown. Remove from the heat and gradually add the stock (which if necessary can be made from a stock cube), stirring after each addition. Return the pan to the heat and stir until the sauce thickens; add the bouquet garni, tomato paste and salt and pepper. Reduce the heat and allow to simmer very gently for 1 hour, stirring from time to time to prevent it sticking; alternatively, cook in the centre of a warm oven (325°F., mark 3) for 1½–2 hours. Strain the sauce, reheat and skim off any fat, using a metal spoon. Re-season if necessary. 1 tbsp. sherry may be added just before the sauce is served, if you wish.

This classic brown sauce is used as a basis for many other savoury sauces.

APPLE SAUCE

1 lb. cooking apples, peeled
  and cored

1 oz. butter
A little sugar (optional)

Slice the apples and simmer gently in a covered saucepan with 2–3 tbsps. water until soft – about 10 minutes. Beat to a pulp with a wooden spoon, then sieve or put in an electric blender. Stir in the butter and add a little sugar if the apples are tart.

Serve with goose.

BARBECUE SAUCE

2 oz. butter
1 large onion, skinned and
  chopped
1 level tsp. tomato paste
2 tbsps. vinegar
2 level tsps. dry mustard

2 level tbsps. Demerara
  sugar
¼ pint water
2 tbsps. Worcestershire
  sauce

Melt the butter and fry the onion for 5 minutes, or until soft. Stir in the tomato paste and continue cooking for a further 3 minutes. Blend the remaining ingredients to a smooth cream and stir in the onion mixture. Return the sauce to the pan and simmer for a further 10 minutes.

Serve with chicken.

141

BÉARNAISE SAUCE

4 tbsps. wine or tarragon vinegar
1 shallot, skinned
A few sprigs of tarragon

2 egg yolks
3 oz. butter
Salt and pepper

Place the vinegar, chopped shallot and chopped tarragon in a small saucepan over a gentle heat and reduce to about 1 tbsp. Stir into the egg yolks in a basin and cook over a pan of simmering water until slightly thickened. Whisk in the butter a little at a time, then season to taste.

Serve with grills.

Note: 1 tbsp. of the vinegar can be replaced by 1 tbsp. water – this gives a slightly less piquant sauce.

BIGARADE SAUCE

½ pint Espagnole sauce
Juice of 1 orange
Juice of 1 lemon

2–3 tbsps. port
A pinch of sugar
Salt and pepper

Heat the Espagnole sauce (see this chapter), stir in the strained fruit juices and the port and simmer (uncovered) for 10 minutes; add a little sugar if the sauce is too sharp and extra seasoning if necessary.

Serve with roast duck.

BREAD SAUCE

1 medium-sized onion
2 cloves
¾ pint milk
Salt

A few peppercorns
¾ oz. butter
3 oz. fresh white bread-crumbs
½ a small bay leaf

Skin the onion and stick the cloves into it, place in a saucepan with the milk, salt and peppercorns, bring almost to boiling point and leave in a warm place for about 20 minutes, in order to extract the flavour from the onion. Remove the peppercorns from the onion and return it to the pan. Add the butter and crumbs, mix well, add bay leaf and cook very slowly for about 15 minutes, then remove the onion. (If liked, remove the onion before adding the bread-crumbs, but a better flavour is obtained by cooking it with the crumbs, as this allows the taste of the onion to penetrate them.

Serve with roast chicken, turkey or pheasant.

CHAUDFROID SAUCE – WHITE

½ an envelope of aspic jelly powder
¼ pint hot water
¼ oz. gelatine (2 level tsps.)

½ pint Béchamel sauce (see p. 140)
⅛–¼ pint single cream
Salt and pepper

142

Put the aspic jelly powder in a small basin and dissolve it in the hot water. Stand the basin in a pan of hot water, sprinkle in the gelatine and stir until it has dissolved, taking care not to overheat the mixture. Stir into the warm Béchamel sauce, beat well and add the cream and extra salt and pepper if necessary. Strain the sauce and leave to cool, stirring frequently so that it remains smooth and glossy.

Use when at the consistency of thick cream, for coating chicken or eggs.

Notes: A simpler Chaudfroid Sauce can be made by adding $\frac{1}{4}$ pint melted aspic jelly to $\frac{1}{2}$ pint warm Béchamel sauce; beat well, strain, cool and use as above.

CHAUDFROID SAUCE – BROWN

$\frac{1}{2}$ an envelope of aspic jelly powder
$\frac{1}{4}$ pint hot water
$\frac{1}{4}$ oz. gelatine (2 level tsps.)
$\frac{3}{4}$ pint Espagnole sauce (see p. 141)
Madeira, sherry or port to taste
Salt and pepper

Put the aspic jelly powder in a small basin, dissolve in the hot water and stand the basin in a pan of hot water. Sprinkle in the gelatine and stir over a gentle heat until it dissolves. Warm the Espagnole sauce and beat in the aspic and gelatine mixture. Add wine to taste and extra salt and pepper if necessary. Strain the sauce and allow to cool, beating it from time to time so that it remains smooth and glossy.

When it reaches the consistency of thick cream, use to coat game or duck.

CHEESE SAUCE

$\frac{1}{2}$ pint white sauce
2–4 oz. strong cheese, grated
A pinch of dry mustard
A pinch of Cayenne pepper (optional)
Salt and pepper

Make the sauce and when it has thickened remove from the heat and stir in the cheese and seasonings. Do not re-boil, or the cheese will be over-cooked – there is sufficient heat in the sauce to melt the cheese.

Serve with eggs.

CHESTNUT SAUCE

$\frac{1}{2}$ lb. chestnuts, peeled
A small piece of onion, skinned
A small piece of carrot, peeled
$\frac{1}{2}$ pint stock
$1\frac{1}{2}$ oz. butter
1 oz. flour
Salt and pepper
2–3 tbsps. single cream

Put the peeled nuts into a pan with the vegetables and stock, cover and simmer until soft, then mash or sieve. Melt the

143

butter and stir in the flour to form a roux, then add the chestnut purée and bring to the boil, stirring – the sauce should be thick, but it may be necessary at this point to add a little milk or extra stock. Season well with salt and pepper, remove from the heat and stir in the cream.

Re-heat without boiling and serve at once, with turkey, etc.

CRANBERRY SAUCE

½ lb. sugar
½ pint water
½ lb. cranberries

Dissolve the sugar in the water and boil for 5 minutes. Add the cranberries and simmer for about 10 minutes. Cool before serving. A little port can be added for additional flavour.

Serve with turkey.

CUMBERLAND SAUCE

1 orange
1 lemon
4 level tbsps. red currant jelly
4 tbsps. port
2 level tsps. cornflour
2 tsps. water

Peel the rind thinly from the washed orange and lemon, cut in strips, cover with water and simmer for 5 minutes. Squeeze the juice from both fruits. Put the red currant jelly, orange juice and lemon juice into a pan, stir until the jelly dissolves, simmer for 5 minutes and add the port. Blend the cornflour and water to a smooth cream and stir in the red currant mixture. Return the sauce to the pan and re-heat, stirring, until it thickens and clears. Drain the strips of rind and add to the sauce.

Serve with venison.

CURRY SAUCE

2 medium-sized onions, skinned and chopped fine
1 oz. dripping or butter
1 level tbsp. curry powder
1 level tsp. curry paste
1 level tbsp. rice flour or ordinary flour
A clove of garlic, skinned
½ pint stock or coconut milk
Salt
A little Cayenne pepper
2 tbsps. chutney
1 tbsp. single cream (optional)

Fry the onions golden brown in the hot fat and add the curry powder, paste and rice or other flour. Cook for 5 minutes, then add the garlic, pour in the stock or coconut milk and bring to the boil. Add the seasonings and chutney, then simmer for 30–40 minutes. This sauce is much improved by the addition of 1 tbsp. cream immediately before use; less curry powder may be used for those who prefer a mild version. The rice or ordinary flour can be omitted, since a curry is thickened by reduction of the liquid and by long, slow simmering.

Use with poultry, game, eggs, etc.

SAUCE DIABLE

2 shallots, skinned and finely chopped
Butter for frying
½ pint Espagnole sauce (see p. 141)

Cayenne pepper
1 level tbsp. French mustard
Tarragon or wine vinegar
Chutney (optional)

Fry the shallots in butter (or margarine) until they are browned. Add the Espagnole sauce, bring to the boil and season with Cayenne pepper, French mustard and a dash of tarragon or wine vinegar, together with a little finely chopped chutney if desired.

GOOSEBERRY SAUCE

½ lb. gooseberries, topped and tailed

1 oz. butter
1–2 oz. sugar

Stew the fruit in as little water as possible, or until soft and pulped. Beat well, then sieve or put in a blender. Add the butter and a little sugar, if the fruit is sour.

Serve with goose.

LEMON SAUCE

Rind and juice of 1 lemon
½ pint white sauce (using half milk and half chicken stock)

1–2 level tsps. sugar
Salt and pepper

Simmer the lemon rind in the milk and stock for 5 minutes; strain and use the liquid to make a white sauce. When it has thickened, stir in the lemon juice and sugar and season to taste.

Serve with chicken.

MADEIRA OR MARSALA SAUCE

Add up to ¼ pint Madeira or Marsala to ½ pint Espagnole sauce (see this chapter) and re-heat but don't re-boil. The juice and extractives from the roasting tin can also be reduced and added, to give extra flavour.

Serve with game.

MORNAY SAUCE

½ pint Béchamel sauce
2 oz. Parmesan or Gruyère cheese, grated

Paprika pepper, salt and pepper to taste

Make the Béchamel sauce and when it has thickened, remove

from the heat and stir in the cheese and seasonings. Do not re-heat or the cheese will become over-cooked and stringy.

Serve with eggs or chicken.

MUSHROOM SAUCE

½ pint white sauce
2–3 oz. button mushrooms, washed and sliced

½–1 oz. butter
Salt and pepper

Make the sauce in the usual way. Lightly fry the mushrooms in the butter until soft but not coloured, fold into the sauce and season to taste.

Serve with eggs.

PARSLEY SAUCE

½ pint white sauce
1–2 tbsps. chopped parsley
Salt and pepper

A squeeze of lemon juice (optional)

Make the sauce using half milk and half stock (if available). When it has thickened, stir in the parsley and seasonings. Don't re-boil or the parsley may turn the sauce green.

Serve with boiled chicken.

PORT WINE SAUCE

¼ pint clear gravy or juices from roast mutton or venison
4 tbsps. port wine

1–2 level tbsps. red-currant jelly

Put all the ingredients in a pan, stir well and simmer for 5–10 minutes, until clear and syrupy.

Serve with venison.

RAISIN SAUCE

2 level tbsps. sugar
2 tbsps. vinegar
½ pint Espagnole sauce (see p. 141)

2 oz. raisins, stoned
Up to ⅛ pint red wine as required

Dissolve the sugar in the vinegar and boil until syrupy and slightly caramelised. Take the pan from the heat and gradually add the sauce and the raisins. Re-heat and simmer for about 5 minutes or until the raisins are plump. This sauce is very rich and tends to be rather thick, so just before serving thin it down with red wine until the desired consistency is obtained.

Serve with game.

SUPRÊME SAUCE

½ pint velouté sauce (see p. 148)
1–2 egg yolks
2–3 tbsps. cream

½–1 oz. butter
A squeeze of lemon juice
Salt and pepper

146

Make the velouté sauce, remove from the heat and stir in the egg yolks and cream. Add the butter, a little at a time, the lemon juice and seasoning to taste. Re-heat if necessary but don't re-boil, or the sauce will curdle.

Serve with poultry.

SWEET-SOUR SAUCE

½ oz. lard
1 small onion, skinned and finely chopped
An 8-oz. can of tomatoes

1 oz. cornflour
½ pint pineapple juice
1 tsp. Worcestershire sauce
Salt and pepper

Melt the fat in a pan. Fry the onion in the fat till soft but not browned. Add the tomatoes. Blend the cornflour with a little pineapple juice to a smooth cream. Add the rest of the juice and the seasonings to the tomatoes and bring to the boil. Stir a little of the hot liquid into the blended mixtures, return it to the pan and bring to the boil, stirring till it thickens. Cook for a further 1–2 minutes.

Serve with poultry.

TOMATO SAUCE
(Made from fresh tomatoes)

1 small onion, skinned and chopped
1 small carrot, peeled and chopped
1 oz. butter
½ oz. flour
1 lb. cooking tomatoes

½ pint chicken stock (made from a cube)
½ a bay leaf
1 clove
1 level tsp. sugar
Salt and pepper

Lightly fry the onion and carrot in the butter for 5 minutes. Stir in the flour and add the quartered tomatoes, the stock, flavourings, etc. Bring to the boil and simmer for 30–45 minutes, or until the vegetables are cooked. Sieve, re-heat and re-season if necessary.

Serve with croquettes, réchauffés, etc.

Note: You can add 2 level tsps. tomato paste to give a full flavour and better colour; 1–4 tbsps. white wine or sherry can also be added just before serving.

TOMATO SAUCE
(Made from canned tomatoes)

½ an onion, skinned and chopped
2 rashers of bacon, rinded and chopped
½ oz. butter
¼ oz. flour

A 15-oz. can of peeled tomatoes
1 clove, ½ a bay leaf, a few sprigs of rosemary (or 1 level tsp. mixed dried herbs)
Salt and pepper

Fry the onion and bacon in the butter for 5 minutes. Stir in the flour and gradually add the tomatoes, also the flavourings and seasoning. Simmer gently for 15 minutes, then sieve and if necessary re-season.

Serve with made-up dishes.

VELOUTÉ SAUCE

¾ oz. butter
¼ oz. (2 level tbsp. approx.) flour
¾ pint light stock

2–3 tbsps. single cream
A few drops of lemon juice
Salt and pepper

Melt the butter, stir in the flour and cook gently, stirring well, until the mixture is pale fawn in colour. Stir in the stock gradually, bring to the boil, stirring all the time, and simmer until slightly reduced and syrupy. Remove from the heat and add the cream, lemon juice and seasoning.

Serve with poultry.

Accompaniments

BACON ROLLS

Choose streaky bacon. Cut each rasher in half, then "spread" it with a knife on a board, roll up and string 2 or 3 together on a skewer. Grill for about 2 minutes on each side.

Use bacon rolls as an accompaniment to roast chicken, or to garnish made-up dishes. For an unusual variation, wrap the bacon round some cooked stoned prunes and grill as above.

BOILED BACON OR GAMMON

Weigh the piece, then calculate the cooking time, allowing 20–25 minutes per lb. plus 20 minutes over. If you are cooking a large joint (e.g. a gammon of 10 lb. or over) allow 15–20 minutes per lb. plus 15 minutes. Cover it with water and allow to soak for about 1 hour. Place the bacon or gammon in a large pan, skin side down, cover with fresh cold water and bring slowly to the boil, skimming off any scum that forms. Time the cooking from this point. Cover and simmer gently.

For extra flavour add 2 onions, quartered, 2 carrots, quartered, 1 bay leaf and 4 peppercorns. When the bacon or gammon is cooked, cut off the outer skin.

Serve as an accompaniment to roast turkey or chicken.

FRIED CRUMBS

Melt 1 oz. butter in a frying pan. Stir in 4 oz. fresh white bread-crumbs until blended and fry until the crumbs are evenly browned.

148

PASTA

Italians would reckon about 3–4 oz. per person, but in this country 1½–2 oz. is considered sufficient by most people. The pasta should be cooked in a large quantity of fast-boiling salted water until *al dente*, or just resistant to the teeth. It should never be mushy or slimy. Drain as soon as it is cooked and serve on a heated dish. A knob of butter or a little olive oil is usually stirred in just before serving and grated Parmesan cheese can be stirred into the pasta or served separately according to taste.

Allow about 10 minutes for noodles, 12–15 minutes for spaghetti, 15–20 minutes for macaroni.

POTATOES

CREAMED: Mash the cooked potatoes with a knob of butter, salt and pepper to taste and a little milk. Beat them well over a gentle heat with a wooden spoon until fluffy. Serve in a heated dish, mark with a fork and sprinkle with chopped parsley.

ROAST: Using old potatoes, peel in the usual way and cut into even-sized pieces. Cook in salted water for 5–10 minutes – depending on the size – and drain well. Transfer them to a roasting tin containing 4 oz. of hot lard or dripping, baste well and bake near the top of a hot oven (425°F., mark 7) for about 20 minutes; turn them and continue cooking until soft inside and crisp and brown outside – about 40 minutes altogether. Drain well on kitchen paper and serve in an uncovered serving dish, sprinkled with salt.

If preferred, do not parboil the potatoes to begin with – in this case they will take about 50–60 minutes to cook.

CHIPPED OR FRENCH-FRIED: Cut peeled old potatoes into ¼–½ inch slices and then into strips ¼–½ wide. (For speed, several slices can be put on top of one another and cut together). Place in cold water and leave for at least ½ hour; drain well and dry with a cloth.

Heat a deep fat fryer of oil until when one chip is dropped into the fat, it rises to the surface straight away, surrounded by bubbles. Put enough chips into the basket to about quarter-fill it and lower carefully into the fat. Cook for about 6–7 minutes. Remove the chips and drain on absorbent paper. Follow the same procedure until all the chips have been cooked. Just before serving re-heat the fat, test to make sure it is hot enough and fry the chips rapidly for about 3 minutes, until crisp and brown. Drain well on kitchen paper and serve in an uncovered dish, sprinkled with salt.

MATCHSTICK POTATOES: Cut potatoes into very small chips of matchstick size. Cook like chips, but as they are very much

149

smaller, allow a shorter cooking-time – about 3 minutes at the first cooking.

GAME CHIPS: Scrub and peel the potatoes and slice very thinly into rounds. Soak them in cold water, dry and fry in deep fat, as for chipped potatoes, but allowing a shorter cooking time – about 3 minutes for the first frying.

Ready-cooked potato crisps may also be used; heat them for a few minutes in the oven.

RICE

Rice sold in unbranded packs or loose should be washed before it is cooked. Put it in a strainer and rinse it under the cold tap until all the loose starch (white powder) is washed off – it is this loose starch which prevents rice drying out into separate grains when cooked.

BOILED RICE – the 1 – 2 – 1 METHOD: For 3–4 servings place 1 cup of long-grain rice in a saucepan with 2 cups water and 1 level tsp. salt. Bring quickly to the boil, stir well and cover with a tight-fitting lid. Reduce the heat and simmer gently for 14–15 minutes. Remove from the heat and before serving separate out the grains gently, using a fork. (The rice will not need draining.)

If a drier effect is required, leave the rice covered for 5–10 minutes after it has been cooked. The grains should then be tender, but dry and quite separate.

Here are some points to remember when using the 1–2–1 method:

Don't increase the amount of water or the finished rice will be soggy.

Don't uncover the rice whilst it is cooking or the steam will escape and the cooking time will be increased.

Don't stir the rice after it has come to the boil – it breaks up the grains and makes them soggy.

When the rice is cooked, don't leave it longer than 10 minutes before serving, or the grains will stick together.

BOILED RICE – ORDINARY METHOD: Allow 1½–2 oz. long-grain per person. Half-fill a large pan with water (about 6 pints to 6 oz. rice) bring to the boil and add 1 level tsp. salt. Add the rice and continue to boil rapidly, uncovered, until the rice is just soft – 15–20 minutes. Drain the rice in a sieve and rinse by pouring hot water through it, then return it to the pan with a knob of butter; cover with a tea towel or lid and leave on a very low heat to dry out for 5–10 minutes, shaking the pan from time to time. Alternatively, spread the drained rice on a shallow baking tray or ovenproof dish lined with greaseproof paper, cover with a tea towel or greaseproof paper and place in a very low oven to dry out.

SAUSAGES

Pork sausages are more expensive and more delicately flavoured than beef, which have a distinctive taste that is not popular with everybody. Each kind is sold both in the normal 8-to-the-pound size and as the thinner 16-to-the-pound chipolatas. The actual mixture is usually the same, but the thick sausages need longer, slower cooking if they are not to split; chipolatas sometimes look more attractive and appeal to those people who like plenty of nice crisp brown "outside".

FRIED: Melt a little fat in the frying-pan, add the sausages and fry for 15–20 minutes, keeping the heat low to prevent their burning and turning them once or twice.

GRILLED: Heat the grill to hot, put the sausages on the grill rack in the pan and cook until one side is lightly browned, then turn them; continue cooking and turning them frequently for about 15–20 minutes, until the sausages are well browned.

BAKED: Heat the oven to fairly hot (400°F., mark 6). Put the sausages in a greased baking tin and cook in the centre of the oven for 30 minutes.

Salads and Salad Dressings

GREEN SALAD

Use two or more green salad ingredients, such as lettuce, cress, watercress, endive, chicory, cabbage and so on. Wash and drain them and just before serving toss lightly in a bowl with French dressing, adding a little finely chopped onion if liked.

Sprinkle with chopped fresh parsley, chives, mint, tarragon or other herbs, as available.

MIXED ENGLISH SALAD

A small bunch of radishes, washed and trimmed
A bunch of spring onions, washed and trimmed
1 lettuce, washed
A bunch of watercress (or a box of small cress) washed and trimmed
4 tomatoes, wiped and sliced
1 cooked beetroot, peeled and diced
1 small piece of cucumber, wiped and skinned (if liked) and sliced
2–4 hard-boiled eggs, sliced
2–4 oz. firm cheese, grated

Cut the radishes into "roses" (see "Other Garnishes," this chapter). Make fine cuts down the length of the onion tops. Put the radishes and onions in iced water and leave until the radishes open and the onions curl. Put a bed of lettuce and watercress or cress on a shallow plate and arrange the remaining ingredients on top, in rows or groups.

ORANGE SALAD

2 oranges, peeled   French dressing
Chopped tarragon or mint

Divide the oranges into sections, removing all the skin, pith and pips, or cut across in thin slices, using a saw-edged knife. Put the slices into a shallow dish, sprinkle with the tarragon or mint and pour the dressing over; allow to stand for a short time before serving. This salad can be served on a bed of watercress, small cress or endive.

TOMATO SALAD

4 tomatoes   Salt and pepper
A small piece of onion (or 2–3   French dressing
    small spring onions)   Chopped parsley or chives

Wipe the tomatoes, skin them if liked and cut in thin slices. Skin and finely chop the onion (or spring onions). Arrange the tomatoes in a dish, sprinkle with the onion and seasoning and pour the dressing over. Allow to stand for a short time and serve sprinkled with the chopped herbs.

To skin tomatoes: Dip in boiling water or put on a fork and hold in a gas flame for about ½ minute, then dip in cold water and peel off the skin.

FRENCH SALAD DRESSING (SAUCE VINAIGRETTE)

¼ level tsp. salt   ¼ level tsp. sugar
⅛ level tsp. pepper   1 tbsp. vinegar or lemon juice
¼ level tsp. dry mustard   2 tbsps. oil

Put the salt, pepper, mustard and sugar in a bowl, add the vinegar and stir until well blended. Beat in the oil gradually with a fork. Use at once – the oil separates out on standing, so if necessary whip the dressing immediately before use. A good plan is to store it in a salad-cream bottle, shaking it up vigorously just before serving.

Note: The proportion of oil to vinegar varies with individual taste, but use vinegar sparingly. Malt, wine, tarragon or any other may be used.

Variations of French Salad Dressing
To the above dressing add any of the following:
A clove of garlic, crushed.
1–2 tsps. chopped chives.
½–1 level tsp. curry powder.
2 tsps. chopped parsley, ½ tsp. dried marjoram and a pinch of
    dried thyme.
1 tsp. chopped parsley, 1 tsp. chopped gherkins or capers, 1 tsp.
    chopped olives.
1–2 tsps. sweet pickle.

1 tbsp. finely sliced or chopped stuffed olives.
1–2 tsps. Worcestershire sauce.
1–2 tsps. chopped mint.
1 tbsp. finely chopped anchovies.
A pinch of curry powder, $\frac{1}{2}$ a hard-boiled egg, shelled and finely
    chopped, 1 tsp. chopped onion (this is called Bombay dressing).
1 oz. blue-vein cheese, crumbled.

LEMON AND OIL DRESSING

2–3 tbsps. oil   1 tbsp. lemon juice
Pepper and salt

Add the oil gradually to the salt and pepper and when they
are well blended, whisk in the lemon juice with a fork.

CLASSIC MAYONNAISE

1 egg yolk $\frac{1}{2}$ level tsp. sugar
$\frac{1}{2}$ level tsp. dry mustard $\frac{1}{4}$ pint (approx.) oil
$\frac{1}{2}$ level tsp. salt   1 tbsp. white vinegar
$\frac{1}{4}$ level tsp. pepper   (or lemon juice)

Put the egg yolk into a basin with the seasonings and sugar.
Mix thoroughly, then add the oil drop by drop, stirring
briskly with a wooden spoon the whole time or using a whisk,
until the sauce is thick and smooth. If it becomes too thick
add a little of the vinegar. When all the oil has been added,
add the vinegar gradually and mix thoroughly.

Notes: To keep the basin firmly in position, twist a damp cloth
tightly round the base – this prevents it from slipping.

In order that the oil may be added 1 drop at a time, put
into the bottle-neck a cork from which a small wedge has
been cut.

Should the sauce curdle during the process of making, put
another egg yolk into a basin and add the curdled sauce very
gradually, in the same way as the oil is added to the original
egg yolk.

Variations of Mayonnaise
Using $\frac{1}{4}$ pint mayonnaise as a basis, add a flavouring as
follows:
CAPER: Add 2–3 tsps. chopped capers, 1 tsp. chopped pimiento
and 1 tsp. tarragon vinegar.
CELERY: Add 1 tbsp. chopped celery and 1 tbsp. chopped
chives.
CREAM: Add 4 tbsps. whipped cream. (Goes well with salads
containing fruit and chicken or rice.)
CUCUMBER: Add 2 tbsps. finely chopped cucumber and $\frac{1}{2}$ level
tsp. salt.

153

HERBS: Add 3 tbsps. chopped chives and 2 tbsps. chopped parsley.

HORSERADISH: Add 1 tbsp. horseradish sauce.

PIQUANT: Add 1 tsp. tomato ketchup, 1 tsp. chopped olives and a pinch of paprika pepper. *Or* add 1–2 tsps. Worcestershire or chilli sauce.

TOMATO: Add $\frac{1}{2}$ a tomato, skinned and diced, 1 spring onion, chopped, $\frac{1}{4}$ level tsp. salt and 1 tsp. vinegar or lemon juice.

BLUE CHEESE: Add 1 oz. crumbled blue cheese.

Note: All these variations can also be made using a basis of bought salad cream.

Garnishes

The first four are used mainly with hot dishes, while the remainder tend to be used more with salads, hors d'oeuvre, galantines and so on.

CROÛTONS

For croûtons to garnish entrees (such as Fricasse of Chicken or Rabbit, Chicken Marengo and so on) cut slices of bread $\frac{1}{4}$ inch thick and cut these into fancy shapes, such as rounds, square, fingers, crescents, heart shapes or diamonds. Fry in hot oil or butter until golden brown on both sides, or cook in deep fat if preferred. Drain well on crumpled kitchen paper and use at once.

For croûtons to serve with soup, make some toast just beforehand, and cut this into small neat dice. If desired, the bread may be lightly buttered before being toasted. As an alternative to toasting, brown the bread dice in a moderate oven (350°F., mark 4) for a few minutes.

FLEURONS

Oven temperature: very hot (450°F., mark 8)

Small fancy-shaped pieces of pastry (usually puff, flaky or rough puff) used for garnishing entrees, ragoûts, mince, etc. Roll the pastry to $\frac{1}{4}$ inch in thickness, then stamp it into crescents with a small round cutter; place the cutter about $\frac{1}{2}$ inch on to the edge of the pastry for the first cut, then move the cutter a further $\frac{1}{2}$ inch inwards and cut again, thus forming a crescent; continue the length of the pastry, moving the cutter $\frac{1}{2}$ inch each time. Alternatively, cut the pastry into rounds, square, triangles, diamonds, etc. Place the fleurons on a baking sheet, brush the tops lightly with beaten egg and bake in the centre of the oven until well risen, golden brown and firm underneath – 7–10 minutes. Use at once, while crisp.

FRIED PARSLEY

Choose several good-sized pieces of well-curled fresh parsley. If it is necessary to wash them, shake them well to remove the water, then dry thoroughly in a cloth. After frying the food to be garnished, draw the pan of fat from the heat and allow it to cool for 2–3 minutes. Then put in the parsley carefully a little at a time, as the fat tends to spit, especially if the parsley is at all wet. Cook for 1 minute or so, until the parsley is crisp, then scoop out, drain well and use at once.

MAÎTRE D'HÔTEL (PARSLEY) BUTTER

1 oz. butter	1 tsp. lemon juice
2 level tsps. very finely chopped parsley	Salt and pepper

Put all the ingredients into a small basin and mix thoroughly into a creamy paste, using a fork or wooden spoon; shape into pats and allow to harden.

Serve with grills.

OTHER GARNISHES

SAVOURY BUTTER: Flavoured or coloured savoury butters may be piped as a decoration on cold poultry. Cream cheese may be used in a similar way.

CARROT: Cooked carrots may be cut into small fancy shapes and used on galantines, etc.

CURLED CELERY: Cut very thin shreds lengthwise from a stalk of celery. Soak in cold or iced water until curled – about an hour. Drain well before using.

CUCUMBER CONES: Cut thin slices of cucumber. Make a cut in each slice from the centre to the outer edge, then wrap one cut edge over the other to form a cone.

CRIMPED CUCUMBER: Working lengthwise, remove strips of the cucumber skin about ⅛ inch wide at intervals of about ⅛ inch, then cut the cucumber crosswise in thin slices.

HARD-BOILED EGGS: Sliced or quartered, these eggs may be used to decorate salads, cold dishes or entrees, especially such dishes as Curried Egg. To make more elaborate decorations the white may be cut in fancy shapes or finely chopped and the yolk sieved.

GHERKIN FANS: Use whole gherkins, choosing long, thin ones. Cut each gherkin lengthwise into thin slices, but leave them joined at one end. Fan out the gherkins, so that the slices overlap each other. A most attractive garnish can be made by combining gherkin fans and radish roses.

155

LEMON BUTTERFLIES OR FANS: Cut $\frac{1}{8}$ inch thick slices of lemon across, to form half circles. Cut the rind again in half, but leave the centre membranes attached, then open out to form butterflies.

MUSHROOMS: Small button ones may be used whole; larger ones are better sliced. Fry gently in butter.

OLIVES: Stuffed olives may be used whole or sliced; plain olives may be stoned, filled with cream cheese and surrounded by an anchovy fillet.

PARSLEY: Used in the form of sprigs or chopped.

RED AND GREEN PEPPERS: These make a good garnish for galantines and other cold meats. Cut the skin of the uncooked peppers into fancy shapes with small cutters, or trim into julienne strips. Dip the pieces into glaze or aspic jelly and place in position.

ROSE RADISHES: Choose round radishes and wash them well, removing any root, but leaving 1 inch or so of the stalk. With a small, sharp knife (or potato peeler) peel the coloured skin down in sections to look like petals, starting at the root end and continuing nearly as far as the stalk; do this all round, leaving the middle of the radish as the flower centre. Soak in water for a short time to make the petals open out. Before using, shake well to remove water.

LILY RADISHES: Select round radishes, trim them and with a small, sharp-pointed knife make V-shaped incisions around each, finally just cutting through the centre of the radish, when the two halves will come apart attractively notched.

TOMATOES: Tomato slices or wedges make one of the simplest and most colourful decorations. To make "lilies", cut small firm tomatoes in half with a zig-zag line, using a sharp knife, to give serrated edge.

WATERCRESS: Used in small bunches or sprigs: separate leaves are sometimes floated in the surface of a light-coloured soup.

Stuffings

Stuffing, sometimes called forcemeat, serves a triple purpose – it fills up the cavity in a boned joint or in a bird, helping to retain its good shape; it adds flavour; it makes a small joint or bird go further.

Most stuffings start with a base of one of the following:

156

1. Sausage-meat.
2. Bread-crumbs: make from white bread 2–3 days old, rubbing it on a grater or through a sieve or putting it in a blender.
3. Rice: Boil in salted water, rinse and dry before using.

To this basis add a fat (butter, dripping, oil or, most commonly, chopped suet); a little moisture and/or egg to bind; herbs and seasonings to give flavour and perhaps vegetables or fruits of various kinds.

Don't have the stuffing too wet or it becomes stodgy, nor yet too dry, or it will become crumbly and fall apart. Season a stuffing very well.

Don't stuff a joint or bird too tightly, for when the stuffing absorbs juices from the flesh during the cooking, it expands and might burst the skin or come out. It is better to cook any surplus stuffing in a separate casserole or baking tin. Sometimes it is rolled into small balls and cooked round a joint.

When stuffing a bird, put the forcemeat in loosely at the neck end, under the flap of skin, taking care to give the breast a plump round shape. Put an onion, a knob of butter or a wedge of lemon in the body of the bird to keep the flesh moist. Truss the bird firmly.

There are several excellent packet stuffings available and these make a good addition to the store-cupboard.

FORCEMEAT BALLS
Form the stuffing mixture into a roll, cut off small pieces and shape into balls; coat with flour, fry in hot fat and drain well.

APPLE AND CELERY STUFFING

2 oz. bacon, rinded and chopped
1 oz. butter
2 onions, skinned and chopped
2 sticks of celery, scrubbed and chopped
4 medium-sized cooking apples, peeled, cored and sliced
3 oz. fresh white bread-crumbs
2 tbsps. chopped parsley
Sugar to taste
Salt and pepper

Fry the bacon in the butter for 2–3 minutes until golden brown and remove from the pan with a slotted spoon. Fry the onions and celery for 5 minutes and remove from the pan with the slotted spoon. Fry the apples for 2–3 minutes, until soft. Mix all the ingredients together.

Use with duck, or (making double quantities) for goose.

APRICOT STUFFING

3 oz. dried apricots
3 oz. fresh bread-crumbs
$\frac{1}{4}$ level tsp. mixed spice
$\frac{1}{4}$ level tsp. salt
$\frac{1}{4}$ level tsp. pepper
1 tbsp. lemon juice
1 oz. butter, melted
1 small egg, beaten

157

Soak the apricots overnight in cold water. Drain off the liquid, chop the fruit, stir in the remaining ingredients and bind with the egg.

Use for stuffing a chicken, or make double the quantity for stuffing the neck end of the turkey.

BACON OR HAM STUFFING

½ oz. dripping
½ a small onion, skinned and chopped
2 mushrooms, chopped
4 oz. cooked bacon or ham, chopped
2 oz. fresh white bread-crumbs

Salt and pepper
A little dry mustard
A few drops of Worcestershire sauce
A little beaten egg or milk to bind

Melt the dripping, fry the onion and add the mushrooms and bacon or ham. Mix well, then remove from the heat and add the crumbs, seasonings and sauce and bind with a little egg or milk.

Use with poultry.

CELERY STUFFING

4 oz. cooked celery, chopped
4 oz. fresh white bread-crumbs
2 oz. suet, chopped

Grated rind of ½ a lemon
1 tbsp. chopped parsley
Salt and pepper
A little beaten egg or milk to bind

Mix the ingredients, seasoning well and bind together with the beaten egg or milk.

Use with poultry.

CHESTNUT STUFFING

2 oz. bacon, rinded and chopped
4 oz. fresh white bread-crumbs
1 tsp. chopped parsley
1 oz. butter, melted

Grated rind of a lemon
8 oz. chestnut purée (see note)
Salt and pepper
1 egg, beaten

Fry the bacon gently in its own fat for about 3–5 minutes, until crisp. Drain and add the rest of the ingredients, binding with the beaten egg.

Use for a turkey.

Note: Chestnut purée may be made from fresh chestnuts. Boil 1 lb. chestnuts for 2 minutes to soften the skins, remove from the heat and peel them while they are hot. Simmer the peeled chestnuts in milk for about 40 minutes, until soft. Sieve them or put them in an electric blender. Alternatively, use dried chestnuts to make the purée, or buy unsweetened canned purée.

158

HERB (PARSLEY) STUFFING

Sometimes called Forcemeat or Veal Forcemeat

1 oz. shredded suet	Grated rind of ½ a lemon
4 oz. fresh white bread-crumbs	1 small egg, beaten
1 tbsp. chopped parsley	Salt and pepper
½ level tbsp. mixed herbs	Milk or stock to bind
	2 oz. bacon (optional)

Mix together the suet, bread-crumbs, parsley, herbs, lemon rind, egg and seasoning, and enough milk or stock to bind the mixture together; if bacon is used, chop it finely and add with the dry ingredients.

Use for stuffing a chicken. Double the quantities for stuffing the neck end of a turkey.

SAGE AND ONION STUFFING

2 large onions, skinned and chopped	4 oz. fresh bread-crumbs
½–1 oz. butter	2 level tsps. dried sage
	Salt and pepper

Put the onions in a pan of cold water, bring to the boil and cook until tender – about 10 minutes. Drain well, add the other ingredients and mix well.

Use with duck and goose (make double quantity for the latter).

SAUSAGE STUFFING

1 large onion, skinned and chopped	1 level tsp. mixed herbs
1 lb. pork sausage-meat	1 oz. fresh bread-crumbs (optional)
1 oz. lard	Salt and pepper
2 tsps. chopped parsley	

Mix the onion with the sausage-meat. Melt the lard and fry the sausage-meat and onion lightly for 2–3 minutes, add the rest of the ingredients and mix well.

Use with chicken; for turkey, double the quantities.

VEAL FORCEMEAT
(Made with Meat)

8 oz. lean veal	2 large mushrooms, washed and chopped
6 oz. lean bacon	
2 onions, skinned and finely chopped	2 tsps. finely chopped parsley
2 oz. butter	Salt, pepper, Cayenne and mace
6 oz. fresh white bread-crumbs	2 eggs, beaten

Pass the mixed veal and bacon twice through a mincer, then beat them well in a bowl. Lightly fry the onion in a little of the butter, until soft but not coloured – 2–3 minutes; add to the

159

meat. Add the bread-crumbs, mushroom, the remaining butter, parsley and seasonings and lastly the beaten egg. Mix well; if the mixture is too stuff, add a little milk.

Use for turkey. (These quantities give sufficient for a 14 lb. bird.)

MUSHROOM STUFFING

4 oz. mushrooms
1 oz. butter
1 clove of garlic, skinned
1 tbsp. chopped parsley

Salt and pepper
2 oz. fresh bread-crumbs
Beaten egg to bind

Prepare and chop the mushrooms and fry in the hot butter. Cut the garlic clove in half and rub the cut side round the inside of the basin you are using for mixing. Put all the ingredients into the basin, including the butter used for frying the mushrooms, and bind together with the egg.

Use as a stuffing to put into a chicken, or roll the mixture into balls and cook in the oven on a greased tray below the chicken for $\frac{1}{2}-\frac{3}{4}$ hour.

If preferred, replace the garlic by 1 small onion, chopped and fried with the mushrooms.

OYSTER STUFFING

1½ doz. "sauce" or canned oysters
6 oz. fresh white bread-crumbs
2 oz. suet, chopped, or 1½ oz. butter

Grated rind of ½ a lemon
1 tbsp. chopped parsley
A pinch of mace
Salt and Cayenne pepper
1 egg, beaten

Beard the oysters and cut them up. Simmer the beards in the oyster liquor to extract the flavour, then strain and discard the beards. Mix all the dry ingredients in a basin, add the oysters, the egg and enough oyster liquor to bind.

Use with turkey, especially for the breast of a boiled turkey.

RICE STUFFING

2 oz. rice, cooked
The liver of the chicken, chopped
1 small onion, skinned and chopped
2 oz. raisins, stoned

2 oz. almonds, blanched and chopped
2 tbsps. chopped parsley
1 oz. butter, melted
Salt and pepper
1 egg, beaten (optional)

Combine all the ingredients, season and bind them well together.

Use for chicken.

Supplement

In these pages we give notes on a variety of subjects connected with the main theme of the book – the choice of poultry and game, the processes of drawing (or paunching), stuffing, trussing, boning and so on, carving and the freezing of poultry, etc. The choice of wine to go with poultry, game, eggs and cheese is also covered, together with the use of wine in cooking these foods.

Choice and Preparation of Poultry and Game

CHICKEN
Available all the year
Choose a bird that looks plump. When buying a fresh (non-frozen) bird, feel the tip of the breast-bone with the thumb and finger. In a young bird this is soft and flexible; if it is hard and rigid the bird is probably too old to roast satisfactorily and will have to be steamed or boiled. Look at the feet also – in a young bird they are smooth with small (not coarse) scales and with short spurs. If the bird has not been plucked, the plumage should look smooth and young.

Many different terms have been used at times to classify chickens, but these are the main categories seen nowadays:
Poussins: Very small chickens, 1–2 lb.; 6–8 weeks old; one serves 1–2 people.
Broilers: Small birds, 2½–3½ lb.; 12 weeks old; one serves 3–4 people. (Frozen chickens are usually broilers.)
Large Roasters: Generally young cockerels or hens, but may be capons. "Young roasters" are 4–5 lb. and one serves 5–6 people; capons weigh up to 8 lb. and one serves 6–10 people.
Boiling Fowls: Older, tougher birds; 4–7 lb. They should be 18 months old, but may in some cases be older. Usually served in casseroles, etc.; allow 3–4 oz. boned meat per person.

GUINEA-FOWL
These are available all the year round, but are at their best from February to June. A guinea-fowl has grey plumage and white spots and is usually of about the same size as a pheasant,

though it can be as large as a small chicken. When choosing one, look out for the same points as in a fresh chicken – especially a plump breast and smooth-skinned feet. An average-sized bird will serve 4 people.

Guinea fowl need to be hung for some time after killing.

All methods for cooking chicken or pheasant are applicable, especially braising and casseroling, but take care to use plenty of fat when roasting guinea-fowl, otherwise the flesh will be dry.

DUCK
Available either fresh or frozen, all the year round.

When buying a fresh bird, look for a young duck, with soft, pliable feet; the feet and the bill should be yellow. Allow about 1 lb. dressed weight per person.

GOOSE
Geese are available all the year round, but are at their best from December to March. A young bird, which has more tender flesh, is recognised by soft, yellow feet and a yellow bill; the fat should be yellow and the flesh pinkish in colour. A 10-lb. bird will serve 7–8 people.

TURKEY
Turkeys are now available all the year round, but are of course especially abundant at Christmas time. Choose a bird that is plump and white-fleshed; short spurs and smooth black legs are signs that it is young. A 10–13-lb. turkey will serve 13–15 people. A 16–20-lb. turkey will serve 20–30 people. A frozen turkey of 9 lb. dressed weight is equivalent to a non-frozen one of 12 lb. undressed weight.

GAME AND OTHER PROTECTED BIRDS
Try to choose a young bird. The plumage is a guide, as all young birds have soft, even feathers. With pheasants and partridge, the long wing feathers are V-shaped in a young bird, as distinct from the rounded ones of an older bird. Smooth, pliable legs, short spurs and a firm, plump breast are other points to look for. Ask whether the bird has been hung (see below), as some poulterers do this.

Seasons for Game Birds
(inclusive of both dates)
Blackgame, 12th August – 10th December.
Grouse, 12th August – 10th December.
Partridge, 1st September – 1st February.
Pheasant, 1st October – 1st February.
Ptarmigan, 12th August – 10th December (in Scotland only).

162

Seasons for other Protected Wild Birds

Under the Protection of Birds' Act, 1954, seasons are also fixed for various wild birds, the best-known of which are:

Capercailzie (or Capercaillye), 1st October – 31st January.

Plover – golden or grey only, 1st September – 31st January.

Snipe, 12th August – 31st January.

Woodcock, 1st September – 31st January (in Scotland), 1st October – 31st January (in England).

The following birds may be shot inland between 1st September and 31st January, or below the high-water mark of the ordinary spring tides up to 20th February:

Wild Duck (e.g., Mallard, Pintail, Teal, Wigeon).

Wild Goose (e.g., Grey Lag, Pinkfoot, Whitefront).

HARE AND RABBIT

Hare is in season August–February; there is no special season for rabbits. Choose if possible a young, plump animal, i.e., one with smooth, sharp claws, ears that are tender and easily torn, and a stumpy, short neck.

VENISON (the meat of the Red Deer)

Buck venison is in season June–end of September; doe October–December. The flesh of the buck is considered the better. The animal is at its best from $1\frac{1}{2}$–2 years. The lean should be very dark and the fat white; plenty of fat shows that the venison is in good condition.

PREPARATION OF POULTRY

In these days of supermarkets and refrigeration, most town housewives buy ready-prepared fresh or frozen poultry, but we include details of the complete preparation.

HANGING AND STORING

Poultry should be hung for 2–3 days after killing before it is cooked. In cold weather it can, if necessary, be hung for about a week, but unlike game it is not kept until it is "high". Poultry is usually plucked before hanging (see below), though this is not essential, but the inside should be left in.

Hang the bird by the feet in a cool, airy larder and protect it from flies, using muslin if the larder is not fly-proof.

If poultry is to be put in a refrigerator, remove the inside and wrap the bird loosely or put it in a covered dish.

PLUCKING AND SINGEING

Poultry is usually plucked, or at least rough-plucked, immediately after killing, as the feathers are much easier to remove

163

while the bird is still warm. If many feathers remain, spread a piece of old sheeting or a large piece of paper on the floor or table and pluck on to this. Holding the bird firmly, take 2–3 feathers at a time and pull them sharply towards the head – that is, in the opposite direction to that in which they lie. Don't try to pluck handfuls at a time, or you may tear the skin. Large wing feathers are firmly attached and need to be plucked singly, with pliers if necessary. After the actual feathers have all been plucked, down (such as that on a goose) and any hairs can be singed off. Hold the bird over an open flame (gas burner, lighted taper or a piece of burning paper), turning it quickly.

DRAWING
In older birds the leg sinews need removing. Cut a small slit with a sharp-pointed knife in the leg just above the claw and parallel with the leg bone, exposing the sinews. Slip a skewer under one of them, then, holding the foot firmly, pull on the skewer to draw out the sinew from the flesh. There are 4–5 sinews in each leg and they must be taken out singly.

Unless the bird is very young, it is usual to cut off the feet and the easiest way of doing this is to sever the leg at the joint, bend the foot back, insert the knife in the joint and cut through. (The feet can be added to the giblet stock.)

To cut off the head, first cut through the skin of the neck about 2 inches from the body. Slip back the skin and cut off the neck close to the trunk. (The neck is kept for stock, but the head is discarded.)

Slit the skin of the neck a little way down the back of the bird – far enough to let you get your fingers inside and to loosen the windpipe and gullet, which simplifies the drawing process. Cut round the vent at the tail end with scissors or a sharp knife, taking care not to puncture the entrails. Make the hole large enough to get your fingers inside the body. Take hold of the gizzard (the large, oval, muscular organ containing food and grit) and draw out all the entrails, including the lungs, windpipe and gullet. Reserve the giblets (heart, gizzard and liver) and any fat – there is always plenty in a goose. Discard the rest of the entrails, burning them if possible. Wipe out the inside of the bird with a clean, damp cloth.

THE GIBLETS
Cut out the gall-bladder from the liver, keeping it intact, and discard it; discard also the flesh on which it rested, as this may have a bitter flavour. Carefully cut through the flesh of the gizzard up to but not through the crop, peel off the flesh and discard the crop.

164

Giblet Stock
Wash the liver, gizzard and heart. Wash and scald the feet, remove the scales and nip off the claws. Put all in a saucepan, cover with water and stew gently for $\frac{3}{4}$–1 hour to make a stock that can be used for gravy or soup.

BONING POULTRY OR GAME FOR A GALANTINE
First cut off the neck and feet as opposite and cut off the end joints of the wings. Commence boning at the neck. Using a small, sharp knife and keeping it close to the bone, separate the flesh from the bone. To bone the wings, cut through from inside where the wing joints the body, then work down the bone, scraping the flesh from it and turning the wing inside out; repeat with the other wing. Continue to work down the body, boning the legs in the same manner as the wings. Finally, turn the bird right side out.

BONING POULTRY OR GAME TO STUFF WHOLE
Prepare the bird as for roasting, but do not truss it. Using a sharp boning knife and starting from the neck, gradually work the flesh away from the bones. Cut through the wing joints and from the inside scrape down the bone, turning the wings inside out. When the wings are completed, work round and round the body, making sure that the skin is not pierced. At the leg joint, cut through from the inside and scrape the meat off the bone, turning the flesh inside out and leaving the bone quite clean. Continue boning to the tail, then sever the skin, and remove any loose bones. Turn the bird to the right side, and it is then ready for stuffing.

JOINTING A CHICKEN
For some recipes it is necessary to divide a chicken into joints (or more accurately, into portions). A bird weighing 2–3 lb. will give 4 good serving portions. If you are using a frozen chicken, let it thaw completely before you attempt to divide it. You can use either a sharp knife or poultry secateurs, as follows:

1. *Using a Knife:* First loosen the legs from the sides of the bird. Cut through the skin between the breast and one leg and ease the leg away from the body till it is at right angles to the bird. Cut through the joint and remove the leg. Repeat on the other side. Trim the legs at the joint. Cut down the centre of the breast and ease the meat from the rib cage on one side as far down as the main wing joint. Cut through this joint and remove the wing, which is attached to the breast. Repeat on the other side.

165

2. *Using Secateurs:* First cut down the centre of the breast, beginning at the neck and continuing along to the vent. Cut along the line of the spine in a similar way. Now divide each half between the leg portion and the wing, so that a small part of the breast is included in each leg portion.

STUFFING AND TRUSSING

Although it is not essential, poultry is usually stuffed for roasting. Fowls and turkeys are stuffed at the breast end and geese and ducks at the tail end. Forcemeat or chestnut, celery, sausage-meat, or other suitable stuffing may be used for turkeys or fowls, and sage and onion stuffing is the one most commonly used for both ducks and geese. (For recipes, see chapter 10, page 139).

The object of trussing is to keep a roast (or boiled) fowl a good shape so that it will be easy to carve. A trussing needle (a long needle with an eye large enough to take fine string) is useful, but failing this, use a skewer and some fine string. First fold the neck skin under the body and fold the tips of the wings back towards the backbone so that they hold the neck skin in position; set the bird on its back and press the legs well into the side, thus raising the breast. Make a slit in the skin above the vent and put the tail (the so-called "parson's nose") through this slit.

Thread the needle with a length of clean string and insert it close to the second joint of the right wing; push it right through the body, passing it out so as to catch the corresponding joint on the left side. Insert the needle again in the first joint of the left wing, pass it through the flesh at the back of the body, catching the tips of the wings and the neck skin, and pass it out through the first joint of the wing on the right side. Tie the ends of the string in a bow. To truss the legs, re-thread the needle, insert it through the gristle at the left side of the "parson's nose" and tie the ends of the string firmly to keep all in place.

When using a skewer, insert it right through the body of the bird just below the thigh bone and turn the bird over on to its breast. First, catching in the wing tips, pass the string under the ends of the skewer and cross it over the back.

Turn the bird over and tie the ends of the string together round the tail, at the same time securing the drumsticks.

PREPARING FROZEN POULTRY

Deep-frozen poultry, whole or cut up, should be allowed to thaw-out at room temperature; the time required depends on the size of the joint or bird – single joints take from about 1 hour and large turkeys up to 24–48 hours. If you need to speed up the defrosting process, hold the bird under cold (not hot) running water.

The giblets are usually wrapped in polythene and placed inside the bird cavity for freezing, so remove them before cooking the bird. Frozen birds are usually sold trussed, ready for stuffing.

BARDING
When the drier types of poultry (and game birds) are to be roasted, the breast is often covered with pieces of bacon fat to prevent the flesh drying up – this is called barding.

LARDING
Very lean birds and also venison are often larded in order to introduce some extra fat into the flesh, so that it will not be too dry to eat.

The process is carried out with special larding needles. If these are not available, however, a pointed knife can be used to push the strips of fat through the flesh.

To lard a bird or a piece of meat, such as venison, first cut strips of fat bacon or pork about ½ inch wide and thread these into the end of the special larding needles. Pierce the point of one of the needles right through the flesh of the bird or meat and slowly draw the fat through, then remove the needle, leaving the fat in place. Repeat the process as many times as necessary, making "stitches" at regular intervals and if desired forming a definite pattern over the surface of the bird or meat with the white fat.

HANGING AND PREPARATION OF GAME BIRDS
All game birds need to be hung up by the legs, without being plucked or drawn, before they are cooked, or the flesh will be tough and tasteless. The time for hanging depends on the weather and on your taste, varying from a week in "muggy" weather to 2–3 weeks in frosty weather.

Keep the bird in a cold, dry, airy place and examine it from time to time, especially if it has been shattered when shot, or has got wet, or has been packed up for any length of time before hanging, as such birds do not keep so well. For most people the bird is sufficiently mature when the tail or breast feathers will pluck out easily. With a pheasant, the flesh on the breast begins to change colour and the bird smells "gamey".

Pluck, draw and truss the bird as for poultry (see above), but leave the feet on and don't draw the sinews from the legs. Some birds, such as snipe, have the head left on and are not drawn before being roasted – see the individual recipes. The larger birds may be jointed like a chicken before cooking.

167

PREPARING HARES

A hare should be hung by the feet (without being paunched) for 7–10 days, to improve the flavour; it is usually sold ready hung, but if you hang it yourself, put a bowl under the nose to collect the blood, which is used to thicken the gravy. In some shops cut joints of hare are sold, but we give notes on jointing.

SKINNING, PAUNCHING AND TRUSSING

Cut off the feet at the first joint. Loosen the skin round the back legs. Hold the end of one leg and bend at the joint – the flesh can then be grasped and the skin pulled off. Do the same with the other legs. Draw off the skin from the head, cutting it through at ears and mouth, and cut out the eyes with a sharp knife. Wipe the whole of the body with a clean damp cloth – don't wash it.

Place the hare on paper. Using kitchen scissors, snip the skin at the fork and cut it up to the breast-bone; open the paunch by cutting the inside skin in the same direction. Draw out and burn the entrails. Reserve the kidneys. Detach the liver, taking care not to puncture the gall-bladder; cut this out from the liver, keeping it intact, and discard; cut away also the flesh on which it rested, as it may be bitter.

Cut the diaphragm and draw out the lungs and heart; catch in a basin the blood which will have collected. Discard the lungs, but keep the heart.

Cut the sinews in the hind legs at the thigh, bring the legs forward and press closely against the body. Bend the forelegs back in the same way. Fix with 2 fine metal skewers or use a trussing needle and string.

JOINTING

Remove the legs. Cut the back into several pieces, giving the back of the knife a sharp tap with a hammer to cut through the bone. Cut off the head and cut the ribs in two lengthwise. (The head, split in two, may be included in a stew, etc.)

PREPARING RABBITS

Rabbits, both fresh and frozen, are usually sold cleaned and skinned; otherwise you should follow the directions given for hares. The paunching should be done within a few hours of killing.

Rabbits may be cooked in almost any way suitable for other types of meat, especially hares, though only very young ones should be roasted or fried. The can be fricasseed, braised or made into a pie.

168

To make the flavour of a rabbit less strong, wash it and soak in salted water for 1–2 hours before it is cut up and cooked.

PREPARING VENISON

As venison tends to be tough, it should be hung in a cool, airy place for 1–2 weeks, according to the weather; wipe it occasionally with a cloth to remove moisture. Test it at intervals by running a skewer through the haunch – as soon as a slight "high" smell is noticeable, the venison is ready for cooking.

The best joints of venison are the saddle, haunch and shoulder. Before cooking they should be marinaded, as the meat tends to be dry.

The usual accompaniments are red currant jelly, braised chestnuts and a port wine sauce.

MARINADE FOR VENISON

2 carrots, peeled and chopped	6 peppercorns
2 small onions, skinned and chopped	Parsley stalks, washed
	A bay leaf
1 stick of celery, scrubbed and chopped	3 blades of mace
	Red wine

Place the vegetables and flavourings in a large container, put in the venison and add sufficient wine to half-cover it. Leave to soak for 12 hours, turning the meat over in the marinade 2 or 3 times.

FLAVOURINGS FOR GAME AND POULTRY

For game there are certain traditional flavourings which would be hard to better. Duck, goose and turkey, too, have long associations with particular herbs and accompaniments. With chicken, however, it is well worth experimenting with new herbs, flavourings such as wines (see pages 176–178), orange, cheese and so on – partly because we use chicken more often than the other birds, partly because modern chicken tends to have a somewhat muted flavour.

In addition to the well-tried parsley, fines herbes (mixed parsley, chervil, chives and tarragon) and bouquet garni (see p. 24), try chervil, thyme and tarragon on their own with chicken dishes. Try also marjoram with any poultry, and winter savory in combination with marjoram and/or thyme for chicken or turkey. (Remember that savory, tarragon and thyme, like sage, need to be used sparingly.) The herbs may be added to casseroles, etc., towards the end of the cooking time, while marinades or basting mixtures are the best way of flavouring grills and roasts. The individual recipes in this book give many other suggestions.

CHICKEN

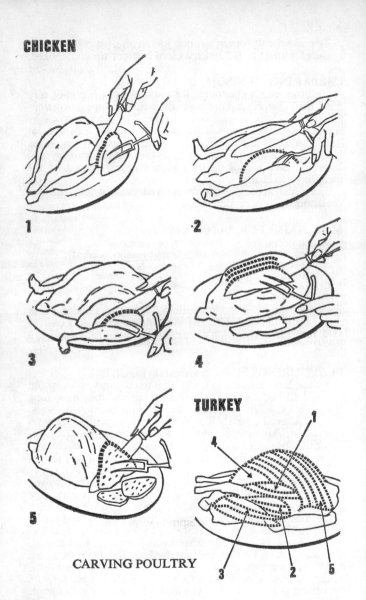

TURKEY

CARVING POULTRY

Carving Poultry and Game

Chicken: Place the bird so that one wing is towards your left hand, with the breast diagonally towards you (if you are left-handed, reverse these directions). Hold the wing with the fork and cut through the outer layer of the breast, judging the direction of the cut so that the knife enters the wing joint. Gently ease the wing away from the body of the bird and firmly cut through the joint gristle. Repeat for the other wing.

Steadying the bird with the flat of the knife held against the breast, prise the leg outwards with the fork, thus exposing the thigh joint – one clean cut through the joint will then sever the leg. It is usual to divide the thigh from the drumstick by cutting through the joint, and in a big bird, the thigh is further divided. Cut the breast in thin slices, parallel with the breast-bone. When stuffing has been cooked in the bird, it is sliced from the front of the breast, the remaining part being scooped out with a spoon. (See figures 1–5 opposite.)

Turkey: See diagram opposite. Begin by slicing the flesh from the drumsticks first at 1, then at 2. Carve the flesh from the main carcase in slices, working from 4, the tail end, towards 5 (or if you prefer, reverse this, working from 5, the breast end, towards 4). Remove the legs as for chicken, above. (You will find this easier to do if you place the bird on its breast.) Carve the remaining flesh from 3.

Serve each person with slices of both light and dark meat.

Game Birds: A pheasant or other game bird, if large, is carved in the same general manner as a chicken. Partridges, pigeons and birds of similar size are usually cut in half. If very small, the whole bird may be served as one portion; woodcock, snipe and quail are among the birds which are served whole, on the toast on which they were cooked. Special scissors (rather like small secateurs) are available for cutting up birds; failing these, use the game carver or a short, pointed kitchen knife, by inserting the point of the knife in the neck end of the breast and cutting firmly through the bird in the direction of the breast-bone and tail.

Venison: Carve as for the corresponding joints of meat.

Poultry and Game in the Home Freezer

All raw poultry and game may be frozen, also stocks, soups, stews, etc.

The birds or joints should of course be in first-class condition – of high quality and freshly killed (except in the case of game), and the preparation and processing should be carried out quickly.

Follow the general directions given with your freezer, but note these special points:

Poultry: Freeze only young, tender birds (if possible, they should be starved for 24 hours before being killed). Hang them in a cool place for 1 day.

Game: All game must be hung prior to freezing for the same length of time as for immediate use, and according to your individual taste.

Preparation: Hang, then draw and clean the bird in the normal way. Joint it if desired. Discard the gall bladder and clean the giblets. Truss the bird as for table, but don't stuff it.

Packing and Storage: Use polythene bags or sheeting, padding any sharp edges of bone with paper or extra polythene to prevent the wrapping being punctured during storage. If the bird is jointed, pack the joints either separately, or in one container, but separated by pieces of paper or polythene. Wrap and freeze the giblets separately (or use them to make some stock and freeze this separately – see below). The maximum storage time is 6–8 months.

Thawing and Cooking: Thaw the poultry or game completely in its package. The time depends on the size, a 4-lb. chicken taking 3–4 hours at room temperature, or 7–8 hours in a refrigerator. For turkeys allow up to 20–30 hours in a cool larder for a bird weighing up to 12 lb. and up to 48 hours for a larger one.

Stocks, Soups, Sauces: Everything is suitable, but remember to use cornflour rather than flour for thickening. Don't add cream or egg thickening to soups or sauces until you thaw and re-heat them. Storage time is 2–3 months, except in the case of highly spiced sauces, which develop an "off" flavour if kept for longer than 1–2 weeks. Either thaw these foods in the container for 1½–2 hours, or place the unthawed pack in a pan and heat slowly, stirring, until the contents come to the boil.

Stews, Casseroles: Make as usual, but under-cook by 20–30 minutes. Cool, pack and freeze. Storage time is about 2 months. For use, heat slowly and simmer for at least 15 minutes.

Cooked Poultry (to Serve Cold): Allow the bird to cool after cooking, then joint or slice it and pack with a piece of waxed paper between the pieces. Storage time is about 2 months. Thaw for about 1 hour, open the pack and lay the pieces on kitchen paper to absorb the moisture; cover and thaw for another ½–1 hour.

Chicken Loaves, etc. (to Serve Cold): Make as usual, cool, pack and freeze. Storage time is about 2 months. Thaw the pack in the refrigerator for 6–8 hours, or overnight.

Chicken, Pastries, Pies, etc. The treatment varies according to whether the pastry is cooked or uncooked, and whether pastry cases are filled or unfilled. The normal storage time is 2 months for baked goods, 1 month for unbaked.

Baked pastry flan cases: unwrap and heat in a fairly hot oven (375°F., mark 5) for 15–20 minutes.

Unbaked pastry flan cases: make as usual. Unwrap and bake in hot oven (425°F., mark 7) for 20–25 minutes.

Pies (filled and baked): To eat cold, thaw for 1¾–2 hours. To eat hot, unwrap and heat in a fairly hot oven (375°F., mark 5) for 30 minutes.

Pies (filled and unbaked): unwrap and bake in a hot oven (425°F., mark 7) for 40–60 minutes.

Freezing eggs

Preparation: eggs cannot be frozen whole because they crack, so they must be broken and the yolks and whites frozen separately. Yolks congeal and are not very satisfactory, but are better if mixed with either a little salt or a little sugar, depending on how they are to be used; for 6 yolks add 1 level tsp. salt or 2 level tbsps. sugar.

Packaging: used waxed cartons or polythene bags.

Thawing: thaw completely in the unopened package for ½ hour.

Preserving eggs

Now that commercially produced eggs are available cheaply and in quantity all the year round, there is little need for most households to preserve them. However, those who live in remote places may still find it useful to have a store of home-produced eggs put by for winter use, so we give the full directions.

For preserving, eggs should for preference be non-fertile, though this is not essential.

Hens' eggs, when freshly laid, are free from harmful bacteria and can safety be preserved by any of the methods outlined below. Duck and goose eggs, on the other hand, even when newly laid, may be contaminated with bacteria. Although egg-preserving solutions prevent the entry of bacilli into the egg, those already within it are not destroyed by their agency. Their by-products, set up over long periods, are harmful, so the preservation of these eggs cannot be recommended, although they are safe to eat when fresh, provided they are properly cooked.

The eggs should be fresh, though not taken straight from the nest: a minimum period of 24 hours should be allowed for the liquid and air inside the shell to reach equilibrium. The older the eggs, however, the greater the risk that bacilli will have found an entry.

Do not wash the eggs, though slightly soiled ones may be wiped over carefully with a clean, damp cloth. Very dirty eggs and those with rough, uneven or very thin shells should not be preserved.

Pickling in Waterglass: as the strength of waterglass varies, follow the directions given on the tin or jar, mixing it with hot water, then diluting it with cold. Put the mixture in the receptacle – a galvanised pail or bin, a stoneware crock or enamel bin, with a lid – and allow it to cool. Add the eggs, arranging them carefully, with the pointed end downwards. The liquid should come three-quarters of the way up the receptacle and should completely cover the eggs.

Preserving in Lime Water: although this method involves rather more trouble, it is preferred by some people. A week before it is required for use the lime water must be prepared; mix 4 parts of finely slaked lime with 20 parts of water; stir the mixture daily, and on the fourth or fifth day add 1 part of salt. Place the eggs in a barrel or something similar and pour the clear solution over them, avoiding the sediment. There should be 2–3 inches of solution over the top layer of eggs. An egg preserved in this way can be told by the roughness of its shell.

Pickled eggs: see page 116.
Frozen eggs: see page 173.

Wine with Poultry, Game, Eggs and Cheese

Although people are nowadays probably less concerned than formerly to serve the conventionally "correct" wines, there are still occasions when it is useful to know the accepted partners. Here are notes as what to serve with the kinds of food discussed in this book.

CHOICE OF WINE

Soups: With piping hot soups avoid chilled wine. If the soup is flavoured with sherry, Madeira or Marsala, match it with a glass of the same wine, unchilled.

Plainly Cooked Chicken, and Guinea Fowl: The drier white wines, still or sparkling, go well with these.

Duck, Goose, Turkey, Game: The red wines of the Rhône, and also the fuller white wines from the Rhineland, counterbalance the fatness of duck and goose. Turkey and unhung game birds go well with a red Bordeaux, but a good big Burgundy is best with grouse or other game which has been hung. Gamey meat, like venison, wild boar and hare, is usually served with a strong, dark red wine but – surprisingly perhaps – is also enjoyable with the fuller hocks, particularly those from the Palatinate.

Curries: Wine and curries don't go. A light lager is better, or simply plain water. If you must drink wine, have a dry white *ordinaire*. Dishes *à l'Indienne* which have some curry powder in their sauce can take a chilled *vin rosé* or *vinho verde*.

Food cooked in wine or beer: The general rule is to match the wine in the food with the wine accompanying it – a full-flavoured Burgundy with poultry cooked in Burgundy, for instance. Carbonnades and other stews, braises or casseroles with beer in them are best served with beer.

Cheese: Individual and national tastes in wines-for-the-cheese vary infinitely and it is true that the milder cheeses are happy with almost any type of wine. For the stronger-flavoured cheeses, red wine, robust and dry, is very good, though many people in Britain still make port their choice.

Eggs: Served in aspic, in mayonnaise, or *en cocotte* as a first course, they need no special consideration, but will take kindly to a light white wine. With a main-dish omelette accompanied

175

by a salad for a simple lunch, a red *vin ordinaire* is companionable. For the more formal occasion when, say a cheese or fish soufflé is on the menu, a good white Burgundy or a mellow hock would be in keeping. When eggs appear in a classic *Quiche Lorraine*, then a white wine of Alsace is an elegant partner. With Scotch eggs for buffet or picnic, beer is as good a drink as any.

Chinese Food: The diverse dishes that make a Chinese meal don't easily lend themselves to a particular wine. The Chinese use quite a lot of wine in cooking (often *Shao hsing*, for which dry sherry can be substituted.) Normally they do not have wines with the food, but sometimes take tea – without milk or sugar – as a break between some courses of a long meal.

COOKING WITH WINE

Probably the most important reason for using wine in cooking is that it gives added flavour and "body" to the food. Wine (or a spirit or liqueur) is a traditional indispensable ingredient in many classic dishes (particularly those of French origin), such as Salmi of Game, Chicken Marengo, Rum Baba, Crêpes Suzette. It will in fact improve the flavour of almost any savoury or sweet dish.

Another specific reason for using wine is that it makes food more tender and moist. It is particularly useful with the tougher kinds of poultry or game, hence its addition to stews and casseroles and its use as a marinade.

Note: When wine is actually cooked with food, most of the alcoholic content is driven off during the process, but the flavour remains, becoming mellower as the cooking proceeds.

Any wine, whether cheap or expensive, can be used. The choice depends to a large extent on what you can afford at the time and what you have in the store-cupboard. Leftovers from the previous night's dinner or from a party can quite well be used. Even sparkling wine that has gone flat need not be wasted.

Careful shopping can enable you to buy very pleasant wines at comparatively little cost – a non-vintage wine or one from the less traditional wine-producing areas (for instance, Yugoslavia, South Africa, Australia) can often cost a fraction of the price asked for its better-known counterpart, yet still be perfectly adequate for both table and kitchen use.

In savoury dishes, a dry wine is usually more suitable than a sweet one and a still one than a sparkling type. Spirits and liqueurs can be added as you wish – apart from the obvious point that sweet, fruity liqueurs are usually restricted to sweet dishes, there are no really definite rules as to their use. It is a good idea to buy half or quarter bottles or even "miniatures"

176

of liqueurs and spirits, to allow you to experiment without spending too much money.

With ale and cider it is economical to buy a large bottle with a screw-top, rather than a small bottle or can – provided you replace the top tightly each time, the ale or cider will keep quite well. Flat beer can quite well be used, so long as it is not actually stale. If you have the remains of a bottle of not-too-sweet sparkling cider, this can be used in cooking, though still cider is preferable.

GENERAL NOTES ON USING WINE

Wine in cooking should always be used judiciously, or it may overshadow the other flavours and spoil the finished dish.

Don't overdo the wine in menu-planning. Just one wine-based main dish is ample. Alternatively, some sherry in the soup and brandy in the sweet, for instance, would give a pleasant balance.

Here are the general methods of using wine in cooking.

1. *In a Marinade:* combined with a bay leaf, peppercorns, lemon rind, herbs, etc., and used to flavour poultry etc., prior to cooking. The poultry is best left for several hours in the marinade; put it in a cool place, or in a covered container in the refrigerator, and turn it over once or twice.

2. *In Stews, Casseroles and Braises:* wine is added at the start of the cooking, usually in the proportion of half wine to half stock.

3. *In Frying or Grilling:* to make a glaze cook the food completely – plain or marinaded – then add the wine to the juices in the pan and heat rapidly for a few minutes. Pour over the hot food and serve.

4. *In Sauce-making:* the wine and any other liquor is reduced considerably and then added to a basic sauce, or it may be simply thickened with egg yolk and cream.

5. *In Flambé dishes:* Gently heat some brandy or other spirit in a ladle, spoon or tiny pan, ignite with a match, then pour the whole over the hot food and let the flame spread by agitating the pan. When the flames have died down a delicious concentrated essence is left.

6. *To Flavour without cooking:* Add sherry, port or Madeira to a clear soup before serving, stirring in a spoonful at a time and tasting for flavour. Port used in moderation gives a subtle taste to aspic jelly.

HOW TO USE THE DIFFERENT WINES

In general, full-bodied red wines such as Burgundies and clarets and the fortified wines such as port, sherry, Madeira and Marsala, together with cider and brown ale, are best in hearty dishes using rich dark meats like game, in spicy sauces for spaghetti and so on. Light, dry white wines and vermouth and cider are excellent in poultry dishes. A few more specific suggestions are given below:

Red Wine: see above; use in such recipes as Chicken Bourguignonne, Coq au Vin, Duck in Red wine, Duck à la Portugaise, Guinea Fowl and Red Cabbage.

White Wine: A few drops of white wine may be added to clear soup or to the sauces to go with chicken. Dry white wine can be used instead of vinegar in salad dressings.

Sherry: This is perhaps the most generally useful wine in cookery. It enhances soups, particularly those made with game, giblets and so on. It should however be added in very small quantities – only a few drops per serving – as the flavour of the sherry should not predominate.

Sherry is used in many sweet dishes, especially those based on egg or custard mixtures. It is the classic wine for trifle and tipsy cake, and may be used instead of water for dissolving the gelatine in souffles and creams. Sweet sauces, such as prune and whipped egg sauces, may include sherry.

Madeira: This may take the place of sherry in soups, and is an improvement to compote of pigeons. It is, of course, an integral part of Madeira sauce.

Port: Port is associated particularly with game dishes such as hare soup, jugged hare and salmis, and with the sauces to serve with game, although other red wines may replace it.

For Reference

HANDY MEASURES

If you have no scales or if you wish to measure out only a small weight of some ingredients, you can follow this table, using an average-sized tablespoon and measuring in level spoonfuls.

1 oz. (approx.)	Level Tablespoonfuls
Bread-crumbs, dry	3
Cheddar cheese, grated	3
Butter, margarine, lard (soft enough to press into bowl of spoon)	2
Cornflour	3
Flour, unsifted	3
Gelatine, powdered	2½
Rice	2
Salt	1¾

CUP MEASURES

The majority of American recipes give the quantities of ingredients in U.S.A. standard cups and spoons. Anyone who does not possess such cups and spoons can convert the figures into British measures with the aid of the following information:

1 American cup holds 8 fl. oz. or ½ American pint (Note: an English or Imperial ½ pint or cup equals 10 fl. oz.)

1 American tsp. = approximately ⅛ oz.

1 American tbsp. = 3 tsps. or ½ fl. oz.

16 American tbsps. = 1 American cup

An American tbs. holds exactly ¼ oz. flour, measured level. You may be able to find a British dessertspoon which holds this amount; if so, mark and keep it specially for use with

American recipes. An American tsp. is smaller than the standard British one, and holds only $\frac{4}{5}$ of the same ingredients.

The first of the following tables shows the approximate weight in both ounces and grams (metric) of a standard American cupful of various common ingredients, especially those used in cake making, etc. The second table, which will help you follow those recipes that are expressed in our own British standard cup and spoon measures, is also interesting to compare with the American one.

Table I

1 *American cup* (8 *fl. oz. capacity*)	*Weight in oz.*	*Approx. Weight in grams*
Butter, margarine, lard	8	227
Suet, shredded	$4\frac{1}{2}$	120
Oil	8	227
Cheddar cheese, grated	4	113
Cream, double	$8\frac{1}{3}$	236
Bread-crumbs – dry	4	113
fresh	1	28
Cornflour	$4\frac{1}{2}$	128
Rice – Patna	$6\frac{1}{2}$	182
Flour – plain, self-raising	4	113
Almonds, whole and blanched	$5\frac{1}{2}$	154
Walnuts – halved	$3\frac{3}{4}$	100
chopped	$4\frac{1}{2}$	128
Gelatine, powdered	$5\frac{1}{3}$	159

Table II

1 *British standard cup* (10 *fl. oz. capacity*)	*Weight in oz.*	*Approx. Weight in grams*
Butter, margarine, lard	$9\frac{1}{2}$	270
Suet, shredded	5	140
Oil	$8\frac{1}{2}$	241
Cheddar cheese, grated	5	140
Cream, double	9	255
Bread-crumbs – dry	$5\frac{3}{4}$	162
fresh	$1\frac{1}{2}$	42
Cornflour	$5\frac{3}{4}$	162
Rice – Patna	$7\frac{3}{4}$	219
Flour – plain, self-raising	6	170
Almonds, whole, blanched	$6\frac{1}{2}$	182
Walnuts – halved	4	113
chopped	5	140
Gelatine, powdered	7	198

METRIC/AVOIRDUPOIS WEIGHTS
1 gram	= 0·035 oz.
100 grams	= 3½ oz. (approx.)
250 grams	= 9 oz. (approx.)
1 kilogram (kg.)	= 1,000 grams or 2·20 lb.
	(approx. 2¼ lb.)

AVOIRDUPOIS/METRIC WEIGHTS
1 oz.	= 28·35 grams
4 oz.	= 113·4 grams
8 oz.	= 226·8 grams
1 lb.	= 453·6 grams (·45 kg.)

EQUIVALENT OF LIQUID MEASURES
1 litre (metric measure) = 1¾ Imperial pints or 35·2 fl. oz.

1 American pint = ⅘ Imperial pint or 16 fl. oz.

COOKING TEMPERATURES
Oven Temperatures: The ovens of most modern electric and gas cookers are thermostatically controlled; once the thermostat has been set, the oven heat will not rise above the selected temperature.

In the case of thermostatically controlled electric ovens, it is usually found that the thermostat scale is marked either in degrees Fahrenheit, or in serial numbers (1, 2, 3, etc.), corresponding with 100°F., 200°F., 300°F. (38°C., 93°C., 149°C.) and so on.

Oven heats in the recipes in this book are described by such terms as "Cool", "Hot," etc., with the corresponding temperatures and the oven settings used in most modern cookers; the table below shows the various equivalents. If in doubt about settings for your own cooker you can ask advice from your electricity or gas showrooms.

Oven Description	Approx. temp. and elec. oven setting		Standard gas thermostat
Very cool	250°F.	(121°C.)	¼
	275°F.	(135°C.)	½
Cool	300°F.	(149°C.)	1, 2
Warm	325°F.	(163°C.)	3
Moderate	350°F.	(177°C.)	4
Fairly hot	375°F.	(191°C.)	5
	400°F.	(204°C.)	6
Hot	425°F.	(218°C.)	7
Very hot	450°F.	(232°C.)	8
	475°F.	(246°C.)	9

Liquid Temperatures
Boiling   212°F. (100°C.)
Simmering   approx. 205°F. (96°C.)
Blood heat, (also called   approx. 98°F. (37°C.)
   tepid and luke-warm)
Freezing point   32°F. (0°C.)

Index

183

184

185

188

189

SPHERE SOLE AGENTS: